Trust

Trust

Forms, Foundations, Functions, Failures and Figures

Bart Nooteboom

Professor, Rotterdam School of Management, Erasmus University Rotterdam, The Netherlands

Edward Elgar
Cheltenham, UK • Northampton, MA, USA

Published by
Edward Elgar Publishing Limited
Glensanda House
Montpellier Parade
Cheltenham
Glos GL50 1UA
UK

Edward Elgar Publishing, Inc.
136 West Street
Suite 202
Northampton
Massachusetts 01060
USA

A catalogue record for this book
is available from the British Library

ISBN 1 84064 545 8

Printed and bound in Great Britain by Bookcraft (Bath) Ltd

Contents

Figures

Tables

Preface

This book developed from some ten years of research of inter-organizational relationships (for a survey, see Nooteboom 1999a). I started that research on the basis of transaction cost economics. Like many others, I was intuitively opposed to the view, expounded by Oliver Williamson, that governance of inter-firm relations should be based on an assumption of opportunism and that in economic relationships there is no basis for trust beyond calculative self-interest (Williamson 1993). He claimed that if trust goes beyond calculative self-interest it would necessarily be blind, and blind trust is unwise and unlikely to survive in markets. This posed a challenge. It took me some time to find out and to specify clearly why Williamson is wrong. I aimed to show how trust could go beyond calculative self-interest without being blind in the sense of being unconditional. Having found what I considered a satisfactory answer, I went ahead with the job of studying inter-firm relations. However, more aspects of trust cropped up. Trust turned out to be a much more complex and slippery notion than I had first thought. Anyone studying trust soon finds that over the past 30 years an enormous literature on the subject has accumulated, in sociology and management. Reading that literature, one encounters a confusing complexity of partly similar and partly different notions and aspects of trust. I found that it was not enough to dedicate only a paragraph to trust in a wider treatise on inter-firm relations. I concluded that it might be worthwhile to dedicate a full book to a comprehensive and systematic treatise of trust, covering all its requisite complexity, while trying to achieve coherence and conceptual clarity. It seems to me that in spite of all that has been written on trust there is still a need for that.

Of course, I build on the work of countless scholars before me, and on discussions with a number of colleagues. Earlier authors will show up in the literature references. Here I want to thank a number of people for their collaboration in research on which this book is partly based, and for comments on an earlier version of this book: Niels Noorderhaven and Hans Berger for our collaboration in two projects of empirical research on buyer–supplier relations at the University of Groningen, funded by the Dutch research foundation NWO. Rosalinde Klein Woolthuis for our collaboration in her PhD research at the Technical University Twente, on the relation between trust and contracts in innovation projects. Gjalt de Jong and Rob Vossen for our collaboration in Gjalt's PhD research at the University of Groningen on causal structures of buyer–supplier relations, and Susan Helper and Mari Sako for allowing us to use their data for it. Tomas Klos and René Jorna for our collaboration in Tomas' PhD project at the University of Groningen in developing an agent-based computational model of the build-up and breakdown of trust. Frederique Six for our discussions relating to her PhD research at the Rotterdam School of Management on 'trust and trouble in organisations'. Irma Bogenrieder at the Rotterdam School of Management for our discussions on the role of trust in learning communities in organizations. Giorgio Inzerilli and Gabriele Jacobs at the Rotterdam School of Management for their comments on an earlier version of the book, and their suggestions for improvement. Giorgio contributed an example on explosives experts; Gabriele demonstrated the relevance and importance of considerations from social psychology. I thank Guido Fioretti for our discussions, and his help in finding some literature references and Geoffrey Hodgson for his endorsement of the book. Of course, I am solely responsible for any remaining errors.

Abbreviations

ACE   Agent-based Computational Economics
ACTCE   Agent-based Computational Transaction Cost Economics
CAS   Complex adaptive systems
ICT   Information- and Communication Technology
TCE   Transaction Cost Economics

1. Aims and foundations

This introductory chapter discusses the aims and the theoretical foundations of this book. In the first part it indicates why trust is important and why it needs to be discussed. There is still much confusion about the notion of trust, on which this book aims to provide a synthesis. An inventory of questions is given, for which the theoretical foundations for answering are presented in the second part of the chapter. Trust entails important issues of uncertainty and learning. To deal with those issues we need a theory of knowledge and learning, which has implications for the theory of the firm. To understand trust in the behaviour of people we need a theory of the causality of action. We can have trust in things, people, organizations and institutions. Institutions also form a basis of trust. For this we need a clarification of the notion of institutions.

1.1 AIMS

Much has been written about trust, especially in the areas of sociology and management. Much insight has been given into the richness of the concept. However, there still is considerable confusion, with partly overlapping and partly conflicting definitions, analyses, explanations, conclusions and recommendations. The aim of this book is to contribute to more conceptual coherence, without surrendering the richness of the concept, in a systematic analysis of dimensions, levels, types, sources, roles and limitations of trust. Only some of the elements used in the analysis are new, but the architecture of how they are connected is. With some pointers to the literature, in a first round review, I specify a series of questions to be answered in this book.

The Importance of Trust

Trust is of all times. It is pervasive and indispensable. It is also open to treachery, and blind, unconditional trust is unwise. In the practice of human relations, it has always drawn attention. Trust is a complex and slippery notion, and many of its intricacies have been recognized throughout history. Behavioural science, however, has had problems in tackling the concept. Social science neglected it until some 30 years ago. Since then, it has produced a kaleidoscope of insights, which now require some ordering for the sake of clarity and analytical grip. Economics has begun to recognize the importance of trust but tends to underestimate its complexity and to misconstrue it. It is high time that a systematic and clear understanding of trust be incorporated in economic analysis.

There has always been interest in trust, if not in theory then in practice. In all its diversity, the practice of human relations shows up in literature, where the making and breaking of trust is a perennial theme. Consider Shakespeare's plays, for example. Even a lighter play such as *Much Ado about Nothing* is about trust and deception. Morton Deutsch, one of the most important writers on the subject of trust, quoted Theognis from his *Sententiae* (666 BC): 'He who mistrusts most should be trusted least'. And Samuel Johnson in *The Rambler* (1750): 'It is happier to be sometimes cheated than not to trust'. And Nicolai Hartmann in his *Ethics* (1930): 'All human relationships . . . are based on faith' and 'It is presumably a communal value; it is the most positive unifying force which welds together a variety of individual persons, with their separate interests, into a collective unit . . .' (Deutsch 1973: 144–5). The nineteenth century Dutch politician Thorbecke recognized another truism on trust: 'It comes on foot and leaves on horseback'. All these insights in trust are important and valid, as we shall see. Thus we see that in the practical wisdom of human affairs there is no lack of insight on the importance and the intricacies of trust.

Deutsch (1973: 144) expressed surprise at the lack of attention to trust in social science prior to his book: 'Despite the obvious significance of trust and other related phenomena, an examination of leading empirical and theoretical works reveals that these phenomena have been largely ignored by the social scientist'. Subsequently, however, there has been a flood of literature on trust in sociology and management, as references presented in the course of this book will testify. In modern economics, on the other hand, a relative neglect of trust has persisted, in spite of the fact that at the origin of modern economics, in the work of Adam Smith, trust was included, in Smith's (1759) 'theory of moral sentiments'.

Let us consider the value of trust in society. Trust can have extrinsic value, as a basis for achieving social or economic goals. It can also have intrinsic value, as a dimension of relations that is valued for itself, as part of a broader notion of well being or the quality of life. Many authors have pointed this out (Blau 1964, Arrow 1974, Jarillo 1988, Buckley and Casson 1988, Bradach and Eccles 1989, Powell 1990, Casson 1991, 1995, Helper 1990, Sako 1992, Gulati 1995, Berger, Noorderhaven and Nooteboom 1995,

Chiles and McMackin 1996, Nooteboom 1996). People may prefer, as an end in itself, to deal with each other on the basis of trust. Most economists tend to think of value in exchange as something that exists independently from the transaction. As formulated by Murakami and Rohlen (1992: 70): 'The value of the relationship itself is typically ignored and the impersonality of the transaction is assumed'. In intrinsic utility, the exchange process itself matters, as does the economic surplus that the exchange yields.

When intrinsic, the value of trust can be hedonic or based on self-respect. Many people would prefer to have trust-based relations rather than relations based on suspicion and opportunism for hedonic reasons. For most people it is more agreeable or pleasurable to have friendly relations than to have to deal with animosity and suspicion. There is also an intrinsic motive of self-respect, based on adherence to internalized norms or values of decent or ethical conduct. There is also a more socially oriented motive, in the will to be recognized, valued and respected by others. Social recognition may be served by accumulating riches, power or glamour, but also by being trustworthy and trusting, and thereby demonstrating adherence to established values, norms or habits of behaviour. This may merge with the earlier motive of self-respect, while analytically it can still be distinguished. Fukuyama (1995: 358) traced the urge for recognition to Hegel: a struggle for recognition, 'that is, the desire of all human beings to have their essence as free, moral beings recognized by other beings'. As indicated, this does not necessarily lead to trustworthiness and trust. Philosophers have also postulated other urges, such as the will to power. However, the point is that under proper institutional conditions and individual dispositions the urge towards recognition can lend value to trust and trustworthiness. When those conditions are lacking, however, it can lead to pathologies such as ethnic discrimination. There, recognition is not derived from benevolence but, on the contrary, from the condemnation and harassment of others (Fukuyama 1995: 361).

The extrinsic, economic value of trust lies in the fact that it enables interaction between people and between organizations and can reduce transaction costs. In the analysis of this, in Chapter 4, I employ elements from transaction cost economics, but in a wider theoretical framework, in recognition of a number of fundamental objections to that theory as developed by Williamson (1975, 1985, 1991, 1993, 1996, 1999). I will discuss transaction cost economics in the discussion of theoretical foundations, in the second part of this chapter. The downside of trust is that it entails risk and can be betrayed, which may endanger the survival of a firm. There can also be too much solidarity, providing an obstacle to change and innovation.

The distinction between extrinsic and intrinsic value is analytical. They are not necessarily perceived as distinct. An important question is how they are related in the perception and behaviour of agents. Extrinsic value is instrumental, which entails calculation, and suggests a focus on self-interest, while intrinsic value can be non-rational, unreflective and other-directed. The question concerning their relation is related to questions whether and how calculative and non-calculative trust can be combined, and whether trustworthiness can go beyond self-interest. These questions are discussed later.

Question 1: Value of trust
What are the value dimensions of trust, such as intrinsic and extrinsic value, self- and other-oriented value, and how are they related?

To indicate the extrinsic, economic importance of trust, here I simply posit that trust is one of several means, but an indispensable one, for conducting economic relations. The arguments are developed later, in Chapter 4. The fact that trust is now gaining more attention, even in economics, can be explained by the fact that interaction between more or less autonomous agents (people, organizations) is now deemed more important for economic success than it was before. There are several reasons for this.

One important and widely recognized current condition is that information and communication technology (ICT) enables interaction in new ways. The application of ICT in 'virtual' relations between people interacting via the Internet rather than face-to-face also raises new issues of trust concerning the verification of identity (Knights et al. 2001). A second, also widely recognized, current condition is that organizational disintegration into more or less autonomous units of activity is now needed more than ever. That yields a greater variety and flexibility in the configuration of activities than units that are rigidly integrated in an organization, with strong and persistent linkages (Nooteboom 1999a, 2000a). That variety and flexibility, in networks or 'industrial districts' of firms, for example, are needed under current conditions of complexity and rapid change in technologies and markets. Such conditions obtain more generally at the upsurge of fundamental new technologies, at the beginning of long economic (Kondratieff) cycles. And indeed, at that stage we have witnessed the emergence of network-type organizational forms, and the 'swarming' of small new firms before, in a series of industrial revolutions. At a later stage in the cycle this tends to be followed by more integration in larger and more stable organizational units. However, due to effects of ICT the present need and opportunity for network structures is greater than ever, as is argued in Chapter 4.

In earlier work, I proposed another, deeper, cognitive reason for relations between a variety of more or less autonomous organizational units (Nooteboom 1992, 1993, 1999a, 2000a). For this I need a theory of knowledge, which will be summarized later, in the second part of this chapter, in the discussion of theoretical foundations. That theory is needed also because it has implications for the relation between trust in people and trust in organizations, discussed in Chapter 3.

Question 2: Economic function of trust
What is the extrinsic, economic value of trust? How does it work? What are the effects? What are the institutional conditions?

To say that trust can foster productive economic relations does not imply that it necessarily does so. Indeed, it can go too far and have negative effects, in making economic relations too exclusive and durable, thereby yielding rigidities and lack of innovation. This is discussed in Chapter 5, where I treat the failures of trust.

Question 3: Failures of trust
How can trust go wrong? What are its possible adverse effects? What are the limitations and boundaries of trust?

Trust, Uncertainty and Calculation

It is not difficult to explain the peculiar fact that in the history of economics the attention to trust did not increase but was sidetracked. That happened not only to trust but to social psychology more in general. In the development of economics after Adam Smith, economics narrowed from the 'Enquiry into the nature and causes of the wealth of nations' to a calculus of rational choice. The machinery of rational choice analysis breaks down when we go beyond risk, in the economist's interpretation as the variance of a distribution of probabilities attached to alternative outcomes.

Beyond risk there is radical uncertainty, in the sense of Knight (1921), which entails lack of knowledge concerning the set of alternative outcomes of a choice and of alternative options for choice. One cannot rationally choose the best from a set of alternatives if that set is not well defined. Yet that kind of uncertainty does arise in human interaction: the set of outcomes of choice and the set of options for choice are open. Some outcomes and options are not given prior to choice but are revealed or produced as a result of choice and action, so that we can see only in retrospect what we could have chosen if only we had known all the options and possible outcomes. As I will argue at length in this book, the importance and nature of trust arise from the unpredictability, or radical uncertainty, of human behaviour. Trust can be ignored only at the price of ignoring uncertainty. Trust can be understood only by recognizing and accepting radical uncertainty.

Trust is not dealt with adequately in mainstream economics because that does not adequately deal with radical uncertainty. Trust can be calculative, but must inevitably go beyond calculation to a wager on behavioural options that are unknowable. We need to act on information we have, but we know that we don't have all relevant information, so we must allow for unforeseeable contingencies. Lazaric and Lorenz (1998), Vandevelde (2000) and Lindenberg (2000) proposed similar views.

A universal intuition about trust is that it is an expectation concerning the behaviour of others. For example, Sako (1992: 32) defined trust as follows: '. . . a state of mind, an expectation held by one trading partner about another, that the other behaves or responds in a predictable and mutually expected manner'. This connects with Luhmann's (1979) influential analysis of trust as predictability (see Grey and Garsten 2001).

A related universal intuition is that trust entails risk, in the sense of a possibility that expectations will not be met. Actual outcomes may be worse than expected, and possibly disastrous, yielding a negative outcome that is larger than the positive outcome hoped for (Deutsch 1962, 1973, Zand 1972). In trust, one submits to vulnerability to the actions of others (Deutsch 1973). This intuition of trust as an expectation that carries risk has bred the widespread notion of trust as a subjective probability of favourable actions and outcomes (Gambetta 1988, Dasgupta 1988, Mayer et al. 1995, Gulati 1995). There is high trust if this probability is high, and hence perceived risk is low. However, that implies that trust is highest when the probability is unity, so that there is no risk left. But another intuition is that trust entails acceptance of vulnerability or risk, so that if there is no risk, we can no longer speak of trust. How is this puzzle to be resolved? This yields the next question, which will be discussed in Chapter 2:

Question 4: Trust and probability
If trust entails risk, how is this to be understood? Can trust be modelled as a subjective probability? Can trust go together with certainty?

In his early work on transaction costs (1975: 108), Oliver Williamson recognized that 'trust is important and businessmen rely on it much more extensively than is commonly realized', and he paid attention to what he called the 'atmosphere' in which transactions take place. This is striking in view of the fact that Williamson proceeded to neglect trust in his later analysis of transactions (1985), and upon yet later analysis (1993) explicitly rejected it. His argument was that if trust does not go beyond calculative self-interest it does not add anything to existing economic analysis, and calculative trust seems a contradiction in terms. However, if trust does go beyond calculative self-interest, it necessarily yields blind trust, which is unwise and will not survive in markets, and is best limited to personal rela-tions of friendship and family. This yields a crucial challenge to the notion of trust and its use in economics and business, and demands a coherent response.

On the level of societies, Hill (1990) argued the opposite: trustful soci-eties will enjoy lower transaction costs and will therefore have a competi-tive advantage and will survive in the long run. I think both Williamson and Hill are wrong, and I will present my arguments in Chapter 3. As in earlier work (Nooteboom 1996, 1999a, c), I will argue that trust does go beyond calculation as well as self-interest. Nevertheless, the issue thrown up by Williamson is an important one and requires an answer: how can trust be non-calculative without being blind and unconditional? A crucial question arises, which is discussed in Chapter 2, with an elaboration in Chapter 3:

Question 5: Calculative and non-calculative trust
How calculative or rational is trust? When it is not calculative, does this nec-essarily lead to blind, unconditional trust? If not, why not, and how does this work? Can calculative and non-calculative trust be combined? How?

As indicated, trust is difficult to deal with in economics, due to the latter's preoccupation with rational choice, and its neglect of psychological and epistemic obstacles to such choice. That currently provides a problem for economists who now recognize that trust can no longer be neglected, but cannot adequately come to grips with it within their theoretical framework. This is reflected in Williamson's more recent (1996: 261) ruling on trust: 'If calculative relations are best described in calculative terms, then diffuse terms, of which trust is one, that have mixed meanings should be avoided when possible'.

As this book will show, trust is indeed a complex concept, but that does not necessarily make it diffuse in the sense of unclear or imprecise. Trust has several dimensions, and entails a complex of meanings and conditions, but that does not necessarily mean that those meanings are mixed in the sense of confused. Trust does seem diffuse from the diversity of treatments found in the literature. However, the barring of concepts for their being diffuse is inherently conservative, because new theory inevitably starts out with diffuse meanings. It is only later in the development of new theory, and novelty in general, that meanings become clear and practice settles down in a 'dominant design' which is amenable to formalization (Nooteboom 2000a). The proper response to diffuseness of a concept is not to excommu-nicate it but to try and reduce its diffuseness by further developing the concept. That is the purpose of this book. In the game of human relations I would rather not hide trust but seek it.

Williamson seems to suggest that an analysis in calculative terms require simplicity. So much the worse for such analysis, if concepts are inherently complex. The crucial point here is that under radical uncertainty, which is inevitable, relations can be calculative only to a limited extent.

Objects of Trust

Perhaps the most basic point in the analysis of trust is that we should systematically recognize the two-sidedness of trust. We should distinguish trust, on the part of the trustor, and trustworthiness, on the side of the trustee. This distinction is needed especially when we consider the foundations of trust, which splits into the reasons for trustworthiness and the sources of trust. They are related, of course. Rational trust is based on an attribution by the trustor of reasons for trustworthiness to the trustee. However, trust also has other, less rational, sources. I will return to this later.

There is a related question concerning the unit of analysis. Is it a person or a relation? Is trust a feature of a person or of a relationship? As indicated, trust entails a subject, a person who trusts, called the trustor, and an object, something or someone that is trusted, called the trustee. In other words, trust is at least a two-place predicate: the subject has trust in the object. In that sense one can say that the relationship is the unit of analysis. Another argument for that is that trust typically evolves in interaction between people. Trust requires a process approach. Experience from interaction is crucial for trust, as will be analysed in Chapter 3. In Chapter 2 I will argue that trust is in fact a four-place predicate: Someone has trust in something, in some respect and under some conditions.

There is also an important, related issue of levels of analysis. Subjects of trust, or trustors, are agents, which can be people but also corporate agents such as organizations. Objects of trust can be objects or people, but also organizations, institutions and socio-economic systems. There is considerable confusion around this level of analysis issue. Systemic trust is an important concept from the work of Luhmann (1979). A socio-economic system can be both the object and the source of trust. One can have trust in the system, or an organization, and the question emerges how this is related to trust in the people in it. System trust can also be the basis for trust in individuals. The trust that one has in people in an organization will depend on the trust one has in the organization. The reliance on contracts depends on the trust one has in the legal system supporting contracts and litigation: laws, the judiciary, the police, and legal counsel. In other words, we need system trust as part of the basis for personal trust. That does not mean that system trust exhausts the sources of trust. There are also more particularistic sources of trust embedded in specific relations.

Here, we are in fact dealing with the familiar issue, in sociology, of structure and agency. The system provides an institutional basis for action, but is reproduced or changed by that action (Giddens 1984, Archer 1995). Trust in the system affects trust in people and our actions towards them. Conversely, behaviour and experience in specific relations have effects on the trust that one has in a system. Personal and system trust mutually affect each other.

There is also an issue of level in the quite different sense of the stakes involved in trust. Is the risk involved large or small, in terms of potential damage? Does one trust a partner not to cause serious or catastrophic damage, or also not to cause minor damage? Does one trust someone to be benevolent, that is non-opportunistic, and not to cheat, steal or expropriate advantage, or also to dedicate himself scrupulously, and not to be careless? One may be willing to take the second risk but not the first. Note that this is not the same as the conditionality of trust. There the issue is under what conditions we trust someone and take the risk, whatever the potential size of loss may be.

As indicated earlier, under the influence of Luhmann (1979), one tradition is to identify trust with predictability (Grey and Garsten 2001, Maguire et al. 2001). However, to leave it at that leads to misunderstanding. One problem is that it overextends trust. Not all predictability yields trust (it can also yield mistrust). There are other sources of predictability than trustworthiness. A second problem is that it leads to a neglect of different aspects of trust. In particular, it is important to make the distinction between trust in someone's competencies and trust in someone's intentions, that is his willingness to operate to the best of his competence, and to be co-operative rather than opportunistic. This distinction goes back to Parsons (Lane 2000: 4). We can increase predictability by increasing someone's competence by technical training, but that by itself will do nothing for his reliability in the sense of being committed and co-operative. So, neglecting the distinction one may conclude that technical training and increased professionalism support trust. In one sense that is valid, but in another it is very misleading. Another illustration may be given on the level of system trust. When we discuss trust in the legal system, for example, it is also crucial to make clear whether we are discussing competence or intentional trust. Competence trust would entail the training and experience of the judiciary, lack of bureaucratic obstacles, but also guarantees for quality of the litigation process, and equality under the law. Intentional trust would entail lack of corruption. A third problem of Luhmann's functionalist approach of trust as predictability is that it neglects the sources of trust (Lane 2000: 12).

Accepting complexity, the literature in sociology and management offers a kaleidoscopic set of insights in trust: what one sees depends on the twist that one takes. My aim is to systematize this seemingly diffuse constellation of insights, and thereby make the notion of trust more precise and amenable to analytical grip. However, I do not wish to reduce the concept too much, and I wish to maintain its essential richness. I aim to add coherence to the many aspects of trust without reducing it to a simplistic notion.

Most authors try to come to grips with the complexity of trust by offering distinctions between different kinds. Sometimes these distinctions are confusing or even yield category mistakes. Sako (1992, 2000), for example, makes a distinction between the following three kinds of trust: competence, contractual and goodwill trust. In my view, this confuses different categories. A partner's competence contributes to his predictability and to one's reliance on him. However, competence is above all an *object* of trust: something one can have trust in. Does one trust someone to be *able* to conform to expectations? In my view, this can be distinguished from intentional trust, which refers to someone's intentions as the object of trust. Does one trust someone to *intend to use* his ability to conform to expectations? Goodwill trust refers to such intentions. Contractual trust, on the other hand, belongs to the category of the *basis* for trustworthiness and trust. It can apply to competence: one can safeguard competence by contractual means, to some extent. It can also apply to intentions: to a greater or lesser extent one can make contractual safeguards against opportunism.

Summing up, to bring more system in the conceptualization of trust, I propose that in categorizing trust we should distinguish between the following dimensions:

- subjects or trustors: agents that have trust
- objects or things that can be trusted, which include:
    - trustees: trusted things or agents on different levels of people, organizations, institutions and systems
    - aspects of behaviour that form the object of trust: competence, intentions and others
- the limits or conditions of trust
- the stakes involved: size of the potential rewards and damage at stake
- the basis or sources of trustworthiness
- the mental, psychological sources of trust.

This yields a number of distinct questions for analysis. One concerns the objects and aspects of trust, discussed in Chapter 2.

Question 6: Objects and aspects of trust
What can we have trust in? Things, people, institutions, organizations? What are the relations between these different levels of trust? What are the aspects of trust: competence, intentions, and what else?

Foundations of Trust

Let me turn to the foundations of trust. An important area of debate concerns the relation between trust and control: are they substitutes or complements, or both (see the special issue of *Organization Studies*: volume 22, 2001, issue 2, and Klein Woolthuis et al. 2001).

Is trust based on the trustor controlling the trustee by means of contractual safeguards, the taking of hostages, power by making the trustee dependent, and reputation? The corresponding enforcement mechanisms are monitoring and threat of litigation, injury of hostages, exit, and gossip or slander? Here, control is based on rewards, incentives, punishments, in short 'deterrence' (Maguire et al. 2001). Many authors feel that such control is foreign to the notion of trust, and that 'genuine' trust is based on other, more social and personal foundations of trustworthiness, such as loyalty, empathy, friendship, reciprocity, a sense of moral duty or obligation, and routinized behaviour.

This is the issue that was already raised before, and led to Question 5: does trust go beyond calculative self-interest? The notion of trust in everyday language seems to suggest that trust goes beyond contractual obligation and profit, or at least immediate profit, and refers to expected cooperation even when it is not specified in a contract, and even when it may require a sacrifice from the partner. Therefore, trust has been defined as the expectation that a partner will not engage in opportunistic behaviour, even in the face of countervailing short-term incentives (Bradach and Eccles 1984, Chiles and McMackin 1996). This issue is discussed in Chapter 3, where I will make a distinction between 'reliance', assurance and trust (in the strong sense). Reliance is a broad term including all bases of expectations. Assurance is based on the trustee's self-interest. Trust in the strong sense goes beyond calculative self-interest, and is based on social norms or values of behaviour, personal affect and routinized behaviour. This will be discussed in Chapters 2 and 3.

If we make this distinction between assurance and trust (in the strong sense), the question still arises whether the two are substitutes or complements. Arguments for the thesis of substitutes would be the following:

- We need less (more) control when there is more (less) trust (in the strong sense).
- An attitude of control is destructive of the basis for trust.

Arguments for the thesis of complements are the following:

- Since contracts can never be complete, and monitoring can never be perfect, we need trust 'to fill the holes', so to speak.

- Since blind, unconditional trust is unwise, under some conditions we may need to revert to control.
- In the process of trust building, we need a certain amount of control, as a basis for reliance, before we hazard into trust in the strong sense.
- We need prior trust before we engage in the costs and hazards of contracting.
- Contracts can yield the clarity of expectations concerning obligations and rights needed to develop trust.

All these propositions have been offered in the literature. I will argue that they are all valid, depending on the conditions, and I will therefore conclude that trust and control are both complements and substitutes (Klein Woolthuis et al. 2001).

Many authors make a distinction between one or more of the following categories: calculus-based, knowledge-based, cognition-based, affect-based and identification-based trust (Macaulay 1963, Zucker 1986, Shapiro 1987, Helper 1990, Larson 1992, Parkhe 1993, Gulati 1995, Zaheer and Venkatraman 1995, McAllister 1995). An important question is how trust develops where there was none before (Sako 2000). According to the influential view of Lewicki and Bunker (1996), adopted by many other authors (Maguire et al. 2001, Das and Teng 2001, Child 2001), trust develops in stages of calculus-based, knowledge-based and identification-based trust.

Here it is especially important to distinguish between trust on the part of the trustor and trustworthiness on the part of the trustee. For trust there are rational reasons and psychological causes. Reasons arise from a rational assessment of the trustee's trustworthiness, based on knowledge of him inferred from reputation, records, established norms and standards, or one's own experience. A psychological cause is empathy, which means that one can identify with someone and thereby understand motives in relation to conditions of action, and can sympathize with them. Here, intrinsic and extrinsic value of a relation become mixed.

Rationality and emotion are not so distinct, however. Rational reasons for trust, based on inferences, entail attributions of competence or motives to the trustee. Those attributions are based on psychological mechanisms that may partly be instinctive, are affected by previous experience, entail prejudice and are mixed with emotion. This is discussed in Chapter 3.

Now, there is confusion, even in the recent literature, concerning knowledge-based and cognition-based trust. Are they the same, as Child (2001), for example, seemed to suggest? Knowledge inferred from observed behaviour of the trustee, or from his reputation, or other outside sources, is the basis for control or for an assessment of the trustee's trustworthiness. Cognition-based trust most often refers to shared cognitive structures, which yield empathy. If that is what it means, how different is cognition-based trust from identification-based trust? As partners interact over a prolonged period of time, they develop shared cognitive, mental structures, by which they come to develop shared perceptions, interpretations and evaluations. In other words: cognitive distance between them is reduced. This can develop into empathy, or identification, or even friendship as a basis for trust (in the strong sense). This is my understanding of identification-based trust.

What remains problematic in the three-stage model of trust development is that calculation-based trust is said to precede knowledge-based trust. Here, 'calculation-based trust' can mean that trustworthiness is based only on calculative self-interest, and that the trustor knows that this is the case. Then, calculation-based trust entails the use of rewards and punishments (Maguire et al. 2001: 303). Alternatively, it could mean trust that is based on a rational assessment ('calculation') of a partner's trustworthiness. Perhaps both meanings are intended. But both require knowledge, either from monitoring to decide on the meting out of reward or punishment, or to assess trustworthiness. How then can knowledge-based trust constitute a separate, subsequent stage? Calculation requires knowledge.

So, perhaps the three stages proposed by Lewicki and Bunker collapse into two stages. In the first, in the absence of a basis for trust (in the strong sense) one must take into account that calculative self-interest may prevail. One needs a limitation of risk, with some measure of control as the basis for assurance. This is essentially what was proposed by classical transaction cost economics as propounded by Williamson. However, Williamson does not recognize any subsequent process of the emergence of trust. In fact, in his early work (Williamson 1975) he recognized notions of the 'atmosphere' of a relation, 'idiosyncratic cognition' in a relation, and 'cognitive spill-overs' between the partners. However, these ideas remained embryonic and were not applied or developed in his later work. As a relationship develops, there may be a convergence of cognition, with a mutual understanding and appreciation of competencies and motives, and an emergence of shared norms, which may yield empathy and identification as a basis for trust. Trust may develop like this, but I do not accept that this is always how trust develops. There are alternative processes and sequences of stages. I return to that in Chapter 3. There, I will also give a re-interpretation of Lewicki and Bunker's three-stage model of trust development.

Question 7: The basis of trustworthiness
On what is trustworthiness of people based? Coercion, self-interest, ethics, friendship, routinization? Does it go beyond self-interest? If it does, can it survive in markets?

Question 8: The mental basis of trust
On what is trust based: knowledge, experience, analysis, emotions, habits,
faith?

As indicated, the mental basis of trust includes reasons, in a rational assessment of trustworthiness (in 'knowledge-based trust'), and psychological
mechanisms that can yield serious errors. Nevertheless, they cannot be
called irrational, and can indeed be shown to have adaptive value, contributing to survival in the face of uncertainty. Rational assessment entails an
evaluation and attribution of a trustee's capabilities, goals, motives, inclinations, and opportunities for actions. This depends on conditions such as
the observability of actions and accomplishments, competitive pressure,
viability and efficiency of contracts, social conditions, personal ties, presence and efficiency of reputation mechanisms, and so on. It can be based
on knowledge obtained from others (as in a reputation mechanism), or on
one's own experience. Affect-based trust includes feelings of friendship or
empathy. The mental basis of trust can include delusions and routinized
behaviour. One may neglect the possibility of things going wrong, due to
blind faith. One may not be aware of the possibility of things going wrong,
due to habit or routine. There are psychological mechanisms involved in
motivation, attribution, empathy, cognitive dissonance and many related
decision heuristics involved in the assessment of probability and causality.
These are discussed in Chapter 3.

Trust typically operates as a default: trustworthiness is often taken for
granted until violated. In routinized behaviour, certain actions in certain
contexts never went wrong, and we lose awareness of the possibility
(Parkhe 1993, Gulati 1995, Nooteboom et al. 1997). In all these cases, of
cognition, affect, routines and heuristics, trust is based on processes of
interaction. Note that interaction has wider consequences than offering
experience and insight in someone's trustworthiness. It affects perceived
goals, norms, values and feelings of friendship, empathy, loyalty, rivalry
and animosity on the part of both trustor and trustee. Therefore, we need
to understand the dynamics of the building and breakdown of trust, in processes of interaction. This is also discussed in Chapter 3.

Question 9: The process of trust
How does the mental basis of trust develop in processes of interaction, and
how does it shape that process? How does the mutual shaping work of trust,
process and trustworthiness?

When the foregoing questions have been answered, and hopefully more
conceptual clarity and coherence have been achieved, the question arises

how we can proceed to empirical tests and more formal models. For empirical tests we need to operationalize a number of concepts so that they can be taken up in interviews, surveys or other forms of systematic observation.

I indicated that trust cannot be modelled as a subjective probability. Is there an alternative model and formalization? Can we model the process of trust? These questions are addressed in Chapter 6.

Question 10: Testing and modelling trust
Can trust be empirically measured and tested? Can it be formalized and subjected to logical or mathematical analysis?

Questions

Table 1.1 collects the questions to be answered in this book, with reference to the corresponding chapters.

Chapter 2 discusses the forms of trust. It addresses the question how we can define trust. Is it a form of behaviour, or a motivation or disposition underlying behaviour? What is its relation to risk, and to subjective probability attached to behaviour of others? Is it calculative, intuitive, or habitual, or all of those? If it goes beyond calculation, or falls short of it, is it then necessarily blind, unconditional and irrational? What is its relation to information, knowledge and experience? The chapter also discusses the possible objects of trust: what can one have trust in? What are the aspects of trust: competence, intentions, and what else? What is the difference between trust and related concepts, of faith, reliance, assurance and confidence? What is the relation between trust in people and trust in organizations?

Chapter 3 discusses the foundations of trust. What are the rational reasons for trust, that is what are the sources of trustworthiness and how can they be assessed? Are the only reliable foundations of trust coercion and other forms of self-interest, or are there also reliable altruistic sources? How does one infer trustworthiness from observed behaviour? What is the psychological basis of trust? How, in what processes, is trust built up and destroyed?

Chapter 4 discusses the economic functions of trust, This yields an elaboration of the economic value of trust, as a means for enabling productive relations and for reducing transaction costs. The chapter summarizes and extends earlier work on the place of trust in the governance of inter-firm relations (Nooteboom 1999a). The central question is what instruments there are for the governance of relations, and whether and how trust fits in. More specific questions are the following. Can trust yield a substitute for other, more costly instruments for the governance of relations, such as contracts? Or does trust form a necessary complement to contracts? Or is trust

Table 1.1   Questions

Questions	Chapters
1: Value of trust What are the value dimensions of trust: intrinsic and extrinsic value, self- and other oriented value, and how are they related?	2: Forms, and 3: Foundations
2: Economic function of trust What is the extrinsic, economic value of trust? How does it work? What are the effects? What are the institutional conditions?	4: Functions
3: Failures of trust How can trust go wrong? What are its possible adverse effects? What are the limitations and boundaries of trust?	5: Failures
4: Trust and probability. If trust entails risk, how is this to be understood? Can trust be modelled as a subjective probability? Can trust go together with certainty?	2: Forms
5: Calculative and non-calculative trust How calculative or rational is trust? When it is not calculative, does this necessarily lead to blind, unconditional trust? If not, why not, and how does this work? Can calculative and non-calculative trust be combined? How?	2: Forms
6: Objects and aspects of trust What can we have trust in? Things, people, institutions, organizations? What are the aspects of trust: competence, intentions, and what else?	2: Forms
7: The sources of trustworthiness On what is trustworthiness of people based? Coercion, self-interest, ethics, friendship, routinization? Does it go beyond self-interest? If it does, can it survive in markets?	2: Forms 3: Foundations
8: The mental basis of trust On what is trust based, and how: knowledge, experience, analysis, emotions, habits, faith?	3: Foundations
9: The process of trust How does the mental basis of trust develop in processes of interaction, and how does it shape that process? How does the mutual shaping work of trust, process and trustworthiness?	3: Foundations
10: Testing and modelling trust Can trust be empirically measured and tested? Can it be formalized and subjected to logical or mathematical analysis?	6: Figures

both a substitute and a complement for contract? How does trust relate to other instruments, such as the use of hostages, symmetry of dependence, reputation mechanisms, the use of third parties or network position? What are relevant institutional conditions for trust? This yields a discussion of different types of institutional systems, and their implications for inter-organizational relations and innovation.

Chapter 5 discusses the failures of trust. When can trust be deceptive? To what extent can we trust trust? What are its limits? What is the pathology of trust; when is trust ill founded? When does trust become counterproductive? What are the implications? Trust may be seen as part of 'social capital' (Powell 1990). But social capital may degenerate into social liability (Gabbay and Leenders 1999).

Chapter 6 discusses the 'figures' of trust. How can we measure it? How can we test its effects, in empirical research? How can we model the process of making and breaking trust under conditions of uncertainty? How can we deal with the limits of trust? Can trust survive under competition? Here, use will be made of earlier work of myself and associates (Nooteboom et al. 1997, Klein Woolthuis 1999, de Jong and Nooteboom 2000, Six 2001). This also includes a recent application of the methodology of 'Agent Based Computational Economics' (ACE) for the simulation of the making and breaking of trust (Klos 2000, Klos and Nooteboom 2001).

Chapter 7 summarizes conclusions and gives directions for further research.

1.2   THEORETICAL FOUNDATIONS

This second part of Chapter 1 discusses some of the theoretical foundations for the analysis of trust. I noted before that I would use elements from trans-action cost economics, while taking into account the fundamental criticism that has been raised against that theory. This criticism concerns the way in which transaction cost theory deals, or fails to deal, with time, uncertainty and learning. It also concerns the idea that transaction costs are only obsta-cles, or constraints, while in fact they also enable action. Also, we need a theory of knowledge, for several reasons. One is to mend the shortcomings of transaction cost economics. A second is that knowledge and learning have implications for the importance, the basis and the functioning of trust. Is reality inaccessible, or can we meaningfully talk of underlying reality? Are people driven by objective conditions or by their subjective constructions of reality, if that is not a contradiction in terms? An analysis of trust also requires a basis in (social) psychology. The theory of knowledge has impli-cations for the theory of the firm, and for the relation between trust in people and trust in organizations. A simple definition of trust is that it is an expectation that things or people will not fail us. This leaves open a wide range of forms of trust, corresponding with the possible causes of failure. There are as many forms of trust as there are causes of behaviour. To analyse this, we need a conceptualization of the causality of action. We will have to deal with trust not only in people but also in organizations and institutions. Institutions are both object and a basis of trust. To analyse that we need to clarify the notion of institutions.

Transaction Cost Economics, Time and Learning

I assume that transaction cost economics is known. One objection to the theory, raised by many, is precisely that it neglects trust in its assumption that in the 'governance' of relations we need to safeguard against opportunistic behaviour. I do not wish to neglect the possibility of opportunism, but I do wish to recognize that next to the possibility of opportunism there is also the possibility of trustworthiness, and that neither should be neglected. Transaction cost economics does not claim that everyone is opportunistic, but that one cannot reliably assess the degree of opportunism so that the possibility of opportunism should be taken into account.

As I argued before (Nooteboom 1996, 1999a), and as has also been argued by Lindenberg (2000), there is a peculiar inconsistency in the way in which classical (Williamsonian) transaction cost economics deals with time, uncertainty and bounded rationality. Williamson claims that his theory is inter-temporal, incorporates the passage of time, and indeed he claims that this is *central* to TCE (1999: 1101). And indeed, up to a point his theory does incorporate intertemporality. It makes a distinction between ex ante considerations, before commitment of transaction specific investments, en ex post considerations, after their commitment. This yields the 'fundamental transformation' from a large to a small number of potential partners. The theory also is intertemporal in the sense of taking uncertainty concerning future contingencies into account. However, TCE is not consistent in this. Williamson (1999: 1101) does claim that: 'governance structures are predominantly instruments for adaptation, it being the case that adaptation . . . is the central problem of economic organization; organization has an inter-temporal life of its own'. He admits, however, that this 'is not to say that it [TCE] has worked all of these out in a satisfactory way. I entirely agree that transaction cost economics stands to benefit from more fully dynamic constructions. But whereas saying dynamics is easy, doing dynamics is hard.' This is quite an admission, after saying that inter-temporality is central to TCE. What is said here is that what is central is not well developed. I propose that nowadays innovation and learning are crucial, and should be in the core of theory.

Let me return to the issue of assessing trustworthiness. Williamson (1985: 59) argued as follows:

> Inasmuch as a great deal of the relevant information about trustworthiness or its absence that is generated during the course of bilateral trading is essentially private information – in that it cannot be fully communicated to and shared with others (Williamson 1975: 31–7) – knowledge about behavioural uncertainties is very uneven.

This may be so. But the argument yields insufficient reason to ignore trust. Why should it be easy to incorporate trust? Even if it is difficult, disregarding it may be worse. As the transaction relation unfolds in time, couldn't one accumulate more or less reliable information about trustworthiness? The sociological literature gives extensive instructions how to infer intentional trustworthiness from observed behaviour (Deutsch 1973). Did the partner act not only according to the letter but also to the spirit of the agreement? Did he give timely warnings about unforeseen changes or problems? Was he open about relevant contingencies, and truthful about his dealings with others that might constitute a threat to one? Did he defect to more attractive alternatives at the earliest opportunity? Or to use Hirschman's (1970) notions of 'voice' and 'exit': how much voice rather than exit did he exhibit? I return to this in Chapter 3.

When Williamson argues for the assumption of opportunism, as a basis for governance, he does not seem to be aware of the price one pays for that. It leads to possibly costly contracting. What is worse, a detailed contract and close monitoring might seriously constrain the freedom and open-endedness of action that is crucial especially when the collaboration is aimed at innovation. And perhaps worse than that, an expression of distrust, based on the assumption of opportunism, is likely to destroy the basis for building up trust as the relation unfolds. There is much evidence in the trust literature that distrust breeds distrust and may even elicit opportunism. Then the assumption of opportunism may become self-fulfilling, with considerable costs of contracting and loss of perspective for a fruitful relationship.

The point here is that if we really appreciate the time dimension, in the development of a transaction relation, then we have to analyse how trustworthiness or opportunism evolves in time and how their extent may be observed or inferred. Furthermore, I will argue later that if one takes intertemporality seriously, there are compelling reasons to see the transaction *relation* as the unit of analysis, rather than transactions, as TCE proposes.

As recognized by many, transaction cost economics neglects innovation and learning. It does so by Williamson's own admission (1985: 144–145).

That neglect is unacceptable at a time when innovation and learning seem to form the very core of what is going on in economies, markets and organizations. To accommodate this, I need a theory of knowledge. That is not the focus of this book, but I will summarize the theory in a following section. It is important to take a dynamic view, including innovation and learning, because there trust is especially important, due to the importance of uncertainty in innovation, and the resulting limitations of contracts in the governance of relations.

Williamson's excuse for not taking a dynamic process approach is that it is easier said than done. That is true. The main attraction of economic analysis of equilibrium outcomes is that it is analytically tractable and relatively simple. However, it is possible to analyse how trust emerges or is broken down, on the basis of experiences in processes of interaction. Here, it is not only a matter of assessing the degree of opportunism, as if that were a stable entity. Opportunism and trustworthiness are themselves subject to change as a function of how a relationship develops, in what Zucker (1986) called 'process-based trust'. This is discussed in Chapter 3.

For a dynamic process analysis one may have to resort to complex computer simulation models, and those have problems of their own, such as, notably, problems of complexity and problems of verification. However, problems of complexity and tractability have been considerably reduced by the development of computers and software. A whole new branch of economics has developed, called 'Agent Based Computational Economics' (ACE). This methodology is currently being used to model the evolution of collaborative or transactional relations, including the building and breakdown of trust, in what is called 'Agent Based Computational Transaction Cost Economics' (ACTCE, see Klos 2000 and Klos and Nooteboom 2001). This is discussed in Chapter 6.

Bounded Rationality

Another fundamental point of criticism against classical transaction cost theory, related to the issue of time, concerns its treatment of bounded rationality and uncertainty. Even in recent work, Williamson (1999) maintains that he fully accepts bounded rationality: there is fundamental uncertainty concerning future contingencies. However, he claims that there is foresight: one can take such uncertainty into account, infer the hazards that follow from it and conduct governance accordingly (in a 'discriminating alignment') and 'efficiently', that is in an optimal fashion (to yield an 'economizing result'). We are not myopic, Williamson claims: we are not so stupid as not to take uncertainties into account when we design governance. And indeed, we can to some extent take risks and uncertainty into account.

Firms can spread risks by participating in different markets, in the same way that investors can spread risks in a portfolio of investments. Beyond that, to deal with real or radical uncertainty we can construct scenarios of possible futures, prepare contingency plans for them, and identify the robustness of strategies across different scenarios.

However, the question of course is what the implications of bounded rationality are for the correct identification of relevant hazards. Doesn't bounded rationality imply that we might be mistaken about them? Williamson (1999: 1103) admits that TCE 'makes only limited contact with the subject of learning', and indicates that we may be mistaken about hazards and may learn about them as events unfold (1999: 1104). And apart from hazards I add the question: how about new options? In spite of great imagination and ingenuity, the scenarios we invented may not include what actually arises. And how about shifts in our preferences? Is it reasonable to assume learning without shifts in preferences? And if new insights in hazards arise, new scenarios, or new options or goals, are we then able to shift from the governance structure engaged upon to an adapted, optimal form? That would always be possible only if there is no path-dependence or lock-in in governance, and that is a strong claim to make. Can one consistently accept, on the one hand, lock-in as a fundamental principle, raising the problem of hold-up, and yet assume perfect flexibility to shift to novel governance as new insights in contingencies arise?

This issue is related to the issue of 'efficient', optimal outcomes. Williamson claims that efficient outcomes are achieved because 'dysfunctional consequences and other long run propensities will not be mindlessly repeated or ignored' (Williamson 1999: 1105). But this begs a number of questions. It implies that dysfunctionality and long-run propensities are stable, so that experience in the past is indicative of the future, and it implies that we know which are stable and which are not. How can we know that? And if we did know, how can one be sure that the firm survives to implement the lesson in time?

Perhaps Williamson is falling back on the notion of selection: 'the market' will select inefficient forms of organization out? That is the usual assumption behind the economist's assumption of efficient outcomes, going back to Alchian (1950). I note that if Williamson's argument is indeed evolutionary, he is deviating from the perspective of the firm strategist, who is talking about the survival of the firm.

As noted by Chiles and McMackin (1996), there are two perspectives in transaction cost economics. The first is the long-term evolutionary perspective, where objective transaction costs determine the survival of the fittest governance forms. The second is a short-term managerial choice perspective, where managers act on subjective costs that are based on varying perceptions

and evaluations of risk. The latter explains why firms in similar circumstances may make different trade-offs in their make-or-buy decision.

The selection argument was already shown to be weak by Winter (1964).
In selection it is not the best possible but the best available in the population that survives. In the presence of economy of scale inefficient large firms
may push out efficient small firms, and in this way inefficiency may survive.
Furthermore, the argument assumes efficient selection, but that cannot be
taken for granted in view of possible monopolies, entry barriers and transaction costs.

The truth of the matter is, I propose, that being an economist Williamson
is almost instinctively tied to the notion of efficiency and optimal outcomes: he finds it difficult to theorize otherwise.

Enabling Constraints

Another objection to transaction cost economics concerns the idea, present
in transaction cost thinking from the beginning, in the work of Coase
(1937), that one could have transactions without costs, and that transaction
costs result from obstacles or 'frictions' in markets. In fact, transaction
costs often result from the enabling of transactions. Without such costs a
transaction would not have been possible under any form of governance,
whether market or organization (Campbell and Harris 1993). Relations
require social and cognitive capital, and that carries costs. This point comes
up most clearly when we do incorporate issues of knowledge and learning.
If for a transaction one needs to make oneself understood concerning the
product one has to offer, or the capabilities that one could contribute to the
relation, and to absorb knowledge from the partner, this carries a cost, but
it also enables the relation. Without that cost the relation would not be
fruitful. Building mutual understanding and trust costs time and carries a
cost, but enables relations that would not otherwise be possible. A similar
oddity arises in the view one often encounters that institutions constrain
behaviour, while in fact they also enable it.

Nevertheless, enablers also carry costs, so that it still makes sense to talk
about the minimization of transaction costs, or the costs of institutions, not
by eliminating the facilitators of transactions but seeking ones that are
effective and yet carry low costs. For an example, consider the transfer of
knowledge. Transfer of knowledge is particularly difficult, time consuming
and costly when the knowledge is tacit, that is not codified and documented
in a formula, blueprint, algorithm or standard operating procedure.
Therefore there is a premium on trying to document it, and thereby reduce
transaction costs, while preserving the value of the knowledge. The question then is whether it is possible to codify tacit knowledge without loss,

and if not, what the trade-off is between loss of knowledge and ease of transmission.

However, in spite of all the fundamental criticism of transaction cost economics, it still contains elements that are useful. As indicated, it still makes sense to talk of transaction costs. Also useful is the notion that relations may require investments that are specific for a relationship, thereby create switching costs, and hence create dependence, with a resulting risk of 'hold-up', which requires attention in the governance of relations. While the theory neglects trust, it does yield insights in possible instruments of governance, next to contracts, such as a balance of mutual dependence, the use of hostages, and the use of third parties in 'trilateral governance' (none of these, however, was particularly new). Also still valid is the consideration that integration in an organization may help to solve problems of dependence. Even though there are problems of asymmetric information, motivation and control also under 'hierarchy', as Williamson recognized, the opportunities for demanding information and imposing a settlement of conflict still exceed those one would have with regard to an independent outside organization. Ultimately, such demands can only be enforced in front of a judge, while within a firm there is much more scope for decision by administrative fiat, under the employment relationship.

Knowledge and Cognitive Distance

Now I turn to the theory of knowledge that I employ. It is a truism to say that information is not the same as knowledge: to become knowledge, information needs to be interpreted in a cognitive framework. I employ a theory of knowledge and language derived from 'symbolic interactionism' in sociology (G.H. Mead), and the view, taken from cognitive psychology, that intelligence is internalized action (Piaget, Vygotsky). In contrast with the dominant 'computational representational' view in cognitive science, this leads to the view of knowledge in terms of 'situated action'. This view is sometimes called 'activity theory'. Knowledge and the meaning of words are not independent from context. They lie partly in the context of use, and they shift from one context to another. For a more detailed analysis, see Nooteboom (2000a).

I take 'cognition' in a wide sense, including perception, interpretation and evaluation, hence including value judgements. In this view, emotions and intellect are connected. The Cartesian separation of mind and body is dropped (Damasio 1995). Thus cognition, in the sense used in this book, includes reasoning, emotion, motivation and motor control (compare Tooby and Cosmides 1992: 65).

The theory states that cognition takes place on the basis of mental categories that are partly developed in interaction with one's physical and social environment. To the extent that interaction between people is sustained and intensive, it will yield shared or similar mental categories (or 'models' or 'schemata'). Such similarity yields a basis for mutual understanding and identification, which can yield empathy. Those categories constitute our absorptive capacity (Cohen and Levinthal 1990), that is our ability to perceive, interpret and evaluate phenomena. Perception, in the transition from data to information, requires assimilation into existing cognitive schemata. We cannot absorb what we cannot assimilate. The obstacle can also be that we do not want to absorb it, due to cognitive dissonance. Interpretation, in the transformation of information into knowledge, entails integration with existing knowledge. This may yield novel combinations (associations) that may yield new insight into logical or causal relations. Those provide the basis for evaluation of utility or value, on the basis of means–goal relations.

This process precludes objective knowledge (or at least any certain knowledge whether or to what extent knowledge is objective). We form perceptions, interpretations and evaluations according to cognitive, or mental categories.

This is called the 'constructivist', 'interpretative' or 'hermeneutic view'. It has important implications for how we conduct research of behaviour of people and firms. Much research uses objective conditions, such as market conditions, technology, events, and the like as direct antecedents or causes of behaviour and its outcomes. We should remain aware that such causality is at best intermediated and at worst seriously distorted in interpretations of those conditions, events and communications by the relevant actors (Noorderhaven 2001). This is particularly important in trust processes. It is not what happens in relations so much as how that is interpreted, and how people infer and attribute competencies and motives to people that matters, in the formation or destruction of trust.

Since our absorptive capacity is to some extent constructed in interaction with our environment, it is to some extent context- and path-dependent. However, this view does not necessarily entail the radical relativism or subjectivism that is exhibited by some post-modern authors. If we construct knowledge from interaction with our environment, this entails that reality is at least a material cause of our knowledge: our knowledge is 'embodied realism' (Lakoff and Johnson 1999). Here, I assume that the environment does exist, which is a reasonable assumption, even though we cannot pretend to know it as it is in itself. Also, to the extent that we share the environment in which our knowledge develops, there will be similarities of cognition, which yields a basis for inter-subjective debate. Since we share the physical environment (including laws of physics) to a greater extent than we share our cultural environment, knowledge constructed from the former is likely to be more common than knowledge constructed from the latter.[1]

The reverse of this coin is, of course, that to the extent that people have developed their knowledge in different environments, and have not been in communication with each other, cognition will differ: there will be greater or lesser 'cognitive distance' (Nooteboom 1992, 1999a). I do not wish to imply that cognition is any simple, one-dimensional construct that allows for simple measurement of distance. In Nooteboom (2000a) I elaborate on cognitive distance in terms of overlap of, and mappings between, different sets of cognitive constructs.

My thesis that cognitive or mental categories develop in interaction with the physical and social environment does not entail the claim that at birth the mind is a 'tabula rasa', without any innate mental structures. Evolutionary psychologists claim that certain psychological features or mechanisms are 'in our genes' as a result of evolution (Barkow et al. 1992). They emerged as features that gave selective or reproductive advantage, over the millions of years that the human species evolved in hunter-gatherer societies. These yield a shared heritage, in the form of common basic psychological and cognitive mechanisms. These are plausible to the extent that they were conducive to survival and procreation in ancient times. For example, survival required the basic ability to identify objects and movement, to categorize natural kinds (plants, animals), distinguish the animate from the inanimate and natural kinds from artefacts (Tooby and Cosmides 1992: 71). On top of that it requires the ability to recognize objects, judge speed and distance, to avoid predators and to catch prey (Tooby and Cosmides 1992: 110). Survival also requires mother-infant emotion communication signals (Tooby and Cosmides 1992: 39). Reproduction is related to the choice of mates, sexual jealousy, seduction, incest taboo and fidelity.

Of crucial importance, especially in the present book, is the thesis that survival in hunter–gatherer societies was also furthered by sociality. In gathering edible plants, roots, nuts, and so on, and even more in hunting, there is a large variance of yields. This, together with problems of durable storage, entails an evolutionary advantage of the willingness to surrender part of one's yield to others in need, in the expectation to receive from them when they are successful (Cosmides and Tooby 1992: 212). This is enhanced by the ability to assess such willingness among others, to signal a credible threat to sanction cheating, and a mechanism for detecting cheating. As explained by Frank (1988), an emotionally based commitment towards retaliation or revenge, and the ability to signal this, would help to make

---

[1] This view is similar to that of 'critical realism' (Lawson 1977, Archer 1995, Reed 2001).

such threats credible when revenge would carry a cost that is disproportional to its economic gain and would hence be implausible on the basis or rational choice. It also entails an ability to 'read' facial expressions of emotion (Tooby and Cosmides 1992: 70), and to attribute, with some validity, motives to people on the basis of observed behaviour and verbal and other expression. All this may yield an evolutionary basis for social reciprocity and trust. Of course, if this evolutionary argument is true, we also have to take the bad with the good: the adverse effects of a drive towards emotion-laden retaliation or revenge.

However, less basic, higher level cognitive categories of perception, interpretation and evaluation have to be geared to a world that is unrecognizably different from ancient hunter–gatherer societies. This requires a plasticity in the formation of cognitive structures, tacked on to deeper level ones derived from evolution, that are apt for the world one is in. In fact, this is based on an evolutionary argument as well: without such plasticity we would not have been able to evolve as we have. In other words, while underlying cognitive abilities, urges and inclinations may be instinctive, inherited from a shared evolution, the superstructure of cognitive categories is developed in interaction with one's current, more individual environment. Nevertheless, it is possible that our species will succumb to an inability to escape from our instincts.

Cognitive distance yields both an opportunity and a problem. The opportunity is that contact with others gives us a possibility to escape from the myopia of our personal cognitive construction, by profiting from the different insights of others, based on different experience. This may still yield a house of cards, but that stands better and reaches higher than a single card. A problem, however, is that the greater the cognitive distance, the more difficult it is to cross it, that is to understand the actions and expressions of a partner. Thus there is an optimal cognitive distance: large enough for partners to tell each other something new, and small enough for comprehension. Absorptive capacity is part of our ability to cross cognitive distance. The other part is communicative capacity, or the ability to help others understand what we do or say. Note that there is a difference between crossing cognitive distance and reducing it. For an elaboration see Nooteboom (2000a). An implication for relations is that investment in absorptive or communicative capacity can be relation-specific and can thereby entail dependence on a relation in order to recoup the investment, along the lines argued in transaction cost economics.

Mental categories or schemata are more or less tacit. This applies, for example, to pattern recognition. That arises in many areas, such as shapes of objects or drawings, physiognomy, practices, conditions and motives of behaviour. In discussions of tacit knowledge there is a tendency to see tacit and codified knowledge as substitutes, as when tacit knowledge is 'externalized' (Nonaka and Takeuchi 1995) into codified knowledge. However, there is also complementarity: underlying, tacit categories are needed to interpret information (externalized knowledge) transmitted in communication. People properly understand each other only if they sufficiently share underlying categories. When those are tacit and incongruent, there is a problem. They may then first have to develop shared categories, by interaction in a 'community of practice' (Brown and Duguid 1996), to establish what Lissoni (2001) called an 'epistemic community'. Alternatively, it may be possible to make implicit, tacit categories explicit, but those, in turn, would need to be interpreted on the basis of underlying categories. At some level, the preconditions for cognition are inevitably tacit: one must take basic notions and meanings in language for granted; one cannot go on defining the terms of a definition. To some limited extent it is possible to make one's tacit categories explicit, but this is not always possible or easy.

There is a difference between declarative and procedural memory (Cohen and Bacdayan 1996). The first has a locational identification in the brain: it can be 'declared' (as one has to do in the basic coding for a computer programme) and retrieved. It typically relates to information on identity, abstractions and formal explanation, disembedded from specific context. Procedural memory, on the other hand, has more to do with practical know-how, relational knowledge of how to combine elements of knowledge in practical procedures. This latter knowledge is more embedded in practice and specific conditions of application. Procedural knowledge tends to be more tacit. For codification it needs to be disembedded from practical procedure, which can be difficult, and entails a loss in abstraction. That is why sharing it may require interaction in a community of practice.

Procedural knowledge may derive from declarative knowledge, as when formal training is applied in practice and then develops into a routine. This generally entails that to yield procedural knowledge, declarative knowledge is embedded in a specific context of use. That is how one may first learn a language on the basis of formal grammar, then apply it, and after a while be able to identify proper and faulty constructions, without any longer being able to specify why, on the basis of what grammatical rules. In this way, knowledge that was once explicit can develop into tacit, routinized knowledge. Practical knowledge does not have to develop in this way. Procedural knowledge may be transferred, by socialization in a community of practice, without first having been formalized into codified knowledge. This is what happens in a master–apprentice relation, and in the learning of one's mother tongue.

In knowledge transfer, a widely recognized problem is that it may be difficult to externalize tacit knowledge. There is a second problem that has not yet been widely recognized. On the end of the receiver tacit knowledge can also create a problem, as follows. Tacit knowledge is taken for granted because it is tacit. It is hard to criticize something that one is not aware of. Thus, tacit knowledge may create an obstacle for the adoption of new technology. To eliminate this, one may first have to make the tacit procedures and underlying assumptions explicit.

> There is less need to formalize and externalize tacit, procedural knowledge in a smaller firm than in a large one. In a small firm, with a team of people in direct contact on a shop floor, there can be coordination by direct supervision (Mintzberg 1983). In a large firm, aimed at economies of scale by specialization, formalization is needed to co-ordinate over larger spatial and organizational distance, by the specification of work processes or skills. This yields advantages and disadvantages for the smaller firm. An advantage is that the lesser degree of bureaucratic regulation allows for greater flexibility, for adapting the product to idiosyncratic demand. A disadvantage is that tacit, undocumented knowledge is vulnerable to loss. If the carrier has an accident or leaves the firm, the knowledge may be lost. A second disadvantage follows from the obstacle to absorption due to unreflective practices and assumptions indicated above. These phenomena explain why it can be difficult or costly to transfer new technology to small firms: there are firm size effects in transaction costs (Nooteboom 1993, 2001).

Next to cognitive considerations in the narrow sense, there are also more emotion-laden considerations from (social) psychology. We infer causes of behaviour and we attribute characteristics and motives to people according to mental categories or schemata. We can identify with people, and have empathy with them, to the extent that there is similarity of such behavioural schemata. Empathy is highly relevant for trust, because it helps us to attribute motives, sympathize with them and perhaps tolerate deviations from expectations. We entertain more or less tacit categories of justice, and trust depends on the extent that others share them. Absorptive capacity may be limited by cognitive dissonance: we may subconsciously resist information that is in conflict with established and cherished views or convictions, particularly if it would require an admission of mistaken choices in the past. Past acts have to be justified to oneself and to others, even at the cost of distorting facts or construing artificial arguments. Deutsch (1973: 357) quoted Festinger as saying that: 'Rats and people come to love things for which they have suffered . . . [they] enhance the attractiveness of the choice that led to the suffering'. For an example, Deutsch pointed to the American involvement in Vietnam. The heavier the casualties, the more the importance of being there had to be inflated. As shown by Deutsch, social-psychological considerations are particularly important to explain the pathologies of trust: of maintaining trust or suspicion in spite of contrary evidence. This is discussed in Chapter 5.

The analysis leads to the notion of organization as a focusing device (Nooteboom 1992). An important function of organization is to create sufficient focus, that is alignment of mental categories, for people to achieve a common purpose. This seems related to the term 'epistemic community'. It is also similar to the earlier notions of an organization as a sensemaking system (Weick 1979, 1995), system of shared meanings (Smircich 1983), or interpretation system (Choo 1998). Arguably, this is more fundamental than the function of a firm to reduce transaction costs, as transaction cost economics proposes. Now, focusing yields a problem of myopia, by which organizations may fail to see or adequately interpret potential opportunities and threats to its existence. To compensate for that, organizations need outside partners for complementary cognition, or 'external economy of cognitive scope' (Nooteboom 1992). That yields the cognitive argument for inter-firm relations hinted at before.

The sharpness or narrowness of the focus of an organization depends on whether the organization, or part of it, needs to concentrate more on efficient exploitation (utilization of existing resources and competencies, including cognitive competencies) or on exploration (development of new competencies). The former requires a sharper focus, with more unity of perception and interpretation for the sake of efficient coordination, while the latter requires more diversity and volatility of linkages for the sake of finding Schumpeterian 'novel combinations'. A narrow focus of behavioural values may be needed to control trustworthiness and thereby establish trust, within and between organizations.

Absorptive capacity is not fixed. When the knowledge involved is codified, absorptive capacity can be increased and maintained by more formal, declarative forms of learning, such as R&D. Often, when firms outsource certain activities, they maintain R&D in that area in order to maintain absorptive capacity (Granstrand et al. 1997). When knowledge is tacit, I propose that absorptive capacity depends more on cumulative experience in absorbing tacit knowledge from a variety of sources. Then communicative capacity also matters more, to help partners to absorb tacit knowledge.

This cognitive theory of the firm helps to understand the relation between trust in people and trust in organizations, which is taken up in Chapters 2 and 3. It also helps to incorporate innovation and learning in the analysis of inter-organizational relations, and the role of trust in them. This analysis is taken up in Chapter 4, in a discussion of the economic functions of trust.

Causality

Chapter 2 discusses different forms of trust, in particular different objects of trust, i.e. things we can trust. A crucial form is of course trust in the behaviour of people, which I call *behavioural trust*. For a further, systematic analysis of objects of trust, we need a causality of action: trust in behaviour can be broken down into trust in the different causes of behaviour and its outcomes. As in earlier work (Nooteboom 1999a, 2000a), I employ a causality of action inspired by the multiple causality of Aristotle. This includes final cause (goals that people have), efficient cause (agency), material cause (inputs used), formal cause (knowledge, skill, methods), exemplary cause (prototypes, role models) and conditional causes that constrain or enable the operation of the other causes. The paradigmatic example is the carpenter (efficient cause) who uses wood (material cause) to make furniture, according to professional know-how (formal cause) or some guiding model (exemplary cause), in order to earn a living (final cause), subject to conditions of law and market structure (conditional cause). Final causality is a conjunction of man's intentionality and external motivating conditions.

I proposed that an organization serves as a focusing device to align perceptions, interpretations and evaluations. This is to say that it brings together actors (efficient cause), with certain common goals (final cause), and perceptions and knowledge of how to do things (formal cause) and/or exemplars to imitate (exemplary cause), and physical means and materials (material cause). Now we can characterize management and organizational culture in these terms. There may be management by hiring and selection (efficient cause), motivation (final cause), the provision of means (material cause), specification and training in ways of doing things (formal cause), setting role models (exemplary cause), creating conditions for ideas and initiatives to arise (conditional cause). Mintzberg (1983) proposed five methods of coordination. One of them was standardization of work processes and another was standardization of skills. In the present taxonomy these would be formal causes.

I am aware that such multiple causality is controversial. I do not deny the possibility that ultimately when we descend into the mind we can reduce even final causality to physical phenomena in the brain. But on the level of action of people it would remain useful to make the distinctions made here.

Institutions, Organizations and Culture

Next to trust in people, we have to consider trust in organizations and institutions. For this some clarity concerning those notions is needed. A definition of institutions, or part of such definition, is that they enable, constrain and guide behaviour. I recall the earlier discussion of the criticism of transaction cost economics that it tends to see transaction costs in terms only of obstacles, rather than also enablers of exchange (Campbell and Harris

1993). It is odd to see a road across a swamp only, or even primarily, as a constraint, while it does of course constrain where you walk (Nelson and Sampat 2000). Another feature of institutions is that they are durable and in a sense inevitable, or not subject to choice: we are subjected to them, or they may be part of our constitution as social, cognitive and psychological beings. This, in turn, relates to the discussion, in social science, between structure and agency (Giddens 1984, Archer 1995). Institutions that form the structure in which agency takes place, thus enabling, constraining and guiding action, are man-made. However, they are a collective outcome of individual actions, which comes about through processes of interaction and communication, and takes time. At any moment, institutions are given and more or less inevitable to individual actors (Archer 1995).

Institutions include basic cognitive categories, in the wide sense of including perception, interpretation and evaluation. This is close, if not identical, to Veblen's notion of institutions as 'settled habits of thought that apply to the generality of people'. This includes norms and underlying values of conduct. These satisfy the conditions of institutions that they enable (without them we cannot think), constrain (perceiving in one way excludes perceptions in other ways; one cannot look in all directions at the same time) and guide (focus and direct) thought, and thereby behaviour. They are also more or less durable and inevitable, that is not subject to choice. This follows from the theory of knowledge discussed above. The inevitability of psychological mechanisms certainly applies to the extent that they are 'in the genes', as evolutionary psychology tells us. In interaction we construct 'higher level' cognitive categories, on the basis of which we perceive, interpret and evaluate the world. Thus they are contingent upon the physical and social environment, including the associated institutions of society. We cannot freely choose fundamental categories. At some level they are tacit and difficult to subject to criticism. However, on the basis of such categories we think. On some levels, such thought is subject to argument and other forms of learning, and there is room for choice in opening up to arguments, and making the effort to follow and understand them, and to learn the capabilities of doing so.

Much has been written on the question whether an organization is an institution. North (1990) defined institutions as the 'rules of the game'. Originally, he emphasized the constraints that they impose, on opportunism, for example, thereby reducing transaction costs. In his view organizations are not institutions but players confronted with institutions. There is merit in this idea: it is useful to distinguish organizations from the institutional environment in which they operate. In transaction cost economics, by contrast, organization is seen as an institution, as an alternative to 'the market', on the basis that it can help to reduce transaction costs. The implicit definition of institution then is anything that reduces transaction costs. We can reconcile these differences by making a distinction between organization as an 'institutional arrangement', and its 'institutional environment' (North and Thomas 1973). The latter conditions, that is, enables, constrains and guides the former.

I adopted the definition of institution as anything that enables, constrains and guides behaviour, and is enduring and not subject to free choice. According to that definition, an organization is indeed an institution. It does enable, constrain and guide behaviour in it. Earlier, I characterized an organization as a device for focusing cognition: perception, interpretation and evaluation. To function as such, the focus cannot be too variable and non-committal. In other words, it must have some stability and requires a certain engagement. Thus it does resemble an institution. However, the focus is not strictly inevitable and devoid of choice. One can decide to leave an organization, depending on the alternatives one may have. Within an organization one may be able to deviate from the established focus of cognition. In fact, one would hope that people within an organization do that to a greater or lesser extent. If the focus of the organization is too tight, this yields too much 'group think', with too little cognitive distance, which jeopardizes the variety that is needed for exploration, that is for innovation and learning in the sense of discovery. So, the tightness of organizational focus is to be decided as a trade-off between, on the one hand, cognitive proximity needed for efficient exploitation and, on the other hand, cognitive distance for exploration. As discussed earlier, one solution here may be to utilize outside relations with other organizations, at a larger cognitive distance, to complement the narrowness of focus needed for efficient exploitation. So, here also I find that an organization is like an institution but is less inescapable and more subject to choice and influence by individuals than other, 'larger' institutions.

Elsewhere (Nooteboom 2000a) I proposed not to define institutions ontologically, in terms of an inventory of institutional entities, but functionally: institutions enable, constrain and guide behaviour, and are stable and engaging with respect to that behaviour. What the specific institutions are depends on the particular situation we are investigating, and on the perspective and purpose of the enquiry. This yields a hierarchy of institutions. Legal systems are institutions for organizations, and organizations are institutions for the behaviour in them.

If institutions are 'enabling constraints', what precisely does that mean? I propose that it means that institutions affect the causality of action. Here also I use the multiple causality derived from Aristotle.

For example, the constellation of property rights, market entry and exit conditions, tax and social security affect the incentives to become an entrepreneur. When social security is low, or discrimination bars people from jobs, unemployed may be pushed into self-employment. This is the 'refuge hypothesis' of entrepreneurship. Laws of bankruptcy affect exit conditions, and thereby affect the incentive for entry: if the venture fails, with how little damage can one get out? There may be lack of finance (seen here as a material cause) due to lack of venture capital institutions. Level of education and training affect how an entrepreneur and his firm will work, and affect transaction costs (Nooteboom 2000a: 97–8). There are also motivators on a deeper level of categories of perception, interpretation and evaluation, such as sense of responsibility, independence and 'locus of control'. The latter concept is familiar in the small business literature. It indicates whether people attribute outcomes of actions to their efforts and initiative or to outside conditions. Note that the conditions interact. If there is little internal locus of control, people may not move into entrepreneurship even under adverse labour market conditions and low social security.

In a hierarchy of institutions we can identify a 'surface' and a 'deep' structure. The first consists of specific institutional structures that enable and constrain activities of firms. The latter consists of underlying, fundamental categories of perception, interpretation and evaluation that are part of culture (in the anthropological sense) and guide, that is focus and direct behaviour. We find this notion of a deep structure also in Schein's (1985) proposal that organizational culture has a deep structure of categories of thought concerning the relation between organization and its environment, reality, truth, the nature of people and their interaction. According to Schein (1985: 14, 88–110) the basic categories that constitute organizational culture concern the following:

- The relationship to the environment: does one dominate it or is one subjugated; is the primary focus technological, economic, political or socio-cultural. The domination/subjugation distinction is similar to the notion of 'locus of control': does control lie in oneself or outside.
- The nature of physical and social reality and truth: is one pragmatic or does one seek validation in a general philosophy, moral system or tradition; does one avoid uncertainty or does one have tolerance for ambiguity. How does one perceive time and space. For example: does one move towards the future or does that move towards one, or is time past duration (compare Lakoff and Johnson's 1980 analysis of 'metaphors we live by'). Is truth universal or context-dependent; absolute or relative; subjective or objective.
- Human nature: is it good, evil, or does it depend on conditions, are people active or passive, perfectible or not, what are sources of motivation.

– Nature of human activity: is it oriented towards being or towards accomplishment, is it self- or other-directed.
– Nature of human relationships: views on power, influence, hierarchy; on intimacy, love, peer relationships; coercive, utilitarian, aimed at goal consensus; degree and source of authority. Here Schein also adds dimensions proposed by Parsons: dimensions of relationships, such as universalistic (equal rights) or particularistic, achievement oriented or based on ascription (family membership, class), oriented to self or collective.

I defined institutions as things that constrain, enable and guide behaviour, and now I consider a separation between surface institutions that do the enabling and constraining, and a deep structure of cognitive and affective categories, including values of conduct, which do the guiding of behaviour. Perhaps we can say that the deep structure guides behaviour, which is enabled and constrained by surface institutions. However, I am not sure that such separation of enablers/constraints and guides is viable.[2] Behaviour is not only enabled and constrained but also guided by surface institutions, such as incentive systems. Cognitive categories, in deep structure, not only guide but also enable and constrain behaviour.

Perhaps it is better to revert to my earlier proposal of using the Aristotelian notion of a multiple causality of action. Surface institutions impinge mostly on material and conditional causes, while the deep structure impinges mostly on the formal and final causes. However, again we would have that a surface institution such as an incentive system operates on the final cause. As I indicated before, final causality is a conjunction of man's intentionality and external motivating conditions. Also, the formal causality of knowledge is affected by surface institutions such as educational systems. Nevertheless, it remains clear that formal and final causality are associated more directly and deeply with fundamental categories of knowledge and purpose than material and conditional causes. They are also more individual, while material and conditional causality are more collective.

Through interaction and communication, agency contributes to the dissemination and individual construction of categories of thought, in the deep structure. Here I point again to my constructivist, interactionist view of knowledge. Agency also yields incremental changes, and occasionally

---

[2] Mathematical programming, a technique for maximizing an objective function subject to constraints, shows that there is duality between objectives and constraints. The satisfaction of constraints can be incorporated in the objective on the basis of 'shadow prices' attached to slack with respect to constraints.

radical changes, in the surface structure of institutions, as a result of commercial or political entrepreneurship. Organizations develop their own specialized cognitive and semiotic systems: cognitive categories, language, symbols, metaphors, myths, and rituals, which guide behaviour. They also develop their own structures, procedures and rules for enabling and constraining behaviour. These are similar for different firms to the extent that they share an institutional environment. However, within that environment they offer specializations, and those differ between organizations to the extent that they have accumulated different experiences, in different industries, technologies and markets.

I indicated that agency can have effects on structure, which tends to be incremental and occasionally is radical. The question then is what the conditions and underlying processes are for radical change of institutions. That goes beyond this book. An analysis of such process of transformational change was given in earlier work (Nooteboom 2000a).

2. Forms

The first part of this chapter reviews definitions of trust and makes a proposal for a distinction between a wide definition of trust, for which I use the term 'reliance', and a narrower, strong definition of 'real' trust. The second part analyzes different forms of trust: its objects and aspects. The objects of trust include, among other things, people and organizations. This raises the question how trust in people and trust in organizations are related.

2.1 DEFINITION

Is trust a type of behaviour, or an underlying disposition? What are the answers to the fourth and fifth questions identified in Chapter 1?

Question 4: Trust and probability
If trust entails risk, how is this to be understood? Can trust be modelled as a subjective probability? Can trust go together with certainty?

Question 5: Calculative and non-calculative trust
How calculative or rational is trust? If it is not calculative, does this necessarily lead to blind, unconditional trust? If not, why not, and how does this work? Can calculative and non-calculative trust be combined? How?

Disposition and Behaviour

In some literature, trust is seen as a form of behaviour, in other literature it is seen as a behavioural disposition, or a subjective state of expectations (see Das and Teng 2001). Milgrom and Roberts (1992) for example, find the first, in the book on *Economics, Organization and Management*.

> The index of the book indicates that trust is discussed on three pages out of 605. There, trust is treated in a game-theoretic framework as something that can be offered or withheld, and the partner in the game then has the options to honour trust by behaving fairly, or not to honour it. Trust here means behaviour that suspends the demand for contractual safeguards against relational risk. In a single-

shot game there is a temptation for the second party not to honour such trust-ing behaviour, and to profit from opportunism. The first party, anticipating that, will not offer trust. In a repeated game, however, reputation effects, combined with costs and imperfections of writing contracts, can yield the offering and the honouring of trust as an equilibrium outcome. The analysis is useful to demon-strate the working of a reputation mechanism.

In social science also, trust has been defined in terms of behaviour. Consider, for example, the definition of trusting behaviour given by Deutsch (1962 quoted in Zand 1972: 230): 'Trusting behaviour consists of actions that (1) increase one's vulnerability (2) to another whose behaviour is not under one's control (3) in a situation where the penalty one suffers if the other abuses that vulnerability is greater than the benefit one gains if the other does not abuse that vulnerability.'

A classic example of a situation where the potential loss exceeds poten-tial benefits is that of hiring a caretaker for a small child. The benefit of being able to go out is far less than the potential cost of harm done to the child, due to negligence or worse. This illustrates what in Chapter 1 I called the scope of trust: the size of potential damage.

Many authors have treated trust not as behaviour but as an underlying disposition towards trusting behaviour. Such a definition of trust was given by Sako (1992: 32), for example: 'Trust is a state of mind, an expectation held by one trading partner about another, that the other behaves or responds in a predictable and mutually expected manner'. Consistent with Sako's definition is the definition offered by Bradach and Eccles (1989: 104): 'a type of expectation that alleviates the fear that one's exchange partner will act opportunistically'

The question whether trust is behaviour or an underlying disposition is easy to answer. For behaviour we use the term 'trusting behaviour' and for the underlying disposition we use the term 'trust' (see Das and Teng 2001). It is important to keep the behavioural perspective in mind, because the process of the build-up and breakdown of trust, with trust as both the basis and the outcome of behaviour, is crucial. Summing up, trust is a disposi-tion towards trusting behaviour, that is behaviour with limited safeguards, accepting vulnerability, based on the expectation that this risk is limited.

Trust entails an information paradox, as was pointed out by Pagden (1988). Trust entails lack of information, which yields risk, but also infor-mation, which limits perceived risk. This suggests that there can be neither trust with complete lack of information, nor with complete information. I will return to this later. If we define trust as a disposition or expectation, the question is on what that is based. That is the subject for Chapter 3.

In trust, is the unit of analysis the person who trusts, that is the trustor? Clearly not. As I indicated in Chapter 1, trust is a predicate with at least two places: the trustor has trust in something or someone (the trustee). One will trust some people less than others. It is very unusual, often a pathology, to trust or mistrust indiscriminately. Is, then, the unit of analysis a relationship between trustor and trustee? That may be. Would that imply that trust must be mutual; that one-sided trust cannot obtain? Trust is indeed highly symbiotic. Trust engenders trust and mistrust engenders mistrust. Mutual trust is enhanced by empathy based on shared categories concerning the motives and conditions of behaviour. Yet trust is seldom completely balanced. Often, it is not symmetric. As we shall see later, trust has different aspects even with respect to a given object: one can trust someone in one respect and not in others. One aspect is competence: is the trustee able to perform? Another is intention: does he intend to perform to the best of his competence? One can trust the one but not the other. Also, trust depends on conditions: one may trust someone in some respect in certain conditions but not in others. One can expect some conditions to exceed his competence or his commitment to perform. Thus, trust appears to be a four-place predicate. Someone (1) trusts someone (or something) (2) in some respect (3), depending on conditions such as the context of action (4). This context of action includes the dynamics of interaction. Trust is, or should be, subject to development, to learning. Fixed trust or mistrust, regardless of evidence or experience, is unreasonable and typically constitutes a pathology. The pathology of trust will be discussed in Chapter 5.

A similar analysis applies to trustworthiness: one is trustworthy with respect to some others, in some respects and under some conditions. One may be loyal to some and opportunistic with respect to others. One may be trustworthy in competence but not in intentions. There are likely to be limits to trustworthiness. There are limits to one's competence, and one may not know those limits until they become manifest. The temptation or pressure to cheat may become too high. Unconditional trustworthiness may exist, even under the greatest temptation or pressure, but it is rare, which is why unconditional trust is generally not wise.

Trust, Risk and Probability

Many authors have connected trust with risk. Not in the (financial) economist's sense of a variance of a probability distribution, but in the sense of what the financial economist would call 'downside risk': the possibility of loss (Luhmann 1988, Gulati 1995, Chiles and McMackin 1996, and many others).

Proceeding from that, trust has been identified with a subjective probability of an action that it is 'beneficial or at least not detrimental' (Gambetta 1988: 217). Dasgupta (1988), Mayer et al. (1995), Gulati (1995),

and others adopted similar views. This brings us to one of the key questions
of this book, identified in Chapter 1:

Question 4: Trust and probability
If trust entails risk, how is this to be understood? Can trust be modelled as a
subjective probability? Can trust go together with certainty?

If trust were a subjective probability, the advantage would be that we could
use probability calculus. Such calculation clarifies, among other things, the
relation between trust as an assessment of risk and the stakes involved, in
the form of possible reward and possible damage.

Let p represent trust as the probability that expectations, or hopes, will
be fulfilled, and let U represent the reward involved. Let L represent the
damage if expectations are not fulfilled (the partner turns out not to be
trustworthy). Then one would rationally engage in the relationship if
expected gain exceeds expected loss:

$$p.U - (1-p).L > 0, \text{ that is } p > L/(L+U).$$

This reproduces the obvious intuition that if potential reward U is high,
one would sooner, with lower trust (p), that is at a higher risk of disappointment, engage in the relationship. At a high potential loss, relative to potential gain, trust (p) must be relatively high. If potential gain and loss are
equal, we should have $p > 50$ per cent. If potential loss is ten times higher
than potential gain, we should have $p > 90$ per cent. Next, with trust as a
probability we could use a (so-called Bayesian) procedure to adapt the
probability as new evidence of trustworthiness arises.

However, trust as a probability raises a puzzle. The notion of a probability would imply that there is high trust if the subjective probability of good
outcomes is high, and hence perceived risk is low. That implies that trust is
highest when the probability is unity, so that there is no risk left. However,
another intuition is that trust entails a wager, an acceptance of risk, so that
if there is no risk, we can no longer speak of trust. As noted before, trust is
seen as submission to vulnerability, so that if there is no vulnerability we
can no longer speak of trust. Under certainty there is no vulnerability or
risk left. As noted, there is a paradox of information. Trust entails both risk
and its limitation, both information and the lack of it.

Pettit (1995a) objected to the idea that there can be no trust under certainty.

Pettit gave the following example. Suppose that in an unknown city you wanted
to get to the city centre by car. One approach would be to follow a bus with the

centre indicated as its destination. Can you trust the bus driver? Does it matter whether or not you tell him that you are following him, and why? Pettit's point is that you may be virtually certain that the driver will indeed take the bus to the centre, regardless of what you do, since that is his duty. Nevertheless, you can be said to trust him to do that. And indeed, if trust is based on certain considerations, then if they lead to certainty, you do not lose those considerations, and in that sense you do not lose your trust. While Pettit does not discuss this, the announcement to the bus driver may matter, as follows. If he is malevolent, for whatever reason, he may spurt through an orange light to leave you locked and lost at the red light. If he is benevolent, he may stop at the orange light. So, can you ever be 100 per cent certain that the driver will behave as you hope he will?

Nevertheless, Pettit's argument is clear: perhaps it is odd to say that one no longer has trust when one is certain. If trust increases with probability, and that is approaching unity, at what point would trust disappear?

Now, either we drop the notion of trust as a probability, and maintain the information paradox, or we accept the notion of probability and drop the information paradox. Earlier, like many others I was inclined to sympathize with the notion of trust as a subjective probability (compare Nooteboom 1999a, 1999c). Now I reject it, for several reasons. Perhaps the most important reason derives from the puzzle indicated above. Subjective probabilities can become unity, if the concept means anything, and that entails certainty, while there is a persistent intuition that there is always residual risk; that we can never be completely certain about another's behaviour; that to speak of trust there must be vulnerability. One reason for this view is ethical: certainty would yield the possibility of perfect predictability of behaviour, which would eliminate freedom of action. Vandevelde (2000) and Verhezen (2000) made similar points. Thus Verhezen (2000: 134, my translation from the Flemish) proposed: 'Trust is a way of dealing with the freedom of others . . . lending trust entails that one leaves another the choice to disenchant or not'.

Certainty concerning behaviour would underestimate radical uncertainty, for both the trustor and the trustee, concerning abilities and future contingencies that may affect choices. This refers back to the discussion of radical uncertainty in Chapter 1. As has been argued before by Shackle, the notion of probability, in any usual sense of satisfying the axioms attached to probabilities with a frequency interpretation, cannot apply under radical uncertainty. There, the set of all the things that could happen is not closed, and unpredictable possibilities arise as we go along. If we talk of beliefs under radical uncertainty, we should drop the term 'probability'. Shackle (1961: 6) formulated his view as follows:

> we think of uncertainty as more than the existence in the decision-maker's mind of plural and rival (mutually exclusive) hypotheses amongst which he has insuffi-

cient epistemic sources of choice . . . Decision is not choice amongst the delim-
ited and prescribed moves in a game with fixed rules and a known list of possible outcomes of any move or sequence of moves. There is no assurance that
any one can in advance say what set of hypotheses a decision maker will entertain concerning any specified act available to him. Decision is thought and not
merely determinate response.

This solves the puzzle. Perhaps we can talk of trust as an expectation, but
not as a probability, because there will always be residual uncertainty about
agency and unforeseeable contingencies, so that there is always a residual
element of risk, in the sense of a non-quantifiable possibility that things go
wrong. This yields an argument against blind or unconditional trust: one
should be aware that there is always a possibility of things going wrong. To
be 100 per cent certain about someone's future behaviour is to rob him of
his freedom. No matter how loyal a friend is, one cannot expect him to
remain loyal and not to betray you under any conditions, such as, say,
torture.

For an illustration, let us return to Pettit's example of the bus driver. Suppose I
tell the driver that I will follow him to get to the centre of the city, and he pledges
to take that into account and to help me. I know that to keep his job the driver
cannot afford not to go to the centre. Perhaps he is my uncle or a close friend. I
still cannot be sure. I may still lose him at a red light, or in the chaos of traffic,
because he simply could not help losing me. Perhaps he could only stop in time
for a light about to jump to red, or stop when I get jammed in traffic, at the cost
of causing a crash. And that he could not afford, in view of his job and his larger
responsibility for his passengers.

Another way to deal with this issue is to go back to the notion of trust
as a four-place predicate. I proposed that trust is conditional, or contingent.
We trust someone with respect to some aspect of behaviour (competence,
intentions) in some conditions, but not in others. If one has trust in
someone with respect to something, under certain conditions, then trust is
as uncertain as the conditions that may obtain. There are two kinds of
uncertainty. The first concerns external conditions that affect outcomes of
actions. The second concerns the limit of someone's trustworthiness. There
may be unconditional trustworthiness, but it is rare and can seldom be
counted on.

Trust and Calculation

A second reason to reject the notion of trust as a subjective probability is that
it seems too rational and calculative, and thereby excludes trust based on
possibly non-rational convictions and routinized behaviour (Nooteboom

1999a, 1999c). By 'calculative' here I do not mean calculation in the arithmetical or mathematical sense. Previously, I claimed that trust cannot be construed as a probability and hence cannot be calculated in that sense. Here I mean calculation in the sense of a rational, reasoned inference. In the present context: a reasoned inference of trustworthiness. This leads to another key question:

Question 2: Calculative and non-calculative trust
How calculative or rational is trust? When it is not calculative, does this necessarily lead to blind, unconditional trust? If not, why not, and how does this work? Can calculative and non-calculative trust be combined? How?

In the literature, there is a persistent intuition that trust entails both calculative and non-calculative elements. One intuition, going back to Simmel (1950), is that 'trust begins where rational prediction ends' (Lane 2000: 6), and 'an element of calculation may be present in most trusting behaviour. The importance of this element changes both with the context and object of trust, as well as varying between the stages of a trusting relationship' (Lane 2000: 7). Let us see whether more clarity can be given to this issue. First, let us explore elements of non-calculative trust.

Apart from a rational, reasoned expectation that things will not go wrong, one may simply not think of things going wrong, or not be aware of that possibility, or ignore it, or deny it. According to Lane (2000: 11) this idea of unreflective trust goes back to Garfinkel (1967). Neglect of risk may be based on naivety. Social psychology tells us that we may be unwilling to face risks precisely because we are afraid of them. Neglect of risk may be based on cognitive dissonance related to friendship or kinship: one does not want to contemplate the possibility of opportunism on the part of friends or family. Particularly in the latter case trust is to a greater or lesser extent based on affect. But also ethics-based trust can be related to affect. People can have an emotional commitment to notions of justice or decency. Trust may also be based on routinized behaviour: things have been going well in the past, so why shouldn't they in future?

This can have a rational basis. Williamson (1993) suggested that non-calculative trust inevitably yields blind trust, but this is not so. There may be two meanings of blind trust here. One is that trust is not based on rational assessment. Another is that trust is unconditional. In routinized behaviour, trust can be blind in the first sense without being blind in the second sense. Unconditional trust would indeed be very hazardous. However, routines may be subject to tolerance levels. As Herbert Simon has taught us, in view of bounded rationality routinized behaviour is rational. It allows us to focus our limited capability of attention and rational evaluation on new things that have priority, while for other activities we adhere to unreflective routines that have proven to work satisfactorily in the past. In the present context, we may trust someone simply because our relation has worked out satisfactorily in the past, or because we have never been duped in other relations. Of course, this expectation is better founded to the extent that this has happened under varying conditions, including ones that required a sacrifice from the partner. Later, in Chapter 3, I analyse in more detail how one can infer trustworthiness from observed behaviour.

Of course, the danger of routinized behaviour is that it is kept up under new conditions where it is not justified and fails. That is why we will often retain a 'subsidiary awareness' of risk, which is shifted into 'focal awareness' when phenomena exceed a certain tolerance level (Polanyi 1962). Emotion, called forth by such intolerable events, serves to break us out of the routine and trigger focal awareness, and put it on the agenda, so to speak (Simon 1983). This is part of the rationality of emotions: they catapult us from subsidiary into focal awareness. The difference between routines and instinct is that the former are in this way susceptible to change, whereas instincts are hereditarily acquired and are 'hard-wired' into our cognitive and physiological make-up. This distinction is probably a bit too stark. Some non-instinctive routines may also become so entrenched as to yield virtually irredeemable inertia.

Lane (2000: 23) noted that 'one falsehood may be reacted to with great emotional intensity and may upset trust forever'. The reason, as proposed by Luhmann, is that people learn to be trusting 'from infancy onwards, by a process of generalizing from isolated experiences, (which) is closely tied up with the self-developing identity of the learner'. Therefore trust is entwined with personality, so that its loss is perceived as very threatening. There is an alternative view from evolutionary psychology, discussed in Chapter 1. An emotion-laden sensitivity to breach of reciprocity may be entrenched in our heritage from evolution, since it contributed to survival in the ancient hunter–gatherer societies in which humanity evolved. An emotional jolting out of routinized behaviour that took reciprocity for granted may be part of such a survival mechanism.

The key notion here is that of trust as a default. On the basis of available knowledge, routine or instinct (if evolutionary psychology is right), one assumes trustworthiness until evidence to the contrary appears. The notion of default arises also in linguistics. In ordinary language, usually no definition of the meaning of a word can be given in terms of necessary and sufficient characteristics. How, for example would one define 'chair'? Legs are not necessary, since there are legless pouch chairs. Chairs have seats, but so do benches, couches, bicycles, and so on. Wittgenstein, in his later work of the 'philosophical investigations' (1976), pointed this out, and proposed that the criteria for judging a proposition to be true, or proper, or adequate, are pragmatic and conventional: something is true if it achieves its operational purpose. In communication and joint action what determines meaning is whether it aligns with common practice, satisfies established rules of the game and performs well in the specific context of action. This is the notion of 'meaning as use', in which a concept is seen as an instrument. For an instrument we would not ask if it is true or what the necessary and sufficient conditions for proper use are a priori. Its adequacy appears in its specific use in a specific context. This is open-ended, and allows for unorthodox but nevertheless adequate use: we may in some conditions use a screwdriver for a hammer, with adequate results. Thus, to identify and categorize objects we use criteria from experience with similar contexts of action in the past, until we run into experience that violates the criteria, and then we change them. Johnson-Laird (1983: 189) employed Minsky's (1975) notion of 'default values' to elucidate how conventional criteria of meaning might work. Characteristics are assumed unless there is evidence to the contrary. They are assumed on the basis of established practice, that is on the basis of what it is possible to think, until contested by new practice, which shifts what we can think. Note that all this emerges from the situated action theory of knowledge that I proposed in Chapter 1.

Wittgenstein offered the idea of 'typical cases' that represent a norm, and we deal with borderline cases by reference to the norm. Different occurrences, in different contexts, do not always share common features, let alone necessary and sufficient features, but sometimes at best only 'family resemblances'. Proximate members of a family may have shared characteristics, but distant members often do not. Members of a class form a chain, with common characteristics at each link, but no characteristic shared by all members of the class. X is in the same class as Y not because they have common characteristics but because they both share characteristics, but different ones, with a third member Z. Others have subsequently proposed similar ideas. Well known is Rosch's (1977) idea of 'prototype', which represents an exemplar of a class that connects others in the class. Class membership is decided on the basis of resemblance to a salient case, or a typical case, which serves as a prototype. This notion of default helps to deal with the open-endedness of uncertainty and the open-endedness of trust as a result of uncertainty concerning human behaviour.

In view of (radical) uncertainty concerning behaviour, we *always* need to allow for the possibility that we do not have complete knowledge. Even when we are rational, or especially then, we can only base our assessment of trustworthiness on available knowledge, recognize that behaviour is subject to radical uncertainty, and that beyond present knowledge a leap of unreasoned trust is always needed. The default entails that under certain conditions we assume trustworthiness, until contrary evidence appears. Note the similarities and differences between default and certainty. A default is like certainty in that one does not continually think about risk or uncertainty and what to do about it. It is unlike certainty in that one knows that one does not know what will happen. We assume rather than know that what will happen will be acceptable. However, in the light of available evidence it is a reasonable assumption. Perhaps one can say that a default acts as if there is certainty, but knows that there is not.

Of course, the default could also be mistrust: we assume lack of trustworthiness until evidence to the contrary arises. There are complications with this, however, especially for powerful people: benevolent, co-operative behaviour can then be interpreted, always perhaps, as other people's submission to the power one has, and hence is not to be seen as evidence of 'real' trustworthiness. Mistrust that leads to avoidance of interaction robs itself of potential evidence that would falsify the lack of trust.

Summing up, there is nothing in the basic notion of trust that indicates that it must be justified or calculated. To allow for a non-calculative basis of trust, such as routinized behaviour, naivety or even sheer stupidity, the definition of trust should be wide enough to include the unreflective neglect of possibilities of things going wrong. This yields the following definition of trust:

Definition 1
Trust in things or people entails the willingness to submit to the risk that they may fail us, with the expectation that they will not, or the neglect or lack of awareness of the possibility that they might.

So far, the definitions of trust were concerned with trust regarding other people's behaviour. The (concise) Oxford dictionary (1991) gives a much broader definition, yielding a wider scope for the objects of trust, as follows: 'A firm belief in the reliability or truth or strength etc. of a person or thing'. In another connotation it mentions 'a confident expectation'. It can also mean 'the resulting obligation or responsibility' as in 'being in a position of trust'.

Like the Oxford dictionary, I allow for trust not only in people but also in 'things'. By that I mean objects, institutions, organizations, and the like. I will expand on that later. Of course, with inanimate objects certain crucial dimensions of trust disappear, such as trust in intentions. In the context of economics and organization, a particularly important question is how trust in organizations is related to trust in people.

A crucial question remains. If trust can be both calculative and non-calculative, how are these apparently contradictory elements to be combined? How can one be calculative and non-calculative at the same time?

Doesn't calculation negate the lack of it? The solution that I propose is to see trustworthiness as subject to limits, and trust as subject to levels of tolerance for deviant behaviour. This is already implicit in the notion of trust as conditional and the notion of trust as a default: we assume trustworthiness under certain conditions, until contrary evidence appears. In the absence of contrary evidence we do not calculate, but when it arises we might, if the evidence triggers awareness that limits of acceptability are exceeded. Thus we can have both calculative and non-calculative trust, with a boundary between them.

The limits of trustworthiness are related to the stakes involved. One of the limits is related to the notion of a 'golden opportunity'. Is it reasonable to expect anyone to remain loyal at any cost? As indicated before, this would rob the other of his autonomy. Is it consistent with friendship to expect one's friend to remain loyal even under torture? One may trust someone up to his resistance to temptation or pressure, which is the perceived, inferred, assumed or intuited limit of his trustworthiness. This forms an upper limit of trustworthiness. 'Don't tie the cat to the bacon' is a Dutch saying. Don't subject your partners to too much temptation of defection or betrayal. Trustworthiness can also have a lower limit. One may not have the capacity or the attention to prevent even the smallest errors or imperfections. One may think that small deceptions and pilferage will not be noticed. Beyond the limits of trustworthiness, it is wise to be aware and think. In this way, trust need not be blind, in the sense of being unbounded or unconditional.

Would this mean that trust is completely calculative, since it entails the awareness of limits? The fact remains that within the limits one may renounce safeguards, and assume trustworthiness as a default. Here one can get on with the job of collaboration, without at every step being preoccupied with monitoring and searching for evidence of untrustworthiness. In other words: without behaving like economists say we do.

Trust has tolerance levels that are connected to the limits of trustworthiness. When one observes or expects behaviour beyond those levels, one is triggered to consider the possibility and the implications of untrustworthiness. At that point one starts to reflect, voice complaints, assess the possibility, causes and conditions of untrustworthiness, and to design preventive or remedial action. It may lead to a downward shift of the perceived limit of maximum trustworthiness, and an upward shift of minimal trustworthiness. In the first case one arrives at the conclusion that the partner is less capable of dealing with crises, or less resistant to temptation or pressure than one thought. In the second case one concludes that the partner has less capacity or attention for accuracy than one thought, or has an inclination to cut corners. This may lead to narrower tolerance levels for deviant behaviour. Those tolerance levels are not necessarily tightly coupled to the perceived limits of a partner's trustworthiness. One may disregard small inaccuracies, or one may be unable to observe them, and prefer to concentrate on 'the big risks'. One may also give the benefit of the doubt and maintain existing tolerance levels for a while longer. Note that in the previous discussion of routinized behaviour there was an implicit tolerance level. Extraordinary events beyond that level trigger awareness, shifting routinized behaviour from subsidiary to focal awareness.

This notion of limits of trust was suggested before by Pettit (1995b). He used it for a discussion of the validity of economics and its limits. Economists may be right when competition is so harsh as to allow for no slack of give and take, in relations, and forces the need to pounce on any small benefit, of whatever kind and at whatever price to others, as soon as it arises, for the sake of survival. Note that the argument against that view is close to the argument against the economist's evolutionary argument for rational choice, discussed in Chapter 1. To the extent that there is slack, due to imperfections of competition, people take the benefit of not having to be continually and unconditionally calculative, untrustworthy and mistrusting. In view of uncertainty, innovation, learning, entry barriers, transaction costs and the fact that competition focuses on being different rather than going for the lowest cost of a homogeneous product, this is the rule rather than the exception. However, the limit to which people or firms can afford to act this way does depend on the intensity of competition.

Self Interest and Altruism

Above, I looked at calculation, in the sense of rational inference, as a basis for trust: to what extent is trust, that is the belief or assumption of trustworthiness, based on rational analysis of behaviour and its motives and conditions. A related question is whether people are trustworthy only on the basis of self-interest, or go beyond self-interest, into altruism.

Question 7: The sources of trustworthiness
On what is trustworthiness of people based? Coercion, self-interest, ethics, friendship, routinization? Does it go beyond self-interest? If it does, can it survive in markets?

Chapter 3 is designed to give a systematic, detailed answer to this question. Here I only look at the broad issue of self-interest versus altruism, and the implications for the definition of trust. Trust, defined as the expectation that 'things will not go wrong' (Definition 1) may be based on contractual safeguards. This will be discussed more systematically in Chapters 3 and 4.

However, here the point is the following. As noted in Chapter 1, a fundamental question is whether expected conformance to expectations on the
basis of contractual obligations and self-interest can properly be called
trust. The notion of trust in everyday language seems to suggest that trust
goes beyond contractual obligation, and refers to expected cooperation
even when it is not specified in a contract, and even when it may require a
sacrifice from the partner. Therefore, trust has been defined as the expectation that a partner will not engage in opportunistic behaviour, even in the
face of countervailing short-term incentives (Bradach and Eccles 1989,
Chiles and McMackin 1996).

Later, in the analysis of the role of trust in the governance of relations,
in Chapter 4, I will employ the notions, developed in earlier work
(Nooteboom 1996, 1999a), of '*opportunities, incentives and inclinations*' to
opportunism'. Opportunities arise from openings for action left in contractual agreements and legal regulations, or imperfect monitoring of compliance with them. Incentives refer to self-interested motives to utilize
opportunities for opportunism. If an agent is himself highly dependent on
the relationship, or is concerned with his reputation, or with the possible
loss of hostages, then he may lack such incentive. Now, trustworthiness as
intended in ordinary language can perhaps be defined as the renunciation
of opportunism in spite of both opportunities and incentives, as a result of
limited inclinations towards opportunism. That can be based on many
things, such as friendship, empathy, ethics, or routinization, to be discussed
more systematically later, in Chapter 3. This leads to a narrower, stronger
definition of trust, as follows:

Definition 2
'*Real' trust, or trust in the strong sense, is an expectation that things or people
will not fail us, or the neglect or lack of awareness of the possibility of failure,
even if there are perceived opportunities and incentives for it.*

Note that there is a similar difference in the definition of trustworthiness:
does it go beyond self-interest or not? Here also, I make a distinction
between reliability, which may be based on coercion or self-interest, and
trustworthiness in the strong sense, which goes beyond that.

There is a source of possibly disastrous misunderstanding here. If in
some exchange situations actors profess, and honestly think, that they can
be trusted, or that someone else can be trusted, very different things can be
meant. Such differences are likely to occur between different cultures and
languages (see Sako 1998). One may mean trustworthiness in the wide
sense, including all kinds of safeguards. One may mean that one can be
trusted because contractually one has no other option, or because it is in

one's interest to stick to the intention of agreements. One may also mean that one will remain loyal and renounce opportunities for opportunism when they occur, even when there are incentives to utilize them, unless temptations or pressures become excessive, and then one will announce the problems and try to solve them together. Misunderstanding about what is meant here can be disastrous.

Therefore, for the sake of clarity, and to avoid confusion, I use the term 'reliance' for the wide notion of trust in Definition 1, as an expectation that 'things will not go wrong', regardless of the basis for that expectation, which can include control by contract or incentives. I use the term 'assurance' when the expectation is based on control on the basis of self-interest (legal coercion, dependence), and the term 'trust' for trust in the strong sense of Definition 2, where the motives for trustworthiness go beyond self-interest. In other words, reliance embraces both assurance and trust in the strong sense. However, this terminology might become somewhat laborious. So, in the following, I may still use the term trust for the broader notion of reliance, not to seem pedantic, but when it matters, I will pick up the distinction between trust in the broader sense of reliance and in the stronger sense of 'real' trust.

2.2   OBJECTS AND ASPECTS

What are the objects of trust, that is what can one have trust in? This was question number 6, identified in Chapter 1:

Question 6: Objects and aspects of trust
What can we have trust in? Things, people, institutions, organizations? What are the aspects of trust: competence, intentions, and what else?

Causes of Failure and Failure of Causes

The definition of trust given before includes the expectation that things or people will not fail us. This leaves open a variety of types or aspects of trust, depending on possible causes of failure. As proposed in Chapter 1, action has multiple causes. There are as many forms of trust as there are (failures of) causes of action. Earlier, I distinguished trusting behaviour and the underlying disposition to trust. Similarly, we can have trust in someone's behaviour, in *behavioural trust*, or in the dispositions underlying that behaviour, or, more generally, the reasons and causes of actions and their outcomes. Causes of failure are mostly failure of causes. In other words, behavioural trust can be broken down into trust in the causes of actions,

Table 2.1   Elements of behavioural trust

Form of trust	Object of trust	Type of cause (Aristotle)
Behavioural trust	An actor	Efficient cause
Material trust	Means, inputs	Material cause
Competence trust	Ability, skills, knowledge, to use technology, methods, language, etc.	Formal cause
Intentional trust	Aims, intentions	Final cause
dedication trust	Dedication/care	
benevolence trust	Benevolence, goodwill,	
(or goodwill trust)	lack of opportunism	
Conditional trust	Outside enablers, constraints	Conditional cause
Exemplar trust	Role models	Exemplary cause
Informational trust	Information	All causes
honesty trust	Truthfulness	

and their outcomes. For a systematic analysis of this I need a theory of the causality of action. For this I use the concept of multiple causality, discussed in Chapter 1, which was derived from Aristotle: efficient (actor), material (means), formal (method, skill, knowledge), final (objectives, motives), exemplary (role models, prototypes, defaults) and conditional (outside conditions that enable or constrain action) causes. For each of these causes there is a corresponding form of trust. This is summarized in Table 2.1.

The object of behavioural trust is an actor (efficient cause). However, his actions and their outcomes entail a number of other causes. One is the means (material cause) required to act according to expectations, that is to prevent failures in material inputs, tools, financial means, and so on. This constitutes *material trust*. Another cause is the competence one needs to achieve expected performance, such as abilities, skills, and knowledge needed to use technology, employ proper methods, communicate and collaborate in teams, plan and co-ordinate activities, and so on. This constitutes *competence trust*. Another cause lies in the intentions of the actor, which includes his aims, motives, and so on to perform according to the best of his competence. This yields *intentional trust*. I already had to take the difference between competence and intentions into account in the earlier discussion. To have intentional trust includes the expectation that the partner will not behave opportunistically. A relatively benign form is lack of *dedication* or care. Here, the partner offers too little, in the way of effort and attention. He shirks, rides free, and fails to admit weakness and to take safety precautions. Here, the stake, in the form of potential loss, is still limited. A more aggressive form, for which I reserve the term *opportunism*, entails that the partner takes too much. This involves cheating, stealing, expropriation, extortion, threats, and power play. It includes the notion of hold-up from transaction cost economics: the use of a partner's dependence to appropriate a larger share in the added value of a relationship, with the threat of exiting from the relationship. Here the stake, in the form of possible loss, can be high or small. The partner may want to capture a big gain, even if that jeopardizes the relationship. He may also think that pilferage and small deceit will remain unnoticed. The opposite of opportunism I call *benevolence* or goodwill.

> I have been challenged on this categorization of trust (with thanks to Giorgio Inzerilli). If a friend uses an umbrella to protect us from the rain, is the umbrella part of my trust in my friend? My answer is that it is. I can mistrust the umbrella, because it looks worn or torn. My trust entails that I expect my friend to protect me from the rain, but the proper functioning of the umbrella is part of it. If I do get wet, this may be due to my friend using the umbrella only to cover himself, or his lack of aim or clumsy handling, or a hole in the umbrella. Which is the case matters for my relationship with my friend. In the first case I may start to doubt his benevolence, in the second his competence and in the third case I may give him a new umbrella.

Another cause lies in the external conditions that enable and constrain actions. This yields *conditional trust*. Recall my proposal of trust as a four-place predicate: One has trust in someone, with respect to something (competence, intentions), depending on conditions. Conditional trust includes the often tacit assumption that no freak accidents will occur that affect outcomes against favourable conditions of means, competence, dedication and benevolence. One could argue that this form of trust is superfluous, since conditional causality operates through the other causes. However, the notion is still useful. It is relevant to consider to what extent outside conditions can contribute to uncertainty. This is especially important with a view to inferences that can be made concerning behavioural causes. The extent to which we can infer lack of competence, dedication or benevolence from disappointing outcomes depends on conditional causality.

Finally, the multiple causality used here employs the notion of an exemplary cause, that is role models or models of outcomes that are to be imitated. This suggests that there may be a corresponding form of trust here as well, which might be called *exemplar trust*. This may appear a bit eccentric at this point, but it will demonstrate its use when the discussion later turns to the relation between personal and organizational trust. Exemplars form an important element of organizational culture, in the guidance of individual action.

I have added an additional category, called *informational trust*, which refers to information that we may have on the different causes mentioned. What is the information available on performance (the outcome of actions) and its causes, such as availability of means, competencies, intentions and conditions. Information cannot be seen as part of material causality, because that refers to the means available to the actor, while here we refer to information *about* the actor and other causes of action. An important aspect of informational trust is *honesty trust* in the truthfulness of the actor, who often is the only source of information, so that we cannot directly verify information and can only fall back on our trust in the truthfulness of the source, that is the actor. As in the distinction between lack of dedication and opportunism, there is a difference of degree, with a lesser and a more aggressive form. In the lesser form, which one may call lack of honesty or incomplete honesty, people fail to give timely signals of weaknesses or impending problems or intentions. In the more aggressive form, which one might call dishonesty, people lie about conditions or intentions. An important difference is that in the first case when challenged people would confess, while in the second case they wouldn't.

Of course, not all the forms of trust in Table 2.1 are new. Many earlier authors have used the notions of intentional trust, benevolence trust (also called 'goodwill trust'), competence trust and honesty trust. The notions of material trust, dedication trust, conditional trust and exemplar trust have not, in my knowledge, been used before. I hope that the results demonstrate the usefulness of this causality of action for a systematic analysis of the objects of trust.

> A simple, everyday example is trusting someone with one's car. This may refer to driving competence, or to dedication to drive carefully and maintain the car well, or to not stealing it. Trust in competence will depend on the tests to which it will be put. One may trust someone's competence in easy driving in good weather and relaxed traffic, but not in conditions of sleet, heavy traffic or at night.

> A more intricate example is the following. It illustrates the difference between competence, dedication and benevolence trust. The source is a private communication from Giorgio Inzerilli.[1] For building roads through mountains, the principal instrument was a big rotating wheel, with a diameter of eleven metres, to carve a tunnel. However, additionally, holes had to be blown with dynamite, for spaces too narrow or steep for the carving machine to reach, such as niches to be made in the tunnel for servicing, parking and emergencies. For that, holes of one metre length were drilled horizontally into the face and then filled with dynamite and a detonator. Two electrical wires connected the detonator to a

---

[1] That, in turn, was based on an interview with a 34 year old student at a Swiss university who, for several years, had worked as a specialized miner.

battery. One wire had blue casing and the other red. All red wires were connected to each other and to a main cable leading to one of the battery poles. The blue wires were similarly connected to the other pole. When the battery was switched on, sparking between the wires in each hole caused the dynamite to explode. For example, to make a niche for parking 240 holes were needed, resulting in 480 wires hanging from the mountain face. There were several risks involved. Handling the detonators was dangerous: if they were struck too hard or exposed to too much heat, they could explode, and this could tear a man's arm off. The main risk, however, was a shared one. Linking all the wires together entailed the crafting by hand of almost 1500 connections. It was a long and tedious job, handling thin wires in poor light, with the risk of making faulty connections. Safety regulations required a complicated, tedious, lengthy procedure. The miners designed shortcuts that considerably reduced time and complexity. However, this entailed that a small mistake anywhere in the string, such as inserting two wires of the same colour, or accidentally touching one end of a wire with the other, would trigger a simultaneous explosion of all the dynamite, killing the whole team. In 1956 six miners had died that way. In this situation, the miners had to completely trust each other. What kind of trust is this? It entails reliance on competence (especially in connecting the wires) and dedication (paying meticulous attention to agreed procedures). Benevolence is not very relevant here, since there is no scope for opportunism: to break trust would entail killing oneself. Conditional trust here entails the trust that no accidents will occur such as, for example, a colleague having a heart attack at some crucial moment.

The distinction between different objects of trust is important, because their breach requires different responses. If lack of competence is the cause, one may respond by bolstering that competence, by support or training, or by subjecting it to less demanding tasks. If lack of means is the cause, one could supply them. If lack of dedication is the cause, one may think of further incentives, an appeal to sense of duty, or threat of replacement. If opportunism is the cause, one may think of penalties, retaliation, replacement, or threats of any of these, or an appeal to ethical behaviour or social duties of reciprocity. When trust in external conditions is broken, one's action will depend on whether a disturbance is seen as incidental or as systematic. When it is an incidental, freak accident, one may have to just accept the loss and perhaps share it among partners. When the disturbance is systematic, one may take out an insurance, or diversify the risk, or revise the design of collaboration to make it more robust under such accidents.

The problem of course is that while the logical distinction between aspects of trust is important, in practice one may not be able to distinguish them (see Bachmann 2000: 308). For example, if someone neglects agreements, does not show up at meetings, exceeds time limits, and the like, this could be due to absent-mindedness (lack of competence) or lack of dedication. If opportunism is the real cause of broken expectations, the perpetrator will not admit it, if he can get away with it. He will claim *force majeure*, and if that cannot be made plausible, he will claim a shortfall of competence, with the promise to catch up, and he may ask for a little help. This is the problem of what may be called the *inscrutability of failure*. When serious failure occurs, it triggers attention. The default of trust is called into question. Awareness of potential problems is triggered. One needs to know what happened and why. Inscrutability of the cause of failure creates discomfort. One may even start to suspect the worst: that one's partner might be behaving opportunistically. In view of that, honesty trust is of crucial importance. It is more important to the extent that causes of unmet expectations cannot be observed. This raises the question how we can infer dispositions from observed behaviour. That will be discussed in Chapter 3, where I will also give a further analysis of the role of honesty.

Competence trust covers many different kinds of competence. One can think of skills and knowledge concerning the production of goods or services, or employing technology, or building and maintaining relations with other people. One can also think of communicative competence: the ability to express oneself and be understood, and to understand others. Earlier, I identified a possible problem in ascribing failure of expectations to lack of competence or lack of intention. Here we have a similar problem. If we identify a failure of truth, is this due to lack of honesty (a lie) or lack of linguistic competence (a misunderstanding)?

In Chapter 1, a distinction was made between exploration and exploitation. Here we can make a corresponding distinction with respect to competence.

> Let us go back to the example of teams of demolition experts, discussed above. One can have trust in a colleague's ability to follow proper procedure, and his dedication to do that meticulously. That is trust in exploitation. One can also have trust in a colleague's ability and dedication to take proper remedial action if an accident does occur. This concerns his competence to improvise, and his dedication to do so, which may require courage, and his benevolence in willing to take risks and make a sacrifice for the benefit of his colleagues. That is trust in exploration.
>
> For another example, consider pilots. In a plane getting ready for take-off one would not like the pilot to deviate from proper procedure in his communication with traffic control in the tower, and deviate from established technical terms. For example, instead of acknowledging receipt and understanding of a message by 'roger', say 'mike'. On the other hand, when in the sky a motor drops from a wing, one would not want the captain to sit back in inaction because this contingency is not covered in his book of standard operating procedures. One would want him to improvise.

Institutions, Organizations and People

In the previous definitions and discussions of trust, the implicit assumption was that trust concerns the behaviour of people, notably partners in exchange. I discussed honesty trust, for example: the trust in someone's truthfulness. This is a special case of trust in information, or informational trust: its factual truth, accuracy, completeness, impartiality, up-to-dateness, accessibility, interpretation, relevance, authenticity, confidentiality and security. These are related to trust in the competencies and honesty of information providers. One can ask what the implications of the Internet will be for the trustworthiness of information, in view of the low threshold for information provision and anonymity of providers. There is a need for authentication, certification, accreditation, licensing and the like (Knights et al. 2001).

There can be trust in many other entities. One can have trust in things: one's car, for example, with an expectation of performance. Here also, there are aspects of trust that underlie expected performance. In the case of the car: its engine, gear, brakes, and so on. Things are less interesting since they have no life or will of their own. Intentional trust does not apply. Trust associated with the actions and motivations of people, that is behavioural trust, is more complicated, interesting and important. When the performance potential or quality of objects is difficult to judge, trust in objects may shift to trust in the provider of the object. In the case of the car this would be the car dealer and the garage. There, intentional trust reappears.

One can have trust in laws of nature and their consequences, such as the weather. One can have trust in God. One can have institutional trust, that is trust in institutions such as the law, police, or government. In Chapter 1, I defined institutions as things that enable, constrain and guide action and are durable and committing, that is more or less inescapable. While institutions are man-made, they are the result of collective action, 'in the long run', and at any one time they are given and more or less inevitable to individual action

This relates to the distinction that Luhmann (1988) made between *confidence* and trust. Confidence relates to bigger or wider systems or entities that we can hardly influence and that are more or less inevitable, such as God, the law, police, government, and so on. In other words: institutions. Then, when something goes wrong, we cannot reproach ourselves for relying on the institution, because we had little or no choice. If we have no confidence, we cannot exit. We can only sit back and hope for the best. Regarding a judge, we would usually speak of confidence (or the lack of it), because we are not usually in a position to choose a judge or influence his judgement, and can only submit to what is imposed on us. If we can choose or bribe a judge, we might speak of trust. Regarding God also it is appropriate to talk of confidence. It would seem hubris to talk of trust, as if we could dodge his influence. Perhaps we could trust the gods of classical Greece, who were much like humans, and could be bribed, seduced or played off against each other. Summing up: we can talk of institutional trust, but mostly that will be a matter of confidence rather than trust, so that it would be better to speak of *institutional confidence*.

Earlier, I identified conditional trust as trust in external conditions that may affect, that is enable or constrain, the outcome of actions, in the use of means and competence according to intentions. Since institutions are also defined in terms of enabling and constraining conditions, there is a link between conditional and institutional trust. Institutions form an important part of conditions for actions. However, institutions do not exhaust all conditions. Those also include laws of nature, for example.

We can speak of self-confidence, self-trust and self-reliance. If we follow the previous definitions, self-confidence would apply when we are inevitable to ourselves: we cannot change and can only hope for the best. This might apply to instincts, cognitive limitations or addiction. Cognitive limitations include the fundamental categories that underlie thought, as discussed before. Self-reliance would apply if there were choice, and trust in our own behaviour is based on a variety of safeguards: duty, conviction, supervision, and coercion. Self-trust would apply if we trust our behaviour in the absence of coercion and against temptations and the weakness of our will. For example, we are resolved to engage in a slimming programme, and we need not ask our partners to hide the fattening delicacies or block ourselves from buying them. We need not surrender our car keys at a party to keep ourselves from drunken driving. This relates to an old definition, in philosophy, of freedom not as lack of constraint but as voluntary restraint. Here I would say: self-trust. We are free if we have a choice to sin, we would derive material or hedonic benefit from it, and yet we choose not to do so.

An important question, relatively neglected in the literature, concerns the relation between trust in people and trust in organizations. How do they differ? Is trust in organizations based on trust in people, or vice versa, or both? For an illustration of the difference between trust in organizations and in people, consider the following example.

> If we trust people to keep a secret, that is just a matter of their individual will, while for organizations the question is whether it can manage to get all the people involved to keep the secret. Professionals, such as researchers, may want to brag about the outcomes of their research at conferences, while the organization wants to keep it a secret. Therefore, trust in an organization to keep a secret may require an appreciation of the interest that the organization has in keeping its promises of confidentiality, and its ability to get its people to keep secrets.

Clearly, one can have behavioural trust in organizations, in the expectation that in our dealings with them, they will not fail us. It is also clear that this can be broken down into: competence trust in the organization's technology, organization and the overall, collective ability of an organization to perform; material trust in the supply of raw materials, components, labour, and so on; intentional trust in its codes and standards of business ethics; honesty trust in the truth of its reporting and public statements; and conditional trust in the effects of the institutional environment and competition. These are inferred from corporate image and reputation, and from experience in one's own dealings with the organization. These foundations of trust will be discussed in Chapter 3.

We should note, however, that in organizations competencies are built up from competencies of people. For these organizational capabilities, March and Simon (1958) used the term 'performance programs' and Nelson and Winter (1982) used the term 'routines'. We need to solve the multi-level problem: how do the levels of people and organizations connect? And beyond an organization, could we trust an entire industry?

In earlier work (Nooteboom 1999f, 2000a) I used the notion of a 'script' to deal with the multi-level problem. A script is an architecture of nodes that represent chunks of lower level, component activity. Scripts have been used to model cognition on the level of people (Shank and Abelson 1977). For example, a restaurant script consists of a typical sequence of typical activities (nodes): entering, seating, food selection, preparation, eating, paying, leaving. Such scripts can also be used to model organizational activities, as the restaurant example already shows. Scripts were used to model organizational processes before, by Gioia and Poole (1984). Individuals substitute activities into nodes of organizational scripts. Scripts can be used recursively on different levels. Organizations can be seen as substituting activities in higher level industry scripts, representing supply chains, for example. Activities substituted by people into organizational scripts can themselves be analysed as scripts. So, one can trust an organization in the sense of trusting its scripts. Trust in organizational scripts concerns the efficacy of those scripts, on the organizational level, given their architectures, and the ability of the organization to co-ordinate the nodes, that is to implement and maintain a script. It also includes trust in the abilities of people to contribute their parts. So, people are included according to the organizational roles they play. However, of course people also participate in many scripts outside their organizational roles. People are more than the organizational roles they play; they are also people 'qua persona' (Smith Ring and van de Ven 1994). Having interactions also outside the organization, their cognitive categories will never become identical to those of other people in the organization. This is a source of both error and innovation, and often the two cannot be distinguished until the outcomes have had a chance to work themselves out.

How does intentional trust in organizations work? Earlier, on the level of people, intentional trust included trust in dedication or care (attention not to make mistakes, effort), and trust in benevolence or goodwill (no opportunism). Can we have these in organizations as well? Can we attribute intentions to organizations? The indication that organizations can have intentions lies in the fact that they issue mission statements and often have a more or less explicit and more or less detailed code of ethics. Firms can certainly accept responsibility and liability. They can engage in contracts, renege on them, and be challenged before a court of law.[2]

We can have trust in the competence of organizations to foster and control the competencies and intentions of the people in it, including their dedication and care, and their inclination towards benevolence rather than opportunism. This can be done on the basis of structures and procedures of control, with organizational scripts, as indicated before. As noted by Mintzberg (1983), there are a variety of coordination mechanisms: direct supervision, standardization of works processes, of in- and outputs, of skills, or by mutual adaptation. As also noted before, organizations have cultural identities. On the surface of organizational culture we find symbols, myths, rituals, styles of behaviour, tall stories, heroes that set examples to be followed. Below that there are more fundamental shared categories of understanding (Schein 1985). These are part of the organization seen as a focusing device (see Chapter 1). Organizational procedures (scripts) and culture can both help us to trust the people in the organization. Intentions are shaped, even if unintentionally, by organizational culture. Underlying values shape ethics. Intentions may be controlled in standard operating procedures, a code of ethics, and written and unwritten cultural codes of behaviour. They may be instilled by symbols and exemplars, in the form of role models that are part of the myths and heroes of organizational culture. All these may be aimed to secure reputation and a corporate identity that are conducive to profit or survival. Thus our trust in people can be enhanced or limited by our trust in the organizations they belong to. For example, our trust in a doctor may be derived from our trust in the hospital he is associated with, on the basis of its reputation.

However, there are malevolent organizations, whose procedures and culture are geared towards opportunism. Procedures and culture may be aimed, explicitly or implicitly, to incite people in the organization to opportunism on behalf of the organization. For the sake of reputation and corporate image this is likely to remain implicit and covert. However, it may be projected as part of the organizations' image, to instil fear, as in the Mafia. Thus it makes sense to talk of the intentions of an organization, in terms of the constraints and guidance of behaviour, generated by procedures and culture.

---

[2] I make a distinction between an organization and a firm. A firm is an organization but also a legal entity, which enables it to own capital, hire people, engage in contracts, and so on. An organizational form which is not a firm is a collaborative relationship between firms, such as an alliance, unless the alliance takes the form of an equity joint venture. Some organizational forms that are not firms have other legal status, such as an association.

Note that it is people acting on behalf of the organization who yield the results. For this they need to be motivated intrinsically or by monitoring plus rewards and/or punishments. People can be more or less trustworthy than their organizational role requires. Thus, to trust an organization, one must look at its interests and intentions as an organization, but also at the way in which those are embedded in culture and embodied and implemented in organizational roles, motivation and control.

Conversely, organizational trust may be based on trust in the people one is involved with. That can be tricky. They may make promises that they cannot keep since those go beyond their organizational competence or influence. Trust in lower echelons may not be backed up by their bosses, and trust in bosses may not be supported by their subordinates or shareholders. Thus one has to look at both the people and their organizational roles. In time, people in organizations may become increasingly socialized to conform to their organizational roles. However, they may also become more and more expert in dodging rules and monitoring procedures, and become perfect embezzlers.

Organizations can also be the subject of trust, that is not the trustee but the trustor. The trust that an organization has in others is built up from opinions, rumours, or facts accumulating inside or outside the organization. It can be based on hearsay and gossip or on a thorough investigation of performance. When conclusions are reached they may be formalized in decisions to stop dealing with no longer trusted partners, special procedures to be followed, or instructions to take special care. The further discussion of the foundations of organizational trust belongs in Chapter 3.

Further, more systematic insight may be derived, here again, from an application of the Aristotelian notion of multiple causality. People constitute an efficient cause in organizations, their motives and intentions constitute a final cause, and their competencies constitute a formal cause. The organization, however, can affect that final cause by means of incentive systems or other forms of motivation, and it can affect the formal cause by training. The organization must supply the means (material cause) for individual action, and the conditions (conditional cause), in the form of organizational structure, procedures and support. An important role of organizational culture is to yield an exemplary cause as guidance for action. This is particularly important when other forms of coordination, such as direct supervision, standardization of work processes, standardization of outputs and standardization of skills are difficult or inappropriate, while one does not want to go so far as to surrender the organization to the lack of direction that would arise from an unlimited scope for mutual adjustment.

Interestingly, Grey and Garsten (2001) pointed at emerging conditions of more autonomous and footloose labour, especially in the case of professionals who work on the basis of short-term assignments or projects, and may work for multiple organizations at the same time. There, the effectiveness of corporate culture as a basis and criterion for individual trustworthiness erodes. For such footloose professionals there is a shift to professional standards as the basis for trustworthiness. A question here is whether that refers only to competence trust or also to intentional trust. Do the corresponding professional associations focus only on competence or also on ethics? Looking only at trustworthiness as predictability, the authors do not make that distinction.

The relation between personal and organizational trust can be summarized as follows. In going from trust in people to trust in the organization they work for, one should take into account whether their perceived intentions are endorsed by the organization, whether the necessary means and organizational conditions are available to perform according to expectations, and whether external conditions (such as competition) give room for it. Conversely, in going from organizational to individual trust, one should consider whether organizational objectives and exemplars are adequately reflected in the individual's intentions and can be implemented with his competencies, and are supported by procedures for monitoring, and motivation or incentive systems. The relation between organizational and personal trust lies in the roles people play in the organization, the conditions and directions given for playing these roles, and monitoring them, in the form of organizational structure, procedures and culture.

We can go beyond organizations to consider industries and institutions more widely. Industries are also said to have 'industry recipes' (Spender 1989): certain procedures that the industry takes for granted and that coordinate different activities in supply chains and the like. As indicated before, scripts also may model these. One can trust the ability of an industry to offer and supply products, protect the environment, and deal with problems. One can trust intentions to be open on product quality, pollution and safety. One may trust them not to engage in anti-competitive practices, such as cartels or the erection of entry barriers. Here, we can apply an analysis that is similar to the previous one. In going from industry trust to organizational trust we should consider to what extent industry standards are adequately reflected in organizational goals, and are secured by organizational competencies, and the role in this of monitoring, reputation, incentives (such as accreditation, licensing, and so on). As already indicated, the behaviour of professionals may be based on professional standards and organizations.

More in general, we can analyse the effects of institutions, that is of the institutional environment on organizations, and of organizations on people, in terms of the multiple causes of action, with corresponding forms of trust. This entails that we consider how competencies, means, conditions and intentions, including dedication, benevolence and honesty, are enabled and constrained by the higher level institutions, and how those, in turn, according to some of the same types of causality, are supported and reproduced by the lower level activities. This brings us back to the discussion of the interaction between structure and agency in Chapter 1.

3. Foundations

This chapter turns to the foundations of trust and trustworthiness. The first part considers the rational reasons and psychological causes of trust and trustworthiness. Reliance can be based on assurance and on trust in the strong sense. Assurance is based on control, with motives of self-interest. Trust in the strong sense is based on altruism. Altruism is likely to be limited, and hence trust in the strong sense is restricted within tolerance levels. Beyond those, one seeks control. Trust may be rational, but is also based on, and biased by, a variety of psychological mechanisms. The second part discusses the process, the dynamics of the production and destruction of trust. How does trust develop where there was none before? When does conflict break trust and when does it deepen it?

3.1 THE BASIS OF TRUSTWORTHINESS AND TRUST

There are rational reasons for trust, based on an inference and attribution of trustworthiness. That comes close to the notions of calculus-based trust and knowledge-based trust in the literature. The analysis is normative, indicating what would be rational to do. In a more descriptive account, trust is also based on psychological causes of affect, routine, lack of awareness or neglect of relational risk, and psychological phenomena such as cognitive dissonance and decision heuristics. Some of that comes close to what in the literature is called affect-based trust.

Question 7: The sources of trustworthiness
On what is trustworthiness of people based? Coercion, self-interest, ethics, friendship, routinization? Does it go beyond self-interest? If it does, can it survive in markets?

Question 8: The mental basis of trust
On what is trust based, and how: knowledge, experience, analysis, emotions, habits, faith?

Sources of Trustworthiness

Here, I focus on behavioural trust, that is trust with regard to people, individually and in organizations, and particularly intentional trust: what will make people dedicate themselves and refrain from opportunism? Analysis of that aspect of trust is arguably the most urgent and the most difficult. In rational, knowledge-based trust, reasons for trust arise from the inference and attribution to a partner of sources of trustworthiness, derived from experience, reputation, records, ratings, publications and the like. Here we return to the question whether calculative self-interest is the only viable basis for trust and trustworthiness, or trust can go beyond coercion and self-interest, to include ethics and loyalty. Or would that entail a foolish, blind, unconditional trust that will not survive in markets, as Williamson proposed?

Table 3.1 gives a survey of different sources of intentional trustworthiness, or, more precisely, reliability, since it includes both sources of self-interest and sources going beyond that. It is adopted and adapted from Williams (1988), who proposed it for the sources of cooperation, which I equate with intentional reliability. I have modified his scheme, adding elements from other literature.

Williams distinguished between 'macro' sources, which apply generally and impersonally, apart from any specific exchange relation. They arise from the 'institutional environment' of laws, norms, values, standards and agencies for their enforcement. They are also called sources of 'thin' trust. The 'micro' sources arise in specific relations, and are therefore personalized. They are also called sources of 'thick' trust. Williams further distinguished between self-interest and altruism as a source of cooperation. Earlier, in Chapter 2, I proposed to use the term 'assurance' for self-interested sources of trustworthiness, and trust in the strong sense for sources that go beyond self-interest, or what here is called 'altruism'. Taken together, in a two by two matrix, this yields four sources of intentional trustworthiness, in the wide sense of 'reliance', discussed in Chapter 2. The altruistic sources go beyond self-interested behaviour, on the basis of established, socially inculcated norms and values (macro), and affect, empathy or identification, and routine-based trustworthiness (habituation) developed in specific relations (micro). These latter sources provide the basis for trust in the strong sense.

Table 3.1 incorporates many elements and intuitions from the literature. The distinction between egotistic and altruistic sources is related to the distinction between what Lindenberg (2000) called a 'gain frame' versus a 'normative' frame. In other words, the table reflects the widespread view that trust (in the wide sense of reliance) includes elements of control,

Table 3.1   Sources of cooperation (intentional reliability)

	Macro	Micro
Egotistic	Sanctions from some authority (the law, god, Leviathan, dictator, patriarch, organization), contractual obligation	Material advantage or self-interest: shadow of the future, reputation, hostages
Altruistic	Ethics: values, social norms of proper conduct, moral obligation, sense of duty	Bonds of friendship, kinship; routines, habituation, empathy

Source: Adapted from Williams (1988).

including both legal coercion and control by incentives and dependence, as well as elements that go beyond control, as a basis for 'goodwill' or 'benevolence'.[1] As noted by Maguire et al. (2001: 286): if we do not include the latter, we conflate trust and power. In yet other words, the table includes the distinction between coercive/remunerative or formal control (Das and Teng 1998), in the first row, and normative or social control by norms, in the second row. I do not wish to suggest that altruism or goodwill operates independently from self-interest or control. The relation between the two is a subject for extensive debate. Some discussion on this was given in Chapter 2, and the discussion will continue in the present chapter. As noted by Bachmann (2000: 303), trust (reliance, as I would say) is a hybrid phenomenon, including both calculation and goodwill.

The table presumes institutional systems as the basis for reliance, in the form of legal systems supporting laws and litigation, and norms of behaviour. This entails that we trust those institutions to support sources of trustworthiness of people and organizations. The notion of social control by norms in society goes back to Parsons' (1951) idea of a suspension of self-interest for solidarity on the basis of institutionalized, shared values, and to Durkheim's (1933) notion of 'organic solidarity'. In the second row, right column I go beyond 'macro' norms of behaviour that are imposed or absorbed in socialization from the institutional environment, to include 'micro' socialization and empathy embedded and developed in specific relations. Next to an institutional level there is an inter-personal level (Bachmann 2000: 307). And I would not call that 'control', since especially the sources of trustworthiness on the inter-personal level are highly volun-

---

[1] For example, see Lane and Bachmann (1996) and the special issue of *Organization Studies on Trust and Control in Organizational Relations*, 22/2, 2001.

Table 3.2   Sources of reliance

	Macro	Micro
Control	Contracts, supervision	Partner's dependence on value, hostages, reputation
Trust (in strong sense)	Norms, values, habits	Habituation, empathy/ identification, friendship

tary rather than imposed. Butler (2001: 369) ended a review of Lane and Bachmann (1996) as follows: 'a fruitful way forward would be to locate the notion of trust more firmly within an institutional framework of both formal regulation and informal tacit relations'. That, I propose, is what Table 3.1 offers.

The distinction between macro and micro sources is also known as the distinction between 'universalistic' or 'generalized' sources versus 'particularistic' sources, made by Deutsch (1973: 55), and between impersonal and personalized sources made by Shapiro (1987), and goes back to the work of Parsons. Social norms and moral obligations, including a sense of duty, following Parsons and Durkheim, were proposed more recently by Bradach and Eccles (1984), Zucker (1986), Granovetter (1985) and Dore (1983), among others. Fukuyama (1995) employed the term of 'spontaneous sociability'. Calculation of self-interest includes reputation (Weigelt and Camerer 1988) and the assessment of future benefits of present cooperativeness ('shadow of the future'), as has been recognized by many (Telser 1980, Axelrod 1984, Frank 1988, Hill 1990, Heide and Miner 1992, Parkhe 1993). Chiles and McMackin (1996) later proposed a taxonomy that is similar in some respects to that of Williams. It included social norms, moral obligations, social embeddedness, sense of duty, rational self-interest and reputation. I have added some of these elements to the original taxonomy proposed by Williams.

Related to the sources of reliability there are sources of reliance. These are specified in Table 3.2. Rational sources of reliance entail an assessment of the sources of reliability. Here we find the duality of (formal) control, in creating reliability on the basis of contracts, supervision, rewards and incentives, and trust that goes beyond that, on the basis of norms, values or bonding that arises within a relation.

An important condition for trust or reliance to arise is of course the need for it. That increases with the need to collaborate. Consider the earlier example of the demolition experts. Blowing holes in a mountain is teamwork and the danger involved creates a high degree of mutual dependence.

Ex ante, this yields a reason to avoid such strong dependence and take another job, but once one is in that situation there is need to trust, and to seek or develop the basis for it. Evidently, a problem arises under asymmetric dependence. The most dependent partner needs to trust most but this is problematic precisely because his partner has a lesser need for trust and trustworthiness. As a result, the more dependent partner will often be suspicious, and that by itself can make it difficult for the trust to develop that he needs so much. One solution is to make dependence symmetrical, by means of control. The choice of instruments for this is discussed in more detail in Chapter 4. Alternatively, the least dependent partner has to show benevolence.

I will now proceed to discuss in more detail each of the sources of reliability, and thereby the sources of rational trust, in the four cells in Table 3.1.

Extension

In Table 3.1, the upper left box contains coercion by institutionalized authority, laws and rules. Coercion by authority is seldom perfect, due to limited or asymmetric information. God of course sees all, but someone's boss in an organization may not. Therefore, trust in people on the basis of organizational safeguards cannot be certain. The trust in people based on trust in the organization they work for depends on the perceived or inferred effectiveness of organizational structure, procedure and culture, along the lines discussed in Chapter 2. Next to the exercise of authority, coercion also takes the form of contractual obligations. These require appropriate and reliable institutions of law and enforcement. Even under the best of institutional conditions, legal ordering cannot be closed, including all relevant future contingencies, to carry their implications to the present ('presentiation') and cover them in the contract (Macneil 1980). This is related to the previous discussion of radical uncertainty, in Chapters 1 and 2. Also, contracts carry costs, and entail economies of scale (Nooteboom 1993), so that they are relatively costly for smaller firms and for small or infrequent transactions. For this reason, Williamson (1985) proposed that for infrequent transactions one may need to resort to 'trilateral governance', where limited, simple contracts are complemented with mediation or arbitration by some third party. Contracts are only useful to the extent that one is able to monitor and judge conformance to them. Between firms, that is even more difficult than monitoring within a firm.

Often, one employs agents precisely because they have a competence that one lacks and cannot judge. I cannot judge the quality of a tax consultant. If I could, I probably wouldn't need him. In other words, his service is a 'credence product'. And even if one can properly assess the execution of agreements, especially small principals may not be in a position to credibly threaten litigation, due to the economies of scale involved. Examples are bad quality of travel or holiday arrangements, insurance, consultancy and accountancy. The risk, effort and cost of litigation, and the difficulty of proving damage, are large relative to the damage incurred. It is not a realistic alternative to personalize such relations, and develop guarantees of personal bonding (Zucker 1986, Shapiro 1987). A reputation mechanism may help, but such mechanisms are not automatic. As a result, there is a host of different types of intermediaries whose task it is to help judge performance and to provide intermediation or arbitration in conflicts. The difference between intermediation and arbitration is that in the first acceptance of a judgement is voluntary, while in the second it is imposed. Shapiro (1987) called these intermediaries 'guardians of trust', Zucker (1986) saw them as part of 'institutions based trust', and Fukuyama used the term 'intermediate communities'. Shapiro (1987: 636) described their functions as follows: 'Procedural norms and structural constraints on trustee roles imitate contract. Agent-selection procedures and policing mechanisms mimic personal social control. Insurance-like arrangements collectively spread risks or offer compensation for failures of social control'.

In the travel example, there is an association of travel agencies that provides insurance and compensation for failed arrangements and bankruptcy of agencies or operators, and an avenue for complaints. There are similar associations for plumbing, insurance, consultancy and accountancy. However, as pointed out by Shapiro (1987), the question arises who guards the guardians. Self-control by professional organizations who claim to control the members on whom they depend is suspect, because they are tempted to go easy on them. There may also be other conflicts of interest.

One example is that accountancy firms who merged with consultancy firms are tempted to go easy on the control of firms who are also customers for large consultancy projects. During the present stock market slump, accusations arise that investment brokers associated with banks have artificially pushed share prices up. In the hype of 'dot-com ventures', they failed to advise sales of stocks of companies that were floated by the investment banking department of the bank they were associated with.

In Table 3.1, the lower left box contains values and norms of social behaviour, in an ethic or custom of conduct. On a deep level of basic values of conduct, these are part of culture in the anthropological sense (see the discussion of culture in Chapter 2). This may apply to countries or professions, but as discussed in Chapter 2 cultural norms also apply to organizations, with their specialized cultures in a wider institutional environment. Norms and values of behaviour tend to be internalized, to a greater or lesser extent, by people as part of tacit knowledge, assimilated in socialization and habitualization. Note that such non-reflective sources of cooperation do belong here, in the discussion of the rational foundations of trust, since one can rationally assess the non-rational, ethical sources of an agent's behaviour.

Of course, one can never be sure ex ante to what extent a stranger without reputation has actually internalized such norms and values. Here, Williamson was right in saying that under such conditions of behavioural uncertainty one must take the possibility of opportunism into account. However, that does not automatically imply that one should go for contractual safeguards, supposing they are feasible and effective. That may have various negative effects, as will be discussed later. An alternative recognized by transaction cost economics is to have specialized intermediaries judge the conformance to norms and standards. Surface level norms that are expressed in ethics and standards of professional practice are often operationalized, guarded and monitored by the guardians of trust discussed above, such as professional organizations. Shapiro (1987: 638) expressed this as follows: 'To facilitate compliance with these norms, measures fashioned by government regulators, professional associations and trustees themselves manipulate the social organization of agency'.

The disposition to observe norms and to follow rules of social behaviour can be motivated by an internalized sense of duty or commitment, or by the desire for social recognition (Fukuyama 1995), as noted in Chapter 1. As quoted by Fukuyama (1995: 359), Adam Smith in his *Theory of Moral Sentiments* already recognized that social recognition more generally is an important driver of behaviour: 'It is the vanity, not the ease or the pleasure, which interests us' (Smith 1982: 50). This desire for social recognition could perhaps be construed as being part of self-interest. Contrary to what Smith said, the intrinsic value of trust-based relationships, with their 'ease and pleasure', can also be a source of collaboration. That can be construed as utility and hence also part of self-interest. Therefore, the different boxes in Table 3.1 may not be as distinct as the table suggests, because there are spillovers or connections between them. In the drive towards social recognition, social conformance to norms may connect with self-interest. Earlier, I identified a link between the boxes of coercion and values and norms, by intermediate 'guardians of trust'. I will return to these spillovers between the boxes in Table 3.1 later.

Now I turn to the micro-level, personalized sources of collaboration, in the right-hand column of Table 3.1. The upper-right-hand box of material self-interest focuses on the condition that one is so dependent on a relationship that one will not hazard opportunistic behaviour, for fear of retaliation. As already indicated, this includes expectation of future rewards from cooperative conduct in the present (the 'shadow of the future'). It also includes the preservation of reputation (Weigelt and Camerer 1988). Note that efficient reputation mechanisms cannot be taken for granted (Hill 1990, Lazaric and Lorenz 1998). They require that malevolent or incompetent behaviour is reliably detected and communicated, and that the culprit has an interest in future relations with potential partners from the community where his reputation is known. The culprit must not be able to engage in hit-and-run, escaping from the community when his malevolence or incompetence is detected. Therefore, one may need intermediate agencies to provide the selection and broadcasting needed for a reputation mechanism. Selection is needed to separate legitimate complaints from gossip and slander, and broadcasting is needed to communicate the complaint to relevant potential future partners. This yields two of the many functions of the 'guardians of trust' discussed before.

Self-interest may also include the need to protect 'hostages' (Williamson 1985). The essence of a hostage is that it has value for the hostage giver but not for the holder. Therefore, the latter would not hesitate to sacrifice the hostage in order to punish the hostage giver in case he reneges on his promise to collaborate, and this would hurt the hostage giver. In business, hostages often take the form of information or knowledge that is sensitive, in the sense that it could cause great damage when leaked to competitors. It can also take the form of cross-participation, or the borrowing of staff, with the threat of poaching them. One problem with hostages is that the holder may refuse to return the hostage at the agreed moment in spite of the fact that the hostage giver has satisfied his obligations. One reason for this may be that the holder wants to maintain his hold over the giver. Another problem may be that after a time the hostage acquires value for the holder, so that he can no longer credibly threaten to sacrifice it. Conversely, the hostage may die or lose its value to both sides.

A classic and mundane illustration of a hostage is the shoe that one leaves with the cobbler. He will not demand payment in advance, since he holds the shoe as a hostage. One will not demand proof of having surrendered the shoe, since it is of no value to anyone else, so that there is no chance that the cobbler will appropriate or sell it. Another illustration is the following. A number of years ago, the Dutch passenger car manufacturer DAF could not survive, and was rescued in a joint venture between Volvo, Mitsubishi and the Dutch government, orchestrated by the then minister of economic affairs Andriessen. The concern of the Dutch government was that one of the foreign partners would take out the design capability from DAF, and leave only a hollow or 'screwdriver' factory. Asked about this on TV, the minister grinned smugly and told of the shoebox he had sitting on his desk, containing the design for the next generation Volvo cars, developed in the Netherlands. This suggested that if Volvo reneged on the agreement and took out the design capability, these designs would be in jeopardy. Of course, meanwhile those cars have appeared on the roads, and the hostage has outlived its usefulness. Ford has now taken over Volvo, and again the question is what will happen to the Dutch design capability.

Intrinsic value of trusting behaviour, liked for its own sake, and preferred to the aggravation of suspicion, is included in self-interest. I noted before that it might be linked to the desire for social recognition of loyalty. It may also be linked to the personalized, affect- or routine-based sources of cooperation. The preference for trust-based dealings may be part of friendship, to which I turn now.

The personalized micro bonds of kinship, empathy, or friendship, in the lower-right-hand box of Table 3.1, yield altruistic sources of trustworthiness that are attached to specific relations ex ante (kinship), or may be built up (or broken down) in the course of relations (empathy, friendship). Here, intrinsic value of the relation is particularly prominent, next to extrinsic value. This requires a discussion of underlying processes, to which I will turn in the second part of this chapter.

As pointed out by Williamson (1993), there is a risk of blindness here. Personal bonds may prevent us from recognising and facing hazards of opportunism, by blindness or cognitive dissonance. Therefore, Williamson argued, they are unwise and will not survive in markets, and should be reserved for non-economic relations of family and friendship. Problems of trust and betrayal in family firms and partnerships between friends can be especially acute because the reliability of personal bonds could not be questioned. Several popular television series have been based on that theme. Therefore, the important question arises how trustworthy affect-based trust is. Can it be genuine without going so far as to be blind and unconditional? Can we establish the limits of such trust without thereby falling back into calculative self-interest?

This issue was discussed in Chapter 2. There, I proposed that trustworthiness is generally, and wisely, seen as subject to limits which represent a partner's resistance to temptation and pressures of survival. These limits depend on affect-based loyalty, but also on survival conditions that derive from competition and demands from capital markets. Within these limits, a partner can be trusted in the strong sense that he/she will not engage in opportunism even if he/she has both the opportunity and incentive for it. As a result, trust is subject to tolerance levels, within which actions will not be safeguarded or scrutinized for opportunism. When events are perceived to transgress those levels, attention to the possibility of opportunism will be triggered. In this way, trust is kept from becoming unconditional. Yet, within those limits it is real, and yields forbearance, give and take, limited safeguards, and so on. This is the first part of my answer to Williamson's claim that behaviour that is not based on calculative self-interested behaviour is blind and cannot survive in markets. I will return to this issue in the discussion of the failures and limits of trust, in Chapter 5.

In the box on micro/altruistic sources in Table 3.1 I have included routinized behaviour, which may also be called 'habituation'. This yields the second part of my answer to Williamson. Routinized behaviour by definition is non-reflective, and thus cannot be called calculative. Nevertheless, as Herbert Simon has taught us long ago, routinized behaviour is rational in view of bounded rationality, since it allows us to focus our limited capacity for attention and rational evaluation on matters that are new and have priority. Routines are rational also in the sense that they are based on proven success in past behaviour. On the other hand, their lack of awareness creates the problem that they may no longer be adequate when conditions change. However, when results or perceived events exceed certain tolerance levels, routines are often summoned back from subsidiary into focal awareness (Polanyi 1962), to be subjected to rational scrutiny. Routines may subside so deeply into tacit knowledge as to become inextricable, like instinct. However, this is likely to occur only after such a long time, in a succession of generations, that the change that makes routines fail must be very drastic and exceptional.

Economists in particular, but also rational choice sociologists, are prone to push everything into self-interest, in order to preserve their theoretical perspective of self-interested, rational choice. However, the point is that even then a conflict remains between different dimensions of such a generalized notion of self-interest. People may be torn between self-interest in terms of direct material advantage, the intrinsic value of trust-based relationships, with what Adam Smith called 'ease or pleasure', and what he called the 'vanity' of social recognition. Such recognition derives from a certain amount of altruism, with a greater or lesser sacrifice in terms of money. Therefore, I prefer to keep it in the category of altruism, in contrast with what I call gain or 'material advantage or interest'. If self-interest is defined so broadly as to include, by definition, everything that motivates behaviour, the thesis of self-interested behaviour becomes unfalsifiable. It also becomes confusing, since it neglects the fact that different more and less 'self-interested' motives are often in conflict. There is a real conflict between taking advantage or remaining loyal to a relation during hardship, and the conflict does not disappear when we define loyalty as self-interest. Even if altruism is pursued for the sake of social recognition, it is still altruism, in the sense that material sacrifices have to be made for it.

In an overview of the different sources of collaboration, in Table 3.1, Williams argued that none of these sources by itself suffices and that, in cooperation, some mix will always be operative, while no universally best mix, regardless of specific conditions, can be specified. Often, trust based on friendship or kinship will not suffice as a basis for cooperation. It may not be sufficiently robust to extremes of temptation. Conversely, material self-interest and coercion are seldom sufficient as a basis for cooperation. One needs trust on the basis of non-egotistic sources to the extent that one cannot fully control the partner's conduct by threat and reward (compare Deutsch 1962, quoted in Zand 1972), to make this fragile basis for cooperation more resilient (Smith Ring and van de Ven 1992). In Chapter 4 I return to this theme of how trust is related to alternative instruments of governance.

People, organizations and countries differ in their orientation, that is their preference and tolerance, towards the different sources of collaboration, as part of their mental categories concerning motives and conditions of behaviour. Some (Americans, perhaps) are more oriented towards legal assurance, others towards assurance on the basis of self-interest, others (Japanese, perhaps) towards trust (in the strong sense) based on social norms, and others (Latin countries perhaps) towards trust based on personal relations. Earlier, I indicated the importance of empathy, resulting from identification on the basis of shared mental categories concerning behaviour. To the extent that this arises, there will be more mutual understanding and tolerance of behaviour, based on the awareness that in the shoes of one's partner one may well have acted as he does. In that way, through empathy, reliance is affected by culture.

Reciprocity

The matrix in Table 3.1 may suggest a hard, clear separation between the cells, while this is not in fact there. As Bachmann (2000: 307) phrased it, they are loosely coupled. There are spillovers or connections between them, with intermediate, mixed forms. Some of these have already been examined. Intermediary 'trust guardians' play a role between, on the one hand, norms and standards of behaviour and, on the other hand, laws and rules of coercion. The observance of social norms of behaviour may be part of a pursuit of social recognition, which may be seen as part of self-interest. The intrinsic value of trust-based relations may be seen as part of self-interest, and it may be connected with both the social recognition just indicated, and the disposition to be loyal to friends, which is here rendered as part of affect-based altruistic motives.

In sociology, there is an extensive literature on reciprocity and the giving of gifts. For a recent discussion, see Vandevelde (2000). Reciprocity may be seen as an intermediate form between self-interest and altruism. It has been characterized as short-term altruism for long-term self-interest (Putnam 2000: 134). In economic exchange, there is a principle of strict 'quid pro quo', where reciprocity in exchange is either immediate or contractually guaranteed, with a specification of future conditions and procedures. As Macneil (1980) argued, this is somewhat of a myth, since future conditions cannot in general be specified (in 'presentiation'), due to uncertainty. Nevertheless, the attempt at guarantees at least is there. In the social giving of gifts, reciprocity is not immediate, not guaranteed, and cannot be demanded. Such demand would invalidate its social function, which is to bond a relationship. Immediate reciprocation would be a signal that the recipient declines to engage in a relationship. Nevertheless, the gift establishes an informal, non-strict obligation to reciprocate, in due time and measure. In view of this, the giver is expected to soften the obligation, by belittling his gift when he is thanked ('you are welcome', 'my pleasure', 'pas de quoi'). It is important to maintain reciprocation as a free choice, and avoid any impression of manipulation, compulsion or purchase of obligation. In social reciprocity, giving must remain spontaneous, surprising and imperfectly predictable. Nevertheless, gift giving with this type of reciprocity often serves our self-interest. It fosters good reputation, gratitude and return gifts. As Vandevelde (2000: 15) formulated it: 'the logic of the gift thus can be reduced neither to disinterestedness or altruism, nor to strict, calculative egotism. Something of both motivations inheres, or even better: the logic of the gift is situated beyond the opposition between egotism and altruism.'

In Table 3.1 social reciprocity may be situated in between the rows of self-interest and altruism. Gift giving can be used for manipulation, imposing a claim for something in return. However, though unusual, gifts or sacrifices *can* be completely disinterested or altruistic, without an expectation or even wish of reciprocity. Then they fall squarely in the lower row. A form of extreme altruism is friendly reciprocation to a hostile action ('turn the other cheek'; compare Vandevelde 2000).

The combination of economic and social reciprocation can be problematic. This is known in labour relations, for example. Extrinsic rewards such as wages on the basis of contracts are part of strict, economic reciprocity. Intrinsic rewards such as uncontracted, largely symbolic rewards or expressions of appreciation can be part of social reciprocity. Often, the two do not mix well. Strict, economic reciprocation can obstruct the building of social reciprocation, and can be destructive of existing ones.

A classic example is the following. A centre for day care of children found that sometimes parents came late in picking up their children. As an attempted remedy, they imposed a financial penalty in proportion to lateness. Then, lateness

Table 3.3   Intermediate sources of cooperation

	Macro		Micro
Egotistic	coercion, fear legal obedience		quid pro quo economic reciprocity
	social hierarchy trust guardians	reputation, social reciprocity	
Altruistic	social conformance social obligation		disinterestedness spontaneous sociality

increased rather than decreased. The interpretation here is that previously there was an ethic of trying the utmost not to be late, out of a sense of solidarity or fair play. When lateness was punished by a financial penalty, this attitude eroded and was substituted by the idea that since lateness was now paid for, it could be seen as part of the deal.

Table 3.1 can be extended to include intermediate and mixed sources of collaboration, across both the vertical and the horizontal boundaries in the matrix. An intermediate form on the horizontal boundary between egotistic and altruistic motives on the micro side is social reciprocity, as discussed above. Reciprocity may also be a mixed form on the vertical boundary between macro and micro sources. The altruistic part may rest on both shared values or norms of behaviour and personal bonds of family, friendship or empathy. An intermediate form on the horizontal boundary on the left side is provided by the intermediary 'guardians of trust' discussed earlier. This yields Table 3.3.

In Table 3.3, I situated reputation on the line between social conformance and economic quid pro quo. With this I try to express the possibility that reputation can have both an extrinsic value in securing a potential for future relations, and an intrinsic value in gaining social recognition. I situated social reciprocity in the middle between 'quid pro quo' or economic reciprocity, altruistic disinterestedness and social conformance. With this I try to express that it can entail a combination of self-interest, personal altruism, social obligation and personal satisfaction derived from that. In between legal coercion and social conformance I added 'social hierarchy' and 'trust guardians'. The latter were discussed before. Social hierarchy obtains in societies with social strata, as in Indian caste society, for example, or medieval western societies. Here, there is a combination of social position, morality and legality. Lower strata are obliged to obey the higher strata, morally and legally, and this may be perceived as a natural or divine order, which is obeyed as a matter of course.

Organizations

Chapter 2 indicated that organizations also could be the object of trust, in both their competence and their intentions. We can trust an organization to behave responsibly, regarding its stakeholders and the environment. Of course an organization itself does not have an intention, but it has interests and can try to regulate the intentions of its workers to serve those interests. The perceived interests of the organization are in turn the result of perceptions and communication of the people in the organization. One's trust in an individual may be based on one's trust in the organization he belongs to. Trust in an organization can be based on trust in the people in it. It can be affected by corporate communication, which aims to project a certain image. But ultimately the proof lies in the performance of its people. Particularly important for the perceptions that underlie trust in an organization are the public conduct of the firm's leadership and roles that connect the firm with customers or outside partners. These are the 'boundary spanners and gatekeepers' such as purchasers, marketers, negotiators, staff exchanged or combined in joint teams with partner firms. In both the foundation of organizational trust on the trust in people and the foundation of personal trust on the trust in an organization, we need to carefully take into account the position and role of those people in the organization. Are their competencies and intentions supported and backed up by the organization? Are the interests and the culture of the organization properly endorsed and implemented by the people? This was discussed in Chapter 2.

In my theory of knowledge, discussed in Chapter 1, I proposed the notion of firm as a focusing device, to align perceptions, interpretations and evaluations sufficiently in order to achieve a common goal. How narrow or sharp and how tight, in the sense of controlled, should that focus be? The wider and looser the focus, the more tenuous the relation between organizational and personal trusts. I indicated a trade-off between a sharp and tight focus, for the sake of efficient exploitation, and a wider and looser focus for the sake of exploration. One way to solve the problem of combining exploitation and exploration is to have a relatively narrow focus in one's own organization, complemented with outside partners at a cognitive distance that is sufficiently large to yield novelty of insight and sufficiently small to yield understanding. Here we see that another reason for a sufficiently sharp and tight scope is to establish a tight coupling between personal and organizational trust.

If the basis for one's trust in an employee is friendship or empathy that has built up in the course of the relationship with him, is this in line with the interest of his firm, and with the norms of conduct that form part of the firm's culture? If not, to what extent can he back up his promises nevertheless, and is there a risk that he will be forced to renege on his promises when found out? Conversely, if one's trust in the organization is based on the fact that its interests demands loyalty to an agreement, can one rely on the person implementing them? Suppose there is personal animosity between you and him. Could he sabotage the agreement and get away with it?

> Lorange and Roos (1992) recounted the case of an alliance between two producers of garden equipment in Sweden and Norway ('Norpartner and Swedpartner'). This was based entirely on a personal relationship between the CEOs of the two companies, as a result of which only limited contractual safeguards were made. A third party, which competed with both, in Sweden and Norway, took over the owner of Swedpartner and ended its alliance with Norpartner, who meanwhile had become so dependent on the alliance that he went bankrupt. In this way the third party eliminated two competitors in one stroke. This case illustrates the point that organizational interests need not be identical to individual interests, and trust in a personal relationship may not be a reliable basis for organizational trust. In this case, one should also have secured a basis for relying on owners, by building in their interests or somehow blocking the possibility of a damaging takeover.

Trustworthiness of organizations depends on survival conditions. For example, to survive it must guard its reputation for quality, its brand names. Such safeguards depend on industry conditions, such as the effectiveness and importance of reputation mechanisms, and the intensity of price competition. The importance of reputation depends on the ability of users to judge quality prior to consumption. Clearly, a firm that is under great pressure to make all the profit it can get and to cut costs where it can, as a matter of sheer survival, can afford less goodwill or benevolence, at the sacrifice of profit, than a firm that is not under such pressure. This yields differences especially between industries.

> In the early nineties, I gave a talk on the governance of inter-firm relations, with an emphasis on buyer–supplier relations, to an audience from the car industry in the Netherlands. There, I presented the results of my efforts to combine considerations of trust with the recognition of hazards of opportunism. The audience scolded me for being so naive as to take trust seriously. Trust, in their view, is naive and not fit for survival in markets (rather like the position taken by Williamson 1993). A few days later I gave a similar talk to the company that explores and produces natural gas in the Netherlands. They took an opposite view, and scolded me for my cynical talk of opportunism. As I drove home afterwards, I realised what lay behind this marked difference. At the time, car sales had slumped, which greatly intensified price competition, and the crisis caused manufacturers to renege on the promises of durable relations to suppliers that had previously been given. The natural gas firm, by contrast, had a tight, government-backed monopoly in their field. They could afford to make life easy for their suppliers and themselves.

In Chapter 2, I proposed that trust may be seen as a default, with the assumption of trustworthiness until evidence to the contrary arises. I added the notion of a limit to perceived or inferred trustworthiness. This allows for the recognition of 'golden opportunities' that may be too good or press-ing for a partner to resist, and a tolerance limit in trust, within which beha-viour is not to be scrutinized for evidence of untrustworthiness. In the rational assessment of trustworthiness, external pressure should be taken into account. Intense competition, due perhaps to a temporary slump in the market, may lower the inferred limit of trustworthiness.

Summing up, in dealing with organizations one has to consider the basis for reliance both of the people one is dealing with and of the organization. What mix of foundations of trust is there on the different levels, of people and organization, and how consistent are they, that is to what extent do they support or compensate for each other? Structure of ownership and control, organizational culture and procedures for guiding, supporting, motivating and controlling people in their organizational roles have a crucial mediating role here, and become part of the basis for organizational trust.

Psychological Sources of Trust[2]

Table 3.2 contains rational sources of reliance in the form of an assessment of the sources of reliability specified in Table 3.1. It is normative, indicat-ing what is wise to base reliance and trust on. More descriptively, next to rational reasons for trust, trust is also based on psychological mechanisms. These include affect: empathy, friendship, love. On the basis of affect one may trust an opportunist. They also include cognitive heuristics for assess-ing the probability of events, for attributing causes, motives and character-istics, and for assigning blame, to others and oneself. These heuristics may be rational, at least in part, in the sense of being adaptive, that is contrib-uting to survival, in view of uncertainty, bounded rationality and the need to make quick decisions and act fast.

As discussed in Chapter 1, evolutionary psychology suggests that a ten-dency towards reciprocity is 'in our genes', since it was conducive to survi-val in the ancient hunter–gatherer societies in which humanity evolved. In gathering edible plants, roots, nuts, and so on, and even more in hunting, there is a large variance of individual success. This, together with problems of durable storage, entails an evolutionary advantage of the willingness to surrender part of one's yield to others in need, in the expectation to receive from them when they are successful (Cosmides and Tooby 1992: 212). This

---

[2] I thank Gabriele Jacobs for her instruction in elements of social psychology. Any errors of interpretation are of course mine.

would solve the problem, often noted in the literature, how in a sequential game of give and take the first move of giving, and thereby making a risky pre-commitment, is made (Simmel 1978, Luhmann 1979, quoted in Lane 2000: 3). The evolutionary argument suggests that we do this instinctively. It also suggests that we have developed a 'cheater detection mechanism' (Cosmides and Tooby, 1992).

However, psychological mechanisms that were conducive to survival in evolution do entail biases that can lead to serious error (Bazerman 1998). These are discussed in Chapter 5, where I analyze the failures of trust. Since I cannot presume to be very knowledgeable in social psychology, I will discuss these psychological mechanisms only briefly. My discussion is sufficient only to indicate their importance and the need for further study of them in relation to trust.

Here we should no longer talk of reasons but of causes of trust. However, the distinction I am making here may suggest a greater cleavage between rationality and emotion than is valid. Like many others, I believe that rationality and emotions are intertwined (Polanyi 1962, Merleau-Ponty 1964, Damasio 1995, Hendriks-Jansen 1996, Lakoff and Johnson 1999). As I indicated earlier, in the discussion of theory of knowledge in Chapter 1, I include in cognition not only perception and interpretation but also evaluation, that is value judgements. Not only value judgements but also interpretations and even perceptions are emotion-laden. In the interpretative or hermeneutic view discussed in Chapter 1, our knowledge is constructed in mental categories, which include psychological mechanisms that may yield serious distortion.

Lakoff and Johnson (1999) offer an evolutionary argument to take into account how cognition is 'embodied in the flesh'. Contrary to the opinion of Descartes, cognition is not separate from the body but is embodied. In evolution, it has been tacked on to bodily processes thrown up by previous evolution. It is rooted in proprioceptive perceptions and mechanisms, reflexes and emotions (Damasio 1995). This bodily embedding of thought was argued before by Merleau-Ponty (1964). It has implications for how cognition works. Thus, Lakoff and Johnson build on their previous work (1980). There, they proposed that to conceptualize abstract notions, such as happiness, goodness, and so on, we can only fall back on more primary bodily perceptions, so that even the most basic categories we use are in the nature of metaphors rather than literal descriptions. For example, goodness, happiness, health, achievement, control are 'up': performance going up, people going up in society, having high standing, feeling up to something, the upper classes, and so on. This is due to the primary experience of standing up when healthy and lying down when ill or dead.

Nevertheless, we can distinguish more or less rational inference of trustworthiness from less reflective causes of trust, based on affect of friendship or kinship, or on routinized behaviour. Earlier, I followed Herbert Simon in identifying the role of emotions in reason, to shift routinized behaviour from subsidiary to focal awareness. Evidence of untrustworthiness may be ignored as a result of cognitive dissonance. As Deutsch (1973: 159) put it:

> A person's perceptions of another will be determined not only by the informa-
> tion he receives, but also by his need to absorb this information in such a way as
> to prevent disruption of existing perceptions, cognitions, or evaluations to which
> he is strongly committed.

Social psychology offers a number of insights into the decision heuristics that people use. In a survey, Bazerman (1998) mentions the following heuristics:

- Availability heuristic: people assess the probability and likely causes of an event by the degree to which instances of it are 'readily available' in memory, that is are vivid, laden with emotion, recent and recognizable. Less available events and causes are neglected.
- Representativeness heuristic: the likelihood of an event is assessed by its similarity to stereotypes of similar occurrences. This is related to the role of defaults and prototypes discussed in Chapter 1. We recognize something according to the likeness of some focal features to those of a prototype, which may be a stereotype, and on the basis of that attribute other features from the stereotype that are not in fact present. This can easily yield prejudice.
- Anchoring and adjustment. Judgement is based on some initial or base value ('anchor') from previous experience or social comparison, plus incremental adjustment from that value. People have been shown to stay close even to random anchors that bear no systematic relation to the issue at hand. First impressions can influence the development of a relation for a long time.

One cannot say that these heuristics are irrational. In view of uncertainty and bounded rationality they may well be adaptive, contributing to survival. Concerning the availability heuristic, in my analysis of routines I noted the importance of an emotional identification of a suspicious event to trigger awareness of the routine and subject it to scrutiny. Perhaps this is connected with the availability heuristic: we pay attention only when triggers are emotion laden. If we did not apply such filters our consciousness would likely be overloaded. Concerning the representativeness heuristic, in Chapter 1 I noted the value of prototypes in language and categorization. Since definitions can seldom offer necessary and sufficient conditions for categorization, and meaning is context-dependent and open-ended, allowing for variation and change, we need prototypes. The mechanism of attributing unobserved characteristics upon recognition of observed ones enables pattern recognition that is conducive to survival. Concerning anchoring and adjustment, under uncertainty cognition does need such an anchor, and taking the most recent value of a variable, or a value observed in behaviour of people in similar conditions with whom one can empathize, may well be rational. The notion of a default entails that one adapt past guidelines for behaviour on the basis of new evidence. Incremental adjustment can be inadequate, but so can fast adjustment. Studies of learning and adjustment have shown that hasty and large departures from existing practices can yield chaotic behaviour (March 1991, Lounamaa and March 1999). Thus anchoring and adaptation may also be a useful and justified heuristic, in view of uncertainty. Nevertheless, these heuristics can yield errors, as will be discussed in Chapter 5.

The relevance of these heuristics to trust is clear, because they affect expectation and attribution of trustworthiness. According to the heuristics, one would develop expectations, explain broken expectations, and attribute trustworthiness according to what is 'available' in the mind, stereotypes, existing norms or recent experience.

Another psychological phenomenon is that people are found to have difficulty to choose between immediate gratification and long-term benefit, yielding a problem of 'the weakness of the will'. This has been explained in terms of people having multiple selves that are at odds with each other, or as a visceral drive competing with a rational inclination. Another interpretation follows the availability heuristic: immediate gratification is more 'available'. Studies of behaviour under uncertainty have shown that people may assess delay in gratification differently when it is near than when it is far ahead, and that sometimes discounting seems to take place not according to an exponential but according to a hyperbolic function. According to that function, the negative utility of a delay of gratification increases as the decision moves to the present. As a result, preferences may reverse at some point in time. The relevance of this phenomenon to collaborative relations is also clear, in the trade-off between loyalty to a partner, which may be in one's long-term interest, and the temptation to defect to another partner who offers more advantage in the short term. One may honestly think one is able to withstand that temptation in the future, and succumb to it when it nears. Again, we cannot unequivocally judge that this psychological mechanism is maladaptive. As noted also by Bazerman (1998), the impulse of temptation may also entail the vision of entrepreneurial opportunity, and too much repression of it may suppress innovation.

'Prospect theory' has demonstrated that people are not risk-neutral, but can be risk-taking when a decision is framed in terms of loss, and risk-averse when it is framed in terms of gain. This 'framing' entails, among other things, that in a relation people will accept a greater risk of conflict when they stand to incur a loss than when they stand to obtain a benefit. Related to this effect is the 'endowment effect': people often demand more money to sell what they have than they would be prepared to pay to get it. In the first case one wants to cover for loss. This may contribute to loyalty and stable relations, as follows. Relations typically end when one of the partners encounters a more attractive alternative, while the other partner wants to continue the relation. The first partner is confronted with a gain frame, the second with a loss frame. This may cause the second partner to engage in more aggressive, risky behaviour, to maintain the relation, than the first partner, who may be more willing to forego his profit and run less risk of a harmful separation procedure. One wonders what the adaptive rationale of this difference between a gain- and a loss-frame is, if any. Perhaps it lies precisely in the effect just mentioned: it reduces defection and thereby stabilizes relationships.[3]

Earlier, I noted the importance of empathy, resulting from identification on the basis of shared categories concerning the motives and conditions of behaviour, including sources of cooperation. This is clearly related to the availability heuristic: behaviour that one can identify with is more 'available'. This affects both one's own trustworthiness, in the willingness to make sacrifices for others, and one's trust, in the tolerance of behaviour that deviates from expectations. One will more easily help someone when one can identify with his need. One can more easily forgive someone's breach of trust or reliance when one can identify with the lack of competence or the motive that caused it. One can more easily accept the blame for oneself. Since one can identify with him, one may sympathise with his action, seeing perhaps that his action was in fact a just response to one's own previous actions.

Another reason to attribute blame to oneself when someone else is in fact to blame, is to reduce uncertainty or establish a sense of control. This works as follows. If it is perceived to be impossible or very difficult to influence someone's behaviour in order to prevent or redress damage from broken

---

[3] I do not wish to imply that stability of relations is always a good thing economically, in the sense that it is always conducive to efficiency and welfare. In Chapter 4 I argue that a certain amount of stability may be needed to recoup specific investments, which may in turn be needed to achieve high added value and innovativeness. However, in Chapter 5 I show that relations can become too stable and exclusive and thereby yield rigidities. The question therefore is how to develop relations that have optimal duration: neither too short nor too long.

expectations, one may attribute blame to oneself. By doing that, one relieves the stress of feeling subjected to the power of others. For people with little self-confidence or a low self-image, this is a move of desperation, and self-blame fits with the preconception one had of oneself. For people with self-confidence, self-blame may yield a sense of control: if the cause lies with oneself, one can more easily deal with it. Of course, that may be an illusion, due to overconfidence in oneself.

Another mechanism is that of a belief in a just world, which gives reassurance. By enacting justice, even anonymously, one confirms its existence by contributing to it, and thereby maintains a sense of security. However, when the sacrifice for another would be too high to accept, in the view of self-interest, then to avoid a self-perception of callousness one may convince oneself that his hardship is his own fault.

Yet another psychological mechanism is that in violation of rational behaviour sunk costs, such as sacrifices made in a relationship, are not seen as bygones that should be ignored in an assessment of future costs and benefits. They are seen as sacrifices that would be seen as in vain if one pulls out after having incurred them. This yields what is known as 'non-rational escalation of commitment'. It is associated with cognitive dissonance: cutting one's losses and pulling out would entail an admission of failure, of having made a bad decision in the past. The phenomenon is confirmed in empirical research, which shows that when someone not involved in the initial decision makes the decision, or when the threat of an admission of failure is removed, the rational decision to pull out is made. Again, one cannot say that this mechanism is always bad, because it also demonstrates perseverance in the face of setbacks, which can be a good thing, and is in fact a trait of many a successful innovating entrepreneur. This phenomenon can also be connected with the effect of a loss frame versus a gain frame, proposed in prospect theory. The person, or group, that made the initial decision experiences a loss frame, with the inclination to accept further risk in order to prevent acceptance of the loss. The decision maker who enters fresh experiences a gain frame, to make a decision that will offer profit in the future, regardless of past sunk costs, and will be less inclined to accept the high risk of continuing losses from sticking to past decisions. The mechanism of nonrational escalation can contribute to the continuation of a relationship where it is not beneficial. I will return to this in Chapter 5.

The escalation phenomenon is not only associated with monetary costs. It can also take the following form, in the 'foot in the door technique' practised by salesmen. Early in a sales talk, the salesman tries to achieve small steps of commitment from his prey, such as asking for a glass of water, or evoking a smile or feelings of sympathy. This makes it more difficult for his prey to extricate himself: having made such concessions and shows of sympathy, it becomes more difficult to go back on them. Having smiled at the salesman, surely this means that one likes him and cannot dismiss him, so one tells oneself.

The need arises to go more deeply into the processes underlying 'trust production', including processes of routinization, habituation, perception, absorption, cognitive dissonance, negation, blindness, and so on. That is done in the second part of this chapter.

This chapter discusses the basis of trust, but it must be noted that we must trust even without a basis in rational evaluation, affect or proven routines. This is due to radical uncertainty of behaviour and the incompleteness of language, or 'inscrutability of reference', as Quine (1960) called it. First, there is the argument of radical uncertainty discussed earlier, in Chapters 1 and 2. Probabilistic calculation of possible actions ignores the possibility of unforeseeable contingencies. Furthermore, from an ethical perspective it robs people of their essential freedom, which includes the option not to satisfy our expectations. Secondly, language and communication cannot work without trust that goes beyond reason and affect. If we demand safeguards, these have to be phrased in some code or language, and if we insist on defining all the terms of the safeguard unambiguously, we would fall into an infinite regress of defining the terms of definitions. Knowledge and meaning are embedded in tacit knowledge that cannot be completely codified without any residual. As noted before, meaning is widely embedded in metaphor rather than literal truth, and for that reason maintains an essential ambiguity. At some point we have to stop and take terms for granted, and that is where trust necessarily starts.

The question is not whether we trust but where we lay its limits. This is part of trust in the strong, narrow sense, defined before, going beyond the assurance of contractual safeguards and other safeguards based on self-interest. It goes even beyond affect from kinship, friendship or love, and beyond routines that may be recalled into focal awareness. It involves tacit, unreflective assumptions that are taken for granted. This point is an extension, perhaps, of the argument of routinization discussed before. Here, however, we are dealing not with routines that we developed on the basis of our personal experience, but with routines that are part of our social inheritance. Perhaps they are even part of our genetic make-up, that go so deep that they cannot be called into focal awareness, for the purpose of revision, and in that sense are more like instinct. Examples are the decision heuristics discussed before. Perhaps, here we should not speak of trust but of confidence, as defined before. Such fundamental, ineradicable, virtually instinctive categories or heuristics are difficult to avoid, and while they may be subject to some correction, at some level they cannot be chosen or rejected.

The argument comes close, perhaps, to Macneil's argument (Macneil 1980 and much of his earlier work), that contract is inevitably embedded in society: 'contract between totally isolated, utility maximising individuals is not contract, but war; contract without language is impossible; and contract without social structure and stability is – quite literally – rationally unthinkable, just as man outside society is rationally unthinkable' (1980: 1).

We have to take for granted, at some point, that people are competent to understand what is said, and will adhere to basic social and linguistic conventions that, as we delve more deeply, become more tacit and difficult to codify. At some level, even the dishonest have to mean what they say.

> When Saddam Hussein broke a fundamental ethical convention by using his own citizens as a shield against attack, he still had to communicate this to the enemy, and adhere to what is meant by the term 'citizen', for his threat to have the intended effect.

Summing up, trust is pervasive and inevitable because future contingencies and motives are never completely known, and language cannot yield certainty of meaning, so that contracts and self-interest always leave a gap of uncertainty. While the extent of this uncertainty depends on states of the world, on people, firms, industries or nations, the fact of its existence does not: to a greater or lesser extent it is always there. At that point, where the gap of uncertainty yawns, we must surrender to trust or die from inaction. At that point trust is blind, in the sense that it is based on tacit assumption, not rational evaluation, let alone calculation, or even affect of love or friendship, or revisable routines.

3.2   THE PROCESS OF TRUST

In the previous paragraph, a number of sources of trustworthiness were identified. The question next is to what extent and how we can infer the existence and reliability of those sources. A question also is how other, more affect-based sources of trust arise and develop. At several points, I identified the need to go into the processes of trust. Here, I deal with the following question identified in Chapter 1:

Question 9: The process of trust
How does the mental basis of trust develop in processes of interaction, and how does it shape that process? How does the mutual shaping work of trust, process and trustworthiness?

Modes of Trust Production

How does one decide the extent to which different sources of trustworthiness are in operation, or are feasible? What is the basis for inferring the disposition of people to obey social norms, and their personal loyalty? We cannot directly observe intentions or capabilities, but only certain personal characteristics and people's actions, and we can listen to what they say. Of course, a pledge of trustworthiness in mere words is cheap and unreliable. Yet, a whole pattern of actions and expressions, and 'relational signalling' (Lindenberg 2000) can give us important clues. Perhaps we can infer something from the way a partner treats a waiter, or his wife and children. The question here is, to use the terminology of Zucker (1986): what are the modes of 'trust production'? To some extent this was discussed in the previous paragraph, where I indicated the role of institutions and third parties, but further analysis is needed.

The term 'trust production' can raise misunderstanding. It is meant to refer to the causes of trust. Literal, conscious production of trustworthiness and trust is problematic. Trust or trustworthiness is not something one can install or inject. The opportunities to 'produce' trust in that sense tend to be overestimated by managers. To force trust is like forcing spontaneity: if it worked it would not be genuine. We can, however, speak of trust-sensitive management (Sydow 2000: 54). Management can take into account how decisions, forms of contracting, monitoring, communication, events, procedures, forms of punishment and reward can affect the development of trust. So, we must now consider what the factors in the development of trust are.

Zucker made a distinction between different modes of trust 'production' that is complementary to the different sources in Tables 3.1 and 3.3, and adds to my previous analysis. They are given in Tables 3.4 and 3.5. For the production of trust, Zucker made a distinction between personal characteristics, institutions and the process in which relations develop. This is reminiscent of Parsons's distinction between particularistic, universalistic sources and personal ascription. In Table 3.4 again I focus on intentional trust, in particular benevolence trust (trust in the absence or limitation of opportunism) and adapt Zucker's scheme accordingly. In Table 3.5 I indicate the result when we focus on competence trust. In that table there is no relation to Table 3.1, since that focuses on intentional, not competence trust.

Zucker (1986) argued that in the US increasingly characteristics-based trust related to family and (local, ethnic or religious) community and process-based trust in ongoing relations have eroded. Communitarianism was replaced by individualism. This yielded a vacuum that had to be filled

Table 3.4   Modes of intentional trust production

Basis	Examples	Connection with Table 3.1
Characteristics-based trust	Membership of family, community, culture, religion	Mostly the altruistic sources of social norms and kinship
Institutions-based trust	Rules, ethics, professional standards	The macro altruistic source of social norms
Process-based trust	Loyalty, commitment	The micro altruistic source of empathy, habituation

Source: Adapted from Zucker (1986).

Table 3.5   Modes of competence trust production

Basis	Examples
Characteristics-based trust	Membership of professional associations, educational achievements
Institutions-based trust	Technical/professional standards, benchmarking
Process-based trust	Mutual adaptation, learning by doing, routinization

Source: Adapted from Zucker (1986).

by means of institution-based trust. In my previous analysis, 'institution-based trust' includes the institutional basis for contracts as a source of reliance, as well as intermediate 'guardians of trust'. This thesis about developments in the US was later repeated and illustrated by Fukuyama (1995) and documented by Putnam (2000).

In the attempt to create conditions for process trust to develop, detailed contracts can be destructive: they can signal mistrust that engenders mistrust, so that mistrust becomes a self-fulfilling prophecy (Macaulay 1963, Zand 1972). In terms of the psychological anchoring and adjustment heuristic discussed before, mistrust may become the anchor, from which only small adjustments are made even when observed behaviour is manifestly cooperative. This does not imply that contracts always or necessarily destroy the basis for trust in the strong sense. Trust and contract can be complementary, as will be shown in Chapter 4.

In what sense can trust be 'produced'? Institutions in the form of values, norms and standards of conduct can be part of the macro sources of cooperation: the institutional environment. But they may also be built up on a meso level, in the institutional arrangement of organization. They can also be built up in specific relations, on the micro level. These levels interact: people build their relationships on institutional arrangements that are built upon the institutional environment, and in due course may shift them (Sydow 1996). People may affect the culture and structure of an organization, which may set an example for others and affect the institutional environment.

Some institutions, such as technical standards or systems of certification, can be developed on the basis of some rational design, although this may take quite some time, since they tend to affect established interests and may require a political process. One can select a partner on the basis of his characteristics, such as being a member of a family or community. However, the association between characteristics and expected trustworthiness is subject to the psychological representativeness heuristic discussed before. It may in fact yield prejudice. One cannot simply buy into characteristics-based trust: one can marry into a family and one can become a member of some communities, but entry selection can be strict and it can take considerable time. Process trust by definition has to grow. Such trust can be facilitated, by creating favourable conditions. Process trust is as much the outcome of a relation as the basis for it. Sydow (1996) approached this from the perspective of Giddens's structuration theory. To the extent that process trust is already available it provides the basis for a relationship. It is reproduced in the relation, if it goes well, and may be further deepened to provide the basis for further extending the relationship. Evidently, we need to investigate processes of building and breaking trust in more depth.

As discussed, to some extent sources of trustworthiness can be inferred from the availability and effectiveness of institutions (such as laws and judiciary, professional standards, control agencies), and personal characteristics of various kinds (such as membership of family or of professional, cultural or religious associations, or educational achievements). However, much is derived as 'process-based trust' in interactions in specific relations.

I doubt the validity, under current conditions, of the claim that this source of trust is eroding further, and that this requires an ongoing extension of institution-based trust. That is probably accurate for an account of recent history, as proposed by Zucker, Fukuyama and Putnam. Currently, however, it seems to me that there is a re-emergence of process-based trust, for several reasons. One is that governance by contract, based on legal institutions, has its weaknesses, which have become more salient under current economic conditions. Under current uncertainty of technology and markets, it has become more difficult to specify reasonably complete contracts and effectively monitor compliance with them. Another reason for this, next to uncertainty, is that in times of radical innovation knowledge tends to have more tacit elements, which resist the codification needed for legally enforceable contracts (Nooteboom 2000a). For radical innovation one needs flexibility for experimentation, and detailed contracts can yield a straitjacket. My suggestion is backed up by the fact that several empirical studies show that contracts have only limited perceived value and effect in the control of relational risk (Macaulay 1963, Berger et al. 1995, see Chapter 6). The discussion of alternative institutional systems and their effects on innovation is continued in Chapter 4.

The question now is how process-based trust works. I proposed before that trustworthiness is subject to limits, and that trust operates within limits of tolerance. In the process of trust these limits are set and revised in the light of experience, and as a result of psychological processes, in interaction with other people. This is subject to psychological heuristics of decision-making, as discussed before. The limits of trust and trustworthiness are different with respect to different people, for a given partner they vary with the aspect of trust (competence, dedication and benevolence), and for each dimension they vary with conditions. This goes back to my proposal, in Chapter 2, that behavioural trust is a four-place predicate: one trusts someone with respect to something, depending on the conditions.

Competence shows itself best when it is stretched. Dedication shows itself best when there is no external pressure for it, that is when there are opportunities for slack. Benevolence shows itself best under opportunities for opportunism and temptations or pressures to utilize them. It is especially important to assess whether loyalty is intrinsic or extrinsic. In the first case loyalty is an internal goal, while in the second case it is a means to pursue self-interest. The first does not require monitoring, and the second does. Loyalty as an internal goal is based on ethics and conscience, based on norms and values, or on emotions of friendship or kinship, routinization, or on the enjoyment of trusting relations. Loyalty as a means to pursue self-interest is based on the lack of opportunity for opportunism, dependence or fear of reputational loss. Connected with this, Deutsch also recognized the notion of 'focus', with three possibilities: focus on results for the other, on warrantable effort (is one seen to be doing one's reasonable best?), or on doing as one is told. Is one genuinely trying to cooperate or is one intent only on legitimizing one's actions?

So, when a supportive action by X is observed, how does one judge whether this is based on benevolence? Table 3.6 gives a sequence of questions that aid such assessment (adapted from Deutsch 1973).

Deutsch noted that one's power can have an adverse effect not only on the trust of others but also on one's own trust. This can be seen from Table

Table 3.6   Attribution of trustworthiness

---

1. Was the outcome intended by X, or was it an unintended result of his action?
2. Did the action entail significant risk to X?
3. Was X aware of the risk, and was it not neglected out of impulsiveness?
4. Did X attach a positive value to this risk, out of masochism, sensation, (self) image?
5. Did X have a choice, or was the action dictated by compulsion or conformity?
6. Was it out of confidence in the system rather than a positive evaluation of the situation?
7. Was it out of enlightened self-interest?
8. Was it out of enjoyment of trust relations?
9. Was it out of ethics, friendship or kinship, habituation?

Source: Adapted from Deutsch (1973).

3.6. If one is very powerful, there is more ground for suspicion that people subjected to one's power are reliable only because they have no choice, not because they are trustworthy in the strong sense. In case of absolute power, the hypothesis that this is the case can never be rejected. Thus power can breed suspicion, and absolute power can yield rampant paranoia. Here, one recognizes stories about Stalin. The problem here is that mistrust tends to feed upon itself even more than trust does. (Mis)trust by X tends to engender (mis)trust on the part of Y, which justifies and deepens X's (mis)trust. While trust can be falsified because it leads to reliance on others that can be disappointed, mistrust cannot, because it blocks trusting action that might disprove it.

Stages of Development

There may be trust prior to an economic relation, based on instinct to engage in reciprocation, an assumption of adherence to social norms, characteristics of the partner, previous experience, kinship, friendship or reputation. An important question, however, is how trust can arise where there was none before (Sako 2000: 89). Shapiro (1987: 625) proposed that: 'Typically . . . social exchange relations evolve in a slow process, starting with minor transactions in which little trust is required because little risk is involved and in which partners can prove their trustworthiness, enabling them to expand their relation and engage in major transactions'. This was later repeated by others (for example Smith Ring and van de Ven 1992). McAllister (1995) proposed two stages of trust development: cognition-based trust followed by affect-based trust. Here we encounter a possible confusion between knowledge-based and cognition-based trust. According to the definitions that I proposed before, presumably what is intended here is not cognition- but knowledge-based trust.[4]

Lewicki and Bunker (1996) proposed three stages of calculus-based, knowledge-based and identification-based trust. As discussed before, in Chapter 1, this seems a little odd, because calculation, in the sense of trying to control a partner's performance, requires knowledge, on the basis of monitoring. Thus, calculation-based trust can hardly precede the acquisition of knowledge. I noted that perhaps the three stages proposed by Lewicki and Bunker collapse to two stages that are very much like those proposed by McAllister.

However, I still see a way of making sense out of a three-stage process. For that, I employ the notions of different aspects of trust, and limits of trustworthiness, combined with tolerance levels of trust, discussed in Chapter 2. The three stages, discussed below, are then summed up as follows:

1. Stage of *control* in the absence of trust
2. Stage of assessing trustworthiness, and *developing tolerance levels of trust*
3. Stage of *widening tolerance levels*, on the basis of identification

In the first stage, in the absence of prior trust, one must take the possibility of lack of competence and of opportunism into account, as transaction cost theory argues. One way to deal with this is to proceed in small steps that yield little risk. Another is to begin with a certain amount of control to manage the risk involved. To manage possible lack of trustworthiness, one may create safeguards based on the partner's self-interest (contracts, supervision, dependence, hostages, reputation, see Table 3.2). As indicated above, this requires knowledge, obtained from monitoring the partner's behaviour (his/her inputs, outputs, efforts, and other actions that might impact on his/her performance), in order to decide about the meting out of rewards or sanctions. In this stage one has little idea about the limits of the partner's trustworthiness, and hence no basis for setting one's tolerance limits of trust. In that sense there is no basis for trust.

In the second stage, one obtains more knowledge and experience, as a basis for inferring limits of trustworthiness, for setting tolerance levels of

---

[4] Recall my proposal to understand knowledge-based trust as the use of knowledge to assess trustworthiness, and cognition-based trust as an alignment of cognitive categories, in a reduction of cognitive distance.

trust. Thereby one allows some scope for trust, while preserving the option to revert to control when such tolerance levels are exceeded. Note that, as discussed in Chapter 2, the object of trust has a number of aspects: competence, intentions, truthfulness, and so on. Also, as proposed before, for each of them trust is conditional: one will trust someone concerning his competence, for example, under some conditions but not others. It takes a considerable amount of experience and knowledge to find out where a partner's weaknesses lie, and under what conditions, to infer his truthfulness and willingness to report his weaknesses or problems in time, the degree to which he has internalized cultural norms of behaviour, and his willingness to accept temporary losses for the benefit of a fruitful development of the relation, in other words, to engage in reciprocity rather than immediate quid pro quo.

In the third stage, it may happen that on the basis of identification and empathy tolerance levels of trust are widened. This is based on the development of shared cognitive frames, that is reduction of cognitive distance, in cognition-based trust. Thereby one may develop empathy for the partner's objectives and weaknesses, and feel affinity with his/her style of collaboration. As a result, one may be prepared to do the following:

- give more benefit of the doubt in judging the partner's actions
- surrender control and accept more control from the partner
- accept more risk, that is potential damage, partly because the relation has meanwhile acquired intrinsic value
- go from direct quid pro quo to reciprocity
- extend the horizon of reciprocity, that is the term within which one expects return benefits from the partner.

In this way, making a distinction between two kinds of knowledge preserves a three-stage model. One is knowledge needed for control, on the basis of monitoring, to decide the meting out of rewards or sanctions, in the first stage. The second is knowledge for assessing the degree and limits of trustworthiness, and for setting tolerance levels of trust, thereby allowing for some surrender of control and some scope for trust, in the second stage.

While I recognize the possibility of this sequence of stages, I do not accept it as the only one. First of all, the stages do not necessarily arise. In the second stage, inference of the partner's limits of trustworthiness may lead to the conclusion that the relationship does not allow for trust, and control has to be maintained. The third stage, of identification, may not arise, and indeed, on the basis of more insight one may narrow rather than widen the tolerance levels of trust.

Second, as I noted, it may be better not to start with control, since that may negatively affect either the flexibility of action needed for innovation, or the basis for trust to develop. One may prefer to proceed with small steps that each carry so little risk that no control is required, and thereby try to jump control and go for the second stage, building up insight in the trust-worthiness of the partner as events unfold, and increase the stakes step by step. This, I think, is the process as described by Shapiro.

However, even these alternatives form just some of several possible sce-narios for the development of a relationship. There is not one universally correct or viable way to develop relationships. There are many ways, and which occurs depends on a range of contingencies concerning conditions, objectives, preferences and histories. Personal affect may never develop, nor mutual identification, while the relation can still be very fruitful. Conversely, people may start on the basis of affect, as in a family firm or a partnership between friends, and become calculative later. That may destroy trust, but it can also deepen it. I recall the psychological mecha-nisms and decision heuristics discussed before, on which the process of trust is based, with the biases that they involve, which may support or thwart the process.

In Chapter 4, I continue the analysis. There, I focus on the strategy of trust, in terms of how to govern relational risk. Here, I focus on the social psychology of trust development: how people give and receive information, exert and accept influence, form and adapt perceptions and evaluations, in the development of trust.

Breach and Deepening of Trust

In Chapter 2, trust, or more widely reliance, included an expectation that things or people will not fail us. However, the disappointment of such expectation does not necessarily yield a breach of trust (or reliance). Remember that trust can have as many dimensions as there are causes of things going wrong. As discussed in Chapter 2, in human relations the aspect of reliance can be a partner's competence, his dedication, his benev-olence (absence or limitation of opportunism), his honesty, the availability of means, or external conditions. One may observe that those external con-ditions rather than a partner's behaviour were the cause of disappointing outcomes. It is possible that this cannot be seen, but is claimed by the partner as an explanation. Will the trustor accept the explanation, or will he/she see it as an excuse for something else: for lack of dedication, or com-petence, or worse, a sign of opportunism? Will he, perhaps, turn a blind eye to the mishap, negate evidence of incompetence or opportunism out of cognitive dissonance or blind trust? Or will he give the partner the benefit of the doubt, but remain alert to future mishaps and their possible causes? Or will he jump to a conclusion of opportunism? Which is the case will depend on a number of things. It depends on the sources of previous trust or suspicion, the history of the relationship, psychological make-up (including self-image), personal experience in other relations, external social and economic conditions (for example intensity of price competition, presence of a reputation mechanism, or of trusted third parties).

People have an inclination to judge: to evaluate actions and attribute attitudes or motives to people, and here we often jump to conclusions. Such evaluations are subject to the decision heuristics discussed before. We may be swayed by vivid experiences, in the availability heuristic, by the representative heuristic, and by the anchoring and adjustment heuristic. When the expectations of trust are not fulfilled, we need to control this inclination to judge, and to grant the benefit of the doubt, and assess what has happened as coolly as possible, avoiding the biases that may be involved in the decision heuristics. This is not simple, because heuristics and emotions are not without reason (Frank 1988). Earlier I adopted the notion from Simon that emotions serve to jolt us out of routine behaviour, and shift awareness of risk from subsidiary to focal. Without emotions we would be vulnerable to the blindness of routine. So emotions serve to waken us, but we must also control them in order to grant other people the benefit of the doubt.

Note that in the light of the theory of knowledge discussed in Chapter 1, with the virtuous role of 'cognitive distance' for the purpose of learning, misunderstanding and conflict of opinion are often creative, in shifting existing views and jointly generating novel insights, in a learning process. This reinforces the idea that the dissatisfaction of expectations does not necessarily break down trust. As Zucker (1986: 59) proposed:

> A violation of expectations 'produces a sense of disruption of trust, or profound confusion, but not of distrust. Distrust only emerges when the suspicion arises that the disruption of expectations in one exchange is likely to generalize to other transactions. To distrust, then, implies an attribution of intentionality that continues throughout all interactions or exchanges, at least of a particular type'.

The joint solution of conflict can enhance and deepen trust, in several ways. One way is that it yields learning, as just indicated, which confirms the value of the relation and thereby increases mutual commitment. Another way is that the fact that problems are solved in itself reduces perceived risk in the relation. The conflict yielded a test of the strength of mutual benevolence and the dedication to 'work things out', in a mutual 'give and take'. The fact that the relation survived the test increases trust in the strength and resilience of benevolence and dedication. It increases empathy. This is how the process of ongoing and successful relations, with solutions of conflicts, can deepen trust.

The positive effect of the solution of conflicts carries force especially because the reverse is so often observed, that under adverse conditions a relation breaks down in mutual recrimination and suspicion. This can easily arise especially when the stakes are high at the beginning of a relation between strangers. As indicated, when things do not go all right, this may be due to accident, lack of dedication, lack of competence or opportunism. If in fact the cause is opportunism, this will not be admitted. Knowing this, one may suspect opportunism even when it is denied, or for the suspicious especially when it is strongly denied. In this delicate stage of a beginning relation with high stakes of dependence, a third party may play a useful role in eliminating such incipient misunderstandings and attributions of fault before they become so large, and evoke such hostile reactions from the unjustly accused partner, that they escalate beyond repair.

Pettit (1995a) introduced the notion of 'trust-responsiveness'. It is related to the desire for social recognition and to the notion of social reciprocity, both discussed before. It is also related to the building of empathy. When offered trust, people may reciprocate 'due to the love of regard or standing in one's own eyes and in the eyes of others' (Pettit 1995a: 203). To the extent that this is true, trust is reciprocated and there is a possibility of an upward spiral of trust. However, the converse may also apply, where mistrust engenders mistrust, and then there may be a downward spiral of suspicion. Which is the case can depend on minor events or misunderstandings. Thus, with such non-linear feedbacks, the trust process can assume the properties of a chaotic system.

This is connected with the idea of trust as a default, discussed before, and the notions of limits of trustworthiness and tolerance limits of trust. In interaction, one may have developed an explicit or implicit assessment of the partner's trustworthiness, and a tolerance limit for deviant behaviour. A positive cycle of reciprocation and increasing empathy can widen the limits of trustworthiness and the tolerance limits of trust. This yields less occasion for mistrust to arise, which further widens tolerance levels. With narrow limits, on the other hand, deviant behaviour sooner triggers awareness of possible foul play and possibly the beginning of suspicion. It may narrow tolerance and narrow the inferred limits of trustworthiness. Events that previously were given the benefit of the doubt, or were even not noticed, may now be scrutinized for evidence of untrustworthiness. As a result, deviant behaviour is sooner perceived, and a spiral of suspicion may be set in motion. Again, intermediaries may play an important role here, to test whether suspicion is justified, and if it is not to stop such a dynamic from getting under way.

Information and Communication

In view of this potential self-reinforcing dynamic of trust and suspicion, honesty and trust in honesty are crucial. Honesty here is openness: giving appropriate, truthful and timely information. 'Appropriate' information here is information that the partner can absorb and helps him to reduce risks. Dishonesty is the withholding or distortion of appropriate information. Honesty and trust reinforce each other, as suspicion and dishonesty do. Honesty serves to deal with deviant phenomena without narrowing tolerance levels and without reducing perceived limits of trustworthiness. They may even widen both, and thereby deepen trust.

When there is no intentional trust (that is trust in dedication and benevolence), one is afraid to be honest, lest the partner will misuse information for opportunistic purposes or to relax the level of his dedication. If there is lack of trust in dedication, one may think praise will cause slack. If there is lack of trust in benevolence, one may think that information on one's needs, opportunities and their limits, or competencies, will be used opportunistically in power play, cheating, expropriation, or treating sensitive information as a hostage (blackmail).

However, when the other side perceives that he is receiving neither trust nor information, he may reciprocate with dishonesty. One elementary lesson is the following. When a disaster is foreseen, one is tempted to keep it secret. This should be resisted. Here is a chance to win trust by announcing the problem before it becomes manifest, asking for help and engaging in a joint effort to redress or mitigate the disaster.

However, there is also a subtle reason for dishonesty that is benevolent. One may withhold criticism out of fear of (further) reducing a partner's self-confidence. A special problem here lies in the situation where collaboration has to develop between partners who are unequal in their dependence on each other (Klein Woolthuis 1999). The most dependent partner may be suspicious because of the one-sided risk he runs, whereby he starts the relation on the basis of mistrust or apprehension, and is on the lookout for signs of opportunistic exploitation of his dependence. His perceived limit of trustworthiness and his tolerance level are narrow. This is a special case of a more general phenomenon that lack of self-confidence engenders mistrust, which breeds mistrust. Here, it can be in one's self-interest to soften criticism of the partner, not to make him/her more apprehensive, defensive and suspicious.

One may go further, not just withholding criticism, but offering compliments. Compliments, both private and public, especially to new staff, can play a role as an explicit act of policy, in trust-sensitive management. The compliments serve to build trust in two ways. First, they increase self-confidence of new staff, and this helps them to grant trust, but not excessive trust, to others. Second, it enhances the trust that others have in the new colleague. It enhances trust-responsiveness between existing and new staff.[5] It is crucial that the compliments are not empty, and backed up by perceived quality of performance. Empty compliments have an adverse effect. They destroy perceived truthfulness, and we saw how important that is.

Deutsch (1973) suggested that there is circular causation between characteristics of participants and the results of interaction. He offered his 'crude law of social relations': The characteristic processes and effects elicited by a given type of social relationship (cooperative or competitive) tend also to elicit that type of social relationship'. This is consistent with the decision heuristics of availability, representativeness and anchoring.

If this is true, then one must be very careful how to start a relationship, because it may be difficult to get out of the initial mode of interaction. This emphasizes the importance of creating mutual trust with regard to new staff, as demonstrated in the study by Six (2001). It also yields a lesson for the development of collaboration in the preparation of an alliance or merger. Often, in the initial situation of bargaining, games are played in the manoeuvring for position regarding ownership and control, which set the relation going in a mode of rivalry, which may then be difficult to turn around into cooperation, in the stage of implementation. The bargainers from the top of the firms throw the problem in the lap of the poor implementation manager, who is confronted with a huge obstacle that can jeopardize the relation before it has properly started. Therefore, those responsible for implementation should be included in the bargaining process, or bargainers should also be made responsible for implementation. Perhaps there is another role for a third party here: to guide negotiations prior to collaboration.

There is another pitfall. Suppose two strangers need to rely on each other, with large dependence and much at stake, and there is no basis for trust from earlier experience, reputation, advice from a third party, kinship, or apparent values and norms of behaviour. Then one may be tempted to make a safeguard in the form of an extensive contract to limit 'opportunities for opportunism'. That is also the idea in the three-stage model of Lewicki and Bunker, discussed before. There are several problems with this, which will be discussed more systematically in Chapter 4. In the present context, the problem is that the relation starts in an atmosphere of mistrust and rivalry, which may be difficult to turn around into one that allows for the building and deepening of trust.

---

[5] This insight derives from current PhD research by Frederique Six.

This brings us back to the idea that a good way to start a relation between strangers, without prior trust, is to take small steps that are likely to yield positive results soon. This yields limited risk, so that an extensive contract against opportunism is not needed, and a basis for trust may soon be built. Continuity of the relation may also be enhanced by the mechanism of non-rational escalation of commitment: past sacrifices are seen not as sunk costs but as an investment that needs to be seen through to achieve positive outcomes. As suggested earlier, process-based trust moves through several stages. Generally, for people who are not acquainted ex ante, at the beginning of the process calculativeness will tend to prevail: the focus is on the generation of material value. The greater this value or its urgency, the more risk one may be willing to take. Partners are given the benefit of the doubt, within certain margins of risk left by incomplete contracts, accepted on the basis of some heuristic that takes into account prevailing ethics, customs, experience, urgency and the intrinsic value attached to trust. Perceived limits of trustworthiness and tolerance levels of trust start out fairly narrow. As the relation begins to generate value, trust in both competence and intention may deepen due to perception and understanding of the sources of both. Next, bonds of friendship and identification may develop, to deepen trust further, and routinization may weaken the awareness of risk. Perceived limits of trustworthiness and tolerance widen, and empathy grows.

Here, a process of shared experiences plays an important role. For example, for trust between production and maintenance staff, perhaps their tasks should not be separated but combined in mixed teams, to allow for ongoing shared experience.

> For another example, let us return to the case of the explosive experts making tunnels, discussed in Chapter 2. The process of trust building, as reproduced by Giorgio Inzerilli, is as follows. The risk here is that if any of the team makes a wrong connection between explosives, detonator and battery, yielding a premature explosion, this would kill the whole team. For the team to function, the members were first subjected to the following sharing of experience, in which they learn to trust and be trustworthy. They are locked into a bunker, where they have to rehearse their actions, with wires, detonators and batteries, but no explosives. None were allowed to leave before all were ready. The premature or unintended explosion of a detonator has much less effect than of dynamite, but can cause damage to people nearby, and in a closed bunker can have a very unpleasant effect of air pressure on people at a distance. Here, the participants not only develop their competence but also their dedication and care, and personal bonding of mutual dependence, and thereby develop the competence and dedication trust and trustworthiness that are needed for them to function. In their practice, social activities, such as eating and drinking together, and a ritual drinking feast reinforce personal bonding after each project. It is also strengthened by other rituals, such as placing a little statue

of Santa Barbara, the patron saint of the miners, at the entrance to the tunnel.
Each day, when entering the tunnel, they crossed themselves in front of the
statue.

To say, as Deutsch did, that the type of relationship tends to reinforce
itself of course does not mean that this is inevitable. A mistrustful, rival-
rous relationship may develop into a trustful, cooperative one, and vice
versa. The latter is more probable than the former, as is expressed in the
saying that 'trust comes on foot and departs on horseback'. The preceding
analysis clarifies this. Consider the attribution of trustworthiness, in Table
3.4. This requires that all conditions specified in the table be met.
Favourable actions have to be intended, go beyond self-interest and entail
a risk or sacrifice, and the partner must have been aware of them, and
he/she must have had other options of action, before one can attribute
trustworthiness, going beyond coercion and self-interest. For complete or
incipient mistrust, or doubts about trustworthiness, or at least lack of an
increase of trust, only one of these tests has to be failed. The escalation of
conflict may be enhanced by the effects of a loss frame identified by prospect theory, as discussed before. The suspicion of loss may trigger an excessive, risky response that calls forth a similar reaction.

Zand (1972) proposed a cycle in which trust engenders openness, yielding information, which provides a basis for the application and acceptance
of mutual influence, which yields the willingness to demand less and accept
more control from the partner, which further engenders trust. In other
words, the provision of information based on trust promotes the responsiveness to trust identified by Pettit, which may already be latent but
requires a trigger of information that has the dual function of demonstrating trust and reducing the risk of trust reciprocation. This can set a positive dynamic of trust going. Thus, Zand (1972: 238) included openness in
the conceptualization of trust as: 'behaviour that conveys appropriate
information, permits mutuality of influence, encourages self-control, and
avoids abuse of the vulnerability of others'.

Here, we see a positive relation between trust and information: A trusts
B and therefore gives information (even if B could use that to the detriment
of A), which makes B trust A and give information in return.

Sako (1998) suggested that there is a paradox in the relation between
trust and information. In her empirical work she indeed observed a positive relation: trust goes together with information exchange. On the other
hand, Sako wrote, trust is widely seen as a substitute for control: if there is
trust there is less need for control. Such control requires information, for
monitoring. Hence, theoretically, if there is more trust there is less control
and hence less information exchange. There is a misunderstanding here.

There is no paradox. To the extent that trust is indeed a substitute for control, and the extent to which this is the case will be discussed in Chapter 4, it means that if A trusts B he will demand less formal control over her. However, as Zand indicated, he may at the same time accept more control from B. Furthermore, his trust in B, and limited demand for formal control over B, is likely to be the result of the fact that B is open and gives appropriate information. Thus all the following propositions can be true at the same time: trust goes together with much information exchange, formal control requires information, and trust can be a substitute for formal control.

Part of the issue lies in the ambiguity of the notion of control. When trust is a substitute for control, this refers to formal, contractual control with an imposition of procedures for monitoring. The information provided voluntarily in trust may also be called a form of (social) control, but this is in important ways quite different from formal control. It is a form of social reciprocity. First, in trust the information is voluntary. It is not based on demand but on reciprocity. One does not need to demand appropriate information on potential or imminent problems and their true causes because that is already offered. Second, it tends to be less codified and explicit, and more tacit and implicit. Third, not being specified as to its conditions for delivery, it is more flexible, geared to unanticipated contingencies, and therefore it is more robust under uncertainty. That is a great advantage, because in formal control such contingencies would generally be impossible to specify completely. Fourth, and most importantly, by assumption the information given in trust is truthful, while in formal control truth would have to be tested. In view of the multiple possible causes of disappointing outcomes, and the possibility to claim accidents as an excuse for failure or a mask for opportunism, this is a crucial benefit.

The analysis is reminiscent of what Hirschman (1970) called 'voice', as opposed to 'exit'. In exit, one walks out when dissatisfied, avoiding argument. One quits from one's job, fires people, sells shares or part of a firm. In voice, the first response is not to walk out, but to seek amends. One reports one's dissatisfaction, asks for an explanation, and asks for and offers help to 'work things out'. The importance of this in inter-firm relations has been indicated and demonstrated in empirical work, in particular by Susan Helper (1990). I applied the notion in an analysis of differences in systems of corporate control (Nooteboom 1999e). In Chapter 4 I apply it for an analysis of systems of innovation. I propose that the process of voice is as described and analysed above. Of course, voice requires trust in the procedural justice of the voice process: the credibility of commitments and honesty underlying institutions.

Organizational Processes

In organizations people have a range of options for including or excluding colleagues to deal with trust and its violation. One can retaliate or voice complaints directly to the antagonist, one can do this privately or in public, one can involve colleagues in gossip or coalitions, or one can go to one's boss and complain or demand action (Wittek 1999, Six 2001). Confrontation in public entails a multiplier effect. Both the loss of prestige involved in being told off or accepting advice, and the gain of prestige in winning a confrontation or giving advice, are multiplied. Because of such effects, in public confrontation conflict can become more acute than when confrontation is effected in private. However, public confrontation may be attractive to muster support and to hide behind group interest, masking the personal interest that is at stake. This can be used to reduce the blame that a victim can voice when put under pressure. In the organization that she studied, Six found in her present research that public meetings yield more 'masculine', that is confrontational and 'scoring' behaviour, while private meetings are more 'feminine', that is caring and supportive.

Deeper understanding of these phenomena can be achieved by going back to the work of Simmel (1950). He argued that a fundamental shift occurs in going from dyadic to triadic relations (Krackhardt 1999). In dyadic relations individuality is preserved, in the sense that no coalitions can occur, and no majority can outvote an individual. In a triad any member by himself has less bargaining power than in a dyad. The threat of exit carries less weight, since the two remaining partners would still have each other. In a triad, conflict is more readily solved. When any two players enter conflict, the third can act as a moderator, eliminating misunderstandings, proposing a compromise, designing a solution that saves face for the antagonists. This argument can help to understand processes of trust and trouble within firms. Krackhardt (1999) shows how people who participate in different cliques can become constrained in their public behaviour, because they have to be seen to satisfy the combined norms or rules of all the cliques to which they belong. The paradox is that their multiple membership puts them in a position of potential power, but also constrains them in their use of it.

How is this connected to Six's finding that in an organization people tend be more 'masculine' in groups and more 'feminine' in dyads? As indicated, part of the explanation certainly is that in groups effects of reputation and prestige arise, which tempt people to 'scoring' behaviour, and make them more sensitive to loss of face, and hence less inclined to accept compromise. The Simmelian analysis adds two things. One is that since in dyads stalemates and conflicts are more difficult to resolve, they have to be carried into groups, where solutions are forced by coalitions. The second is that while a boundary spanner, involved in multiple cliques, can play a conciliatory role in the privacy of bilateral contacts, he cannot afford to do so in groups that mix the cliques. There, he cannot afford to be conciliatory or sympathetic in public to either of the sides. In other words, dyads drive conflicts into groups, and there conciliation is more difficult. This leads to confrontation and the need to force issues. This may have nothing to do with gender (masculine, feminine), but with social dynamics.

If the above arguments are correct, a dilemma arises concerning group resolution of conflict. On the one hand a group may be needed to resolve stalemates and conflicts, by the use of coalitions, which cannot be resolved in dyads. On the other hand, in groups the loss of face in losing a conflict is enlarged. Also, in public group meetings boundary spanners, which are often managers, may not be able to commit themselves to one of a number of interest groups. The solution may be straightforward: resolve conflicts in the minimal group size needed, with as little publicity as possible. However, that leads to backroom deals that have a bad name in democratic culture.

Speaking more generally, when 'something goes wrong', that is expectations are not met, the identification and attribution of causes can be enabled, but also blocked and distorted, by organizational conditions and processes. Using third party informants can help but can also yield destructive gossip that confirms rather than corrects prejudice and mis-attribution. If Deutsch's 'crude law of social relations', discussed above, is valid, then co-operative or competitive types of relationships can become part of organizational culture, which confirms and propagates such types of relationships. The trust cycle proposed by Zand, discussed above, with its conveyance of appropriate information, mutuality of influence, encouragement of self-control, and avoidance of the abuse of the vulnerability of others, can be enabled or obstructed in many ways by organizational structures and processes.

The study of such processes and organizational effects and influences forms an important area for further research.

4. Functions

The previous chapter discussed the question what the basis for trust is. The present chapter turns the question around. For what does trust serve as a basis? What is its role in society, and how does that work? In the absence of all trust, in the wide sense of reliance, all action would stop. For action we depend on things and on people, and we can never be certain that our expectations will be met. Our confidence in natural laws is seldom broken, but our reliance on institutions and people often is. If we are not prepared to accept any uncertainty, we will not be able to act. If we do not have any trust, we will not engage in relations, and thereby we rob ourselves of the opportunity to find that there may be a basis for trust. If, on the other hand, we begin with trust and it is betrayed, we learn to adjust it. Blind trust may prevent such learning. Such failure and pathology of trust will be discussed in Chapter 5. Trust is indispensable in private life, in politics and government, and in economics and business. In personal life, there is relatively more scope for the micro, altruistic sources of cooperation, indicated in Chapter 3. In politics and government, the focus lies more on the macro sources of legality and social values and norms. There, one may want to avoid the micro sources, in both altruism and self-interest, to avoid nepotism, clientism and corruption. In economics and business, I propose, all sources are relevant: legal regulation, social values and norms, material self-interest and sources of altruism in specific relations. In economics, trust has an intrinsic value next to extrinsic value, as a dimension of utility, in the way in which people would like to conduct relationships, as argued in Chapter 1. This chapter focuses on the extrinsic value of trust, in economics and business. It addresses the following question, identified in Chapter 1:

Question 8: Economic function of trust
What is the extrinsic, economic value of trust? How does it work? What are the effects? What are the institutional conditions?

The chapter consists of two parts. The first part analyses the role of trust in the governance of economic relations. The second part considers the institutional conditions for trust to arise, and the results, in terms of the performance of 'innovation systems'.

4.1 GOVERNANCE

This paragraph analyses how trust enables relations, in economics and business, and reduces transaction costs by reducing relational risk. Such reduction of relational risk is the purpose of 'governance'. I take this term from transaction cost economics. As a basis for the discussion, a brief review is given of some of the relevant concepts from transaction cost theory. As discussed in previous chapters, trust is related to the availability of information. Therefore, the chapter begins with a brief analysis of the relation between transaction costs and information and communication technology (ICT). Relational risk consists of risks of dependence and risks of spillover (loss of appropriability). Trust does not operate on its own, but in varying combinations with other instruments of governance, such as contracts, mutual dependence, hostages, reputation mechanisms, intermediaries and network position. It is discussed how trust relates to these instruments. For example, is trust a substitute for contracts, or does it complement contracts, or both?

Transaction Costs, ICT and Trust

Transaction costs are costs of economic exchange. These occur in different stages of a process of exchange, which I identify as contact, contract and control, as illustrated in Figure 4.1.

I will argue that trust is needed to reduce transaction costs. In every stage of the process of exchange, in Figure 4.1, there is uncertainty, and the more uncertainty there is the more we need trust. ICT also reduces transaction costs. Since ICT improves information, reducing uncertainty, the question arises whether in the 'new economy' perhaps there is less need for trust.

Let me analyse the effects of ICT in more detail. Generally speaking, ICT reduces transaction costs, and this tends to intensify competition. Reduction of transaction costs has been a feature also of previous industrial revolutions. Steam engines and their use in trains and ships have reduced transportation costs, which are part of the costs of contact. Telephone and telegraph reduced communication costs, which are also transaction costs, in contact and control. So what is special about the current revolution based on ICT? It reduces a variety of transaction costs, in contact, contract and control, by reducing the costs of communication. It reduces transportation costs by yielding a tool to optimize the content, routing and timing of transport, and by sending information electronically instead of in print. Its indirect effect, however, is to also increase the volume of goods and information sent, and the net effect may be in doubt.

process of exchange

transaction

————————— ——————————— * ———————————

contact	contract	control
search	evaluation	monitoring
marketing	negotiation	bickering
transportation	contract	re-negotiation
		sanctions

Figure 4.1   Transaction costs

Consider, for example, the effects of electronic shopping. This may entail a larger number of movements in motorized transport for the delivery of goods. The present visits to shops by consumers on foot, or their collection of a basket of goods in one car ride, may be replaced by frequent motorized home delivery of small batches of goods, yielding a net increase of movements.

In search, in the stage of contact, we had the telephone and corresponding directories, including yellow pages. Now we can search supply on the Internet in much more detail, with easier access to more complete information, to find what we specifically want. Furthermore, a novelty is that not only suppliers but also users can put themselves up on the Internet, with a specification of their demand, for suppliers to search. While this is hardly viable in consumer markets, it is important when the user is a firm. This is one of the reasons why the Internet is having more impact in business markets than in consumer markets.

In the stages of contract and control, ICT also reduces costs and enables new forms. It can be used for easy access to information on financial reliability of partners. It can be used to access databases of a partner to monitor contract execution. It can be used for flexible and tailor-made, interactively crafted price offers and contracts.

Consider insurance. The design and communication of conditions, fees and the insurance policy, as well as the submission, control and processing of claims can be speeded up and supported by much more information, tailored to individual histories and conditions. This can be used for tailoring policies to individual insurance customers, and limit the problems of 'adverse selection' and 'moral hazard' that are typical for insurance.

However, the easier and cheaper provision of much more information does not by itself increase the reliability of information. In fact, uncertainties concerning information may increase due to ICT. For example, we need special measures to authenticate the identity of senders of information on the Internet, and to establish their reliability (Knights et al. 2001).

The effects of ICT go beyond communication, extending into production and design. Programmable production machinery, just-in-time delivery, and computer-integrated manufacturing make production more flexible. Virtual prototyping, in computer-aided design, and testing, in computer simulation, greatly increase the flexibility and reduce the time of developing new products. This increase of flexibility reduces the transaction specificity of investments for differentiated products, and thereby reduces transaction costs due to the 'hold-up' problem. On the other hand, I will argue later that as the emphasis shifts to innovation and learning, people and firms may have to make more specific investments in mutual understanding. As I will argue in more detail below, the limitation of the viability of contracts is largest in innovation, since it is paradoxical to specify detailed rights and obligations when the outcome is uncertain as by definition it is in innovation. Therefore, trust may play a role especially in innovation. When trust is not in place prior to a relation, it has to be built up, and this also may constitute a specific investment.

In conclusion, while, like trust, ICT reduces transaction costs, this does not imply that in an 'information society' trust is less important.

In all stages of the process of exchange, we need information, and the question arises whether we can trust it. If it cannot be verified directly or through third parties, this may require trust in the honesty of the supplier or customer. In the stage of contact a user needs information on the availability of products, and a supplier needs information on the demand for them. Here and subsequently, the term 'product' refers to both goods and services, that is anything with added value. Users need to evaluate the quality of supply. The difficulty of this varies across different types of products.

Here we can use the well-known taxonomy of 'search products, experience products and credence products'. With search products one can assess quality prior to purchase and use, with experience products one assesses quality during use, and with credence products one cannot assess quality even after use.

Examples of search products are houses, cars, appliances, etc., for those who know about them. Examples of experience products are concerts, holidays and other forms of entertainment or recreation. Examples of credence goods are tax and other consultants: if one could judge their performance one probably would not have needed them in the first place. To what class does teaching belong? Attempts are increasingly made to turn it into a search product, with public ratings of business schools for example. The question of course is what dimensions of quality such ratings measure, and how reliably they do so. Teaching is to some extent an experience product, as measured by student response. It is also to a greater or lesser extent a credence product: students may not find out about its value until much later, and then it is so combined with other teachings and embedded in personal experience that it is hard to retrieve.

Clearly, uncertainty is higher, and trust is more needed, to the extent that quality is more difficult to judge ex ante. Of course, many attempts are made to facilitate the judging of quality. Health authorities monitor the quality of food and drugs. The mad cow disease slipped through, causing a drop of trust in meat. Consumer bodies conduct and publish quality ratings of cars, appliances and recreational facilities. Art and theatre critics help customers to evaluate exhibitions and performances prior to buying tickets. Estate agents are hired to judge the quality of houses, and form membership associations to suggest a guarantee of their own quality. Medical doctors and consultants are inherently more difficult to judge, so their quality may get judged by not so relevant characteristics such as the height of their fee, prestigious customers or the smoothness of their appearance. Major problems remain.

Due to asymmetric information, many aspects of quality cannot be judged even of goods that look very much like search goods. There may be hidden problems of functioning or safety. Firms use brand names and corporate image to enhance trust in quality. This is more needed the less quality can ex ante be judged by users. Simply the fact that producers have invested so much in building brand name or corporate image by itself already gives some guarantee, because opportunism or lack of care can jeopardize that investment. The fact that once trust is broken it is difficult and slow to build up again enhances this assurance. This is an important part of the reason why branded products fetch a higher price, as an insurance premium. A problem for firms here lies in the gap between trust in the firm and trust in people, discussed in previous chapters. No matter how important it may be for a firm to maintain quality, procedures for safeguarding it in work processes is seldom perfect. Monitoring is not likely to be perfect, and must be complemented by less extrinsic, more internalized social safeguards of commitment and motivation.

Problems deepen when we move on in the exchange process. In the stage of contract one needs to anticipate potential problems after specific investments have been committed to the exchange relationship. These problems, constituting relational risk, are of several kinds. One is that goals of quality, cost and time are not achieved. If that happens, how does one identify the cause, as a basis for remedial action? The cause might be lack of competence, lack of dedication, opportunism, or some outside cause, like an accident. How can one assess proper execution of the agreement? How can we assess trustworthiness? Here we run into the full range of problems discussed in previous chapters. As discussed in Chapter 2, there is a range of causes of actions and their outcomes, and each is a possible aspect of trust: competence, means, benevolence, dedication, honesty, outside conditions. These appear on both the level of individual people and the level of their organization. As discussed in Chapter 3, in assessing intentional reliability there are many possible sources to be taken into account: legal coercion, material self-interest in the relation, social values and norms, personal bonding and habituation in the relation. These sources provide the basis for instruments of governance. I will focus on the governance of inter-firm relations, but later I will briefly say something also about the governance of labour relations within an organization.

In my analysis of inter-organizational relations, I include learning: the utilization of complementary sources of knowledge between actors, and the joint production of new knowledge. A central feature in this is the management of cognitive distance. This notion was discussed in Chapter 1. In order to achieve a common purpose, one needs sufficient cognitive alignment, of perceptions, interpretations, evaluations and goals, that is limited cognitive distance. The 'tightness' of the focus, or cognitive proximity required, depends on the need for efficient exploitation of existing competencies relative to the need for exploration of new ones (Nooteboom 2000a). This depends on the industry, the need and rate of innovation, and the place of a firm in the industry. This yields the notion of a firm as a focusing device. However, such focus or cognitive proximity yields a risk of myopia, and one needs complementary cognitive competence in outside relations, at sufficient cognitive distance. This distance has to be sufficiently large to yield novel insights, but not too large to preclude mutual understanding.

All this has implications for where one should locate the boundary of the firm, how to coordinate activities within the firm and how to coordinate across boundaries of the firm. We cannot effectively deal with coordination in terms of two separate issues of intra- and inter-firm coordination, as if the boundary of the firm is given and fixed. Issues of coordination and the boundary of the firm constitute one integrated issue. As conditions change, both modes of coordination and the boundary of the firm are subject to shift.

As indicated in Chapter 1, when interaction requires the sharing of tacit knowledge, typically in the form of underlying categories of perception, then mutual understanding requires intensive interaction. This may require organizational integration, but that is not necessarily the case. It may be achieved in temporary joint teams, or 'communities of practice' (Brown and Duguid 1996), to develop 'epistemic communities' (Lissoni 2001). One would want to combine this with the preservation of cognitive distance for the sake of variety and novelty of knowledge sources, plus flexibility to shift to novel sources when the need arises. In other words, we are facing the need to have sufficient integration for mutual understanding but also sufficient disintegration to preserve novelty and variety. The conclusion concerning the boundary of the firm and modes of coordination is not evident.

There are further contingencies and dilemmas. Teece (1986), Chesbrough and Teece (1996) and Langlois and Robertson (1995) claimed that when innovation is systemic, that is we are dealing with a system of mutually coupled elements, change of the elements must occur in step to maintain systemic coherence, and this technical need for coordination requires organizational integration. I contest this, for two reasons (Nooteboom 1999a, 2000a). First, it applies only when innovation is incremental. When innovation is radical, in the sense of breaking up systemic coherence, such integration may be a liability rather than a benefit. Second, even if innovation is incremental, it is not a priori impossible to achieve the necessary coordination in some consortium of different firms. However, I grant that such coordination does have implications for the depth, durability and organizational form of the inter-firm relationships involved. If such coordination across firms is technically feasible, it has the advantage over full integration of preserving maximal variety of knowledge and flexibility of configurations.

Relational Risk

Next to exigencies of cognitive distance, variety, flexibility and systemic coherence there are issues of coordination in the more special sense of the governance of relational risk. There are two kinds of relational risk: risks of dependence ('hold-up') and risk of loss of knowledge ('spillover').

The risk of dependence or 'hold-up' is taken from transaction cost economics. In spite of the fundamental objections to that theory, discussed in Chapter 1, here the theory is still useful. When one is unilaterally dependent on a partner, he/she may be tempted to take opportunistic advantage of that and extort a greater share in added value. Can we trust the partner not to do this? On what could such trust be based?

Dependence arises especially from switching costs: switching from the present partner to another. Such costs arise, in particular, from investments which are specific for the partner, or the relationship, cannot be recouped and have to be made anew in another relationship. Such investments have to be made up front, and once they are made one is 'locked in'. Classic cases of specific investments are location-specific assets, assets in the form of dedicated machines or tools, human asset specificity in training and assets for excess volume of production that could not be sold elsewhere. An example of location specificity is a facility on the doorstep of the partner, in a location where no other potential partners are near.

To these classic cases I add specific investments in crossing cognitive distance: in building appropriate absorptive capacity and capacity to make oneself understood by the partner. This may have a large generic component, but also a specific component, particularly when the knowledge involved is tacit. Tacitness of knowledge tends to arise especially in early stages of innovation, where one has hit upon new ways of doing things without knowing why or even how, precisely, this works (Nooteboom 2000a). Knowledge is more procedural than declarative, and as discussed in Chapter 1, the former tends to be more difficult to formalize or even specify. As indicated before, this arises especially in small firms, which allow for direct supervision of work, requiring lesser codification of knowledge to coordinate by the specification of work processes (Mintzberg 1983). I also add the building of process trust as a specific investment. By definition the process of interaction on which the building of personalized process trust is based, as discussed in Chapter 3, is specific to the relationship.

The mutual exchange of information, to achieve understanding and to utilize complementary cognitive competencies, also creates a second type of risk: the risk of 'spillover' to competitors of core competence, which can jeopardize competitive position. Of course, the whole point of utilizing complementary sources of knowledge is to create and utilize knowledge flows between partners. This may even occur between competitors, to jointly produce new technology, to set technological standards in order to conquer markets, or to jointly provide more extensive packages of goods or services to customers. Nevertheless one wants to prevent spillovers that may occur beyond that purpose and defeat it. Between competitors one needs to consider the trade-off between risks and benefits of knowledge flows. In other relations one needs to assess the risk that sensitive knowledge spills over via partners to competitors. That risk depends on whether those partners have relations with one's competitors. One may control for this by demanding exclusiveness of the relation: for a given type of activity during the period of cooperation the partner is not allowed to have relations with one's competitors.

There is a danger of being too protective of knowledge, of myopically attaching too much weight to appropriability, while neglecting the dynamic of new knowledge creation in a network of firms, and the development of communicative and learning capacity. Of course this does not imply that appropriability no longer plays any role at all, but we should consider when spillover constitutes a real problem. Spillover risk depends on a number of other factors. One is the degree to which the knowledge involved is tacit. Obviously, tacit knowledge flows less easily than documented knowledge. But this does not mean that it does not spill over at all. If it is embodied in individual people or teams these may be poached. If people have more allegiance to their profession than to their firm, their knowledge may spill over when they are stationed at other firms, or when they do joint research, or when they meet at conferences. If knowledge is embodied in the structure and culture of a division it can still be expropriated by take-over. However, then the question is how quickly and effectively that culture can be integrated in the acquiring firm, that is how cognitive distance can be sufficiently reduced to yield efficient exploitation. There may be several other reasons why there is no significant risk. Note that, as discussed in Chapter 1, the problem of tacit knowledge lies not only on the side of the sender but also on the side of the receiver of information. He may not have the absorptive capacity to make sense of it. Cognitive distance may be too large and difficult to cross. Another possibility is that the knowledge spilled over is too far from core competence to cause damage. Or the partner may not be able to employ the knowledge for effective competition, with his present technical competencies and organization. Finally, the speed of one's knowledge change may be so high that by the time it has reached a competitor and he is able to effectively absorb and implement it, it will have changed.

When the problem of spillover does arise, it entails issues of trust. To what extent are partners, or other members of one's network, motivated not to steal competitive advantage? To what extent are they competent and committed to guard against accidental spillover to the partner's competitors? Information and knowledge can play the role of 'hostages'. They yield the recipient power: he may threaten to divulge it to your competitors. He may use this, for example, to keep you away from contacts with his competitors. Conversely, the information you receive from a partner may limit your access to other parties that are potential competitors to the focal partner.

> Knowledge may be valuable for other than own use in a different way. Smith-Doerr et al. (1999) showed, on the basis of an empirical study of patenting in biotechnology, that the most important role of patents may not be the potential for own production or licensing fees but the increase of attractiveness as a network partner for others. In terms of the present analysis: it extends one's cognitive range.

When spillover does present a serious risk, the question is to what extent one can monitor it for the sake of control. That depends on the type of knowledge, product and technology involved. Monitoring is more difficult to the extent that knowledge involved is tacit. Then it might have to take the form of constraints on interaction between personnel of one's partner and personnel of one's competitors, or on the attendance to conferences. In contrast, when the knowledge one provides gets embodied in products, one can monitor spillover by taking apart one's competitors' products to see whether it shows up there (Lamming 1993). That would show that in breach of agreement one's partner has allowed spillover to take place. However, when it is feasible, such spillover control is not necessarily desirable. Exclusiveness has the disadvantage of reducing variety. One foregoes the opportunity that one's partner may have of learning from relations with one's competitors, which may be to one's own advantage (Nooteboom 1998).

In this trade-off between benefits and risks of spillover the strategic challenge is to limit spillover control to where it is absolutely essential to preserve the distinctive core competence that constitutes one's competitive advantage. In other words: spillover control should have as narrow and sharp a focus as possible, in order to maximize the scope allowed for variety and flow of knowledge.

Summing up: modes of coordination and the location of firm boundaries should take into account the issue of cognitive distance, the role of systemic coherence in innovation, the type of knowledge involved, and the implications for opportunities of monitoring, and ways to control risks of hold-up and spillover. Now we turn to an analysis of instruments for the control of these two types of risk.

Governance

An enormous literature has been produced on the governance of inter-firm relations. A systematic discussion of that literature is beyond the scope of this book. I will make use of my own previous work (Nooteboom 1996, 1999a), which gives such a discussion, and which develops a method and a set of instruments for the analysis and design of inter-organizational relations. Those instruments are derived from the sources of cooperation discussed in Chapter 3, Table 3.1. Sources of cooperation may be used to achieve collaboration and ensure reliability. I provide a survey to show what role trust plays next to other instruments for governance (control). Does trust operate on its own, or in combination with control? What mixes of trust and control are there, under what conditions?

I focus on the governance of problems related to intentional trust, that is intentions to perform and honour agreements. This includes trust in benevolence (absence of opportunism) and in commitment or care. I do this in terms of risk control: the control of the two central risks of hold-up and spillover indicated before.

For forms of governance, it is customary to distinguish between integration under a 'hierarchy' that can settle disputes, obligational contracting and relational contracting. Each in its own way employs some form or several forms of reliance. Integration within an organization, under 'hierarchy', may entail all sources of reliance discussed in Chapter 3: labour contracts, norms and values, advantage, bonding and habituation. Obligational contracting entails trust in the legal infrastructure. Relational contracting is a very wide form of governance, where reliance may be based on several sources: norms/values, advantage, bonding and routinization. Beyond these wide and general forms of governance, here I consider more detailed strategies of governance.

To mitigate risks of dependence one may eliminate the cause of dependence, or exert direct control on possible opportunistic actions, or reduce 'opportunities for opportunism', associated with scope for action left in incomplete contracts and monitoring of compliance, or reduce 'inclinations to utilize such opportunities' (Nooteboom 1996, 1999a). The latter can be based on incentives of self-interest or on loyalty. The only new dimension here, compared with transaction cost economics, is loyalty, as a basis for trust in the sense of strong or 'real' trust, rather than assurance on the basis of control, as discussed in Chapter 2. Reliance covers all sources of cooperation, including coercion and self-interest. Trust as it is ordinarily understood goes beyond that. As defined in Chapter 2:

Definition 2
'Real' trust is an expectation that things or people will not fail us, or the neglect or lack of awareness of the possibility of failure, even if there are perceived opportunities and incentives for such failure.

We can now deduce the following instruments for governance. One solution of course is to prevent the risk from arising: do not engage in specific investments that give rise to the risk of hold-up, do not give information that may constitute a threat of spillover. I call this 'evasion'. If one does accept specific investments and information exchange, and the risk involved, one may control risk by direct control of actions, by choosing integration under a 'hierarchy' as the form of governance. Alternatively, one may relinquish such centralized control, and try to settle risks of transactions between autonomous parties. One way to do this is to reduce 'opportunities for opportunism', with obligational contracting as the form of governance, by means of formal, legal contracts and the monitoring needed to enforce them. However, as indicated already in transaction cost economics, complete contingent contracting is generally impossible due to uncertainty. If opportunities for opportunism cannot be eliminated, one can aim to reduce inclinations to utilize such opportunities by reducing the incentives to do so, in the governance form of relational contracting. For this one may use symmetric mutual dependence, shared ownership of specific assets, hostages and reputation mechanisms. This is relational contracting on the basis of self-interest. Perhaps relational contracting can also be interpreted to include social reciprocity rather than only economic quid pro quo. However that may be, what I add here is governance beyond self-interest, on the basis of trust, in the narrow, strong sense of 'real' trust. Here one reduces inclinations to utilize opportunities for opportunism on the basis of some degree of loyalty, which may be based on ethics, friendship, empathy, kinship or habituation/routinization.

One may wonder how trust can be seen as an instrument of governance, since it cannot be installed like a machine or injected as an ingredient. This is the problem of trust 'production', discussed in Chapter 3. If trust is not already in place prior to transactions, it can only be developed in time, in an ongoing relationship. Yet it can be seen as an instrument, in two ways. First one may select one's partners on the basis of characteristics-based ex ante trust (Zucker 1986), or from a community one is familiar with, on the basis of kinship, friendship or reputation. Second, one may design the relation and plan its progress so as to build up trust in the process, as discussed in Chapter 3 (Zucker 1986, Gulati 1995, Nooteboom et al. 1997).

Risks of hold-up and spillover depend on one's position in a network of relations, and one may therefore control those risks by selecting an appropriate position in such a network, or designing the network around one's position. This strategy does not seem to fit in any of the existing forms of governance (integration, obligational and relational contracting). Perhaps it constitutes a fourth form of governance, which we might call 'positional governance'. However, perhaps one can argue that it is a special form of relational contracting. Finally, one can also make good use of intermediaries, or third parties or go-betweens. The instruments for risk control are summarized in Table 4.1. They are discussed in more detail, and evaluated, in the next and later sections.

The instruments of governance all have their limitations; their advantages and disadvantages. In the context of learning by interaction, evasion entails that one does not yield sensitive knowledge and does not engage in specific investments for the set-up of knowledge exchange. One tradition in organizational science is to design and explain organizations on the basis of the avoidance of dependence (for example Thompson 1967). Dependence entails subjection to power, which is seen as risky and hence to be avoided. However, from the perspective of social capital and learning,

Table 4.1   Instruments for control of relational risk

Instrument	Description
Evasion	Don't yield sensitive information and don't engage in specific investments
Integration	Unified administrative control, i.e. by merger or acquisition
Obligational contracting	Contracts to control hold-up, and patenting to control spillover
Relational contracting with incentives from self-interest economic reciprocity	Use of mutual dependence, ownership of assets or information, hostages, reputation mechanisms
Relational contracting with loyalty as a basis for trust (in the strong sense), social reciprocity	Based on values and norms of conduct, personal bonds, routinization
Network structure	One's position, in terms of density, centrality, spanning holes
Roles of a go-between	Trilateral governance, solving the revelation problem, monitoring, hostage keeping, sieve and amplifier of reputation

the avoidance of dependence can be highly detrimental: the price of social capital is dependence, and while that in itself tends to be a liability, there may be a positive net advantage. Power can also be beneficial: partners can open up new opportunities. As discussed above, the advantage lies in the creation and utilization of complementary competencies, by means of specific investments and knowledge sharing, for differentiated products, learning and innovation. Thus, rather than evading dependence, as a goal in itself, the challenge is to maximize the returns and minimize the risks of dependence.

The advantage of integration is that different parties are brought under 'unified governance': there is an overarching authority that can establish monitoring backed up by enforceable demands for information, and can impose resolution of conflict, by administrative fiat. Of course, even within an organization there are limitations to this, but the scope for problem solving by authority is larger within than between independent firms, where the last resort is a court of law. However, as argued in transaction cost economics, integration in the firm surrenders the 'high powered incentives' that apply to an independent producer who has his own responsibility for survival, and it may renounce economy of scale in specialized outside production. It can be hazardous to try and integrate different cultures. Integration reduces flexibility in the configuration of activities, unless firms are easy to break up. Integration improves the control of spillover, but can cause cognitive inbreeding: the loss of variety of experience and learning on the basis of cognitive distance.

As indicated, the advantage of obligational contracting between firms is that it constrains 'opportunities for opportunism'. It should be noted that most of the time there will be a contract of some form. The question is not so much whether there is a contract but what its content is and how elaborate it is. One problem with contracting is that it is not always possible, due to uncertainty concerning future contingencies. Secondly, formal contracting and patenting make sense only if compliance and the lack of it can be observed, and sanctions are credible. The set-up costs of contracts and monitoring systems can be significant, which makes the cost relatively high for smaller firms. A third problem is that contracts may form a straitjacket that blocks the utilization of unforeseen opportunities that arise especially in innovation. It is paradoxical to specify in detail all tasks, rights and obligations for something that is new and unpredictable. Furthermore, detailed contracting to prevent opportunism sets a relation off on a basis of mistrust, and may frustrate the building of trust. Patents may not be possible or effective, for small firms the costs of monitoring infringement are high and the threat of litigation may not be credible, and patent information may reveal too much.

Management by relational contracting with incentives from self-interest has the advantage that it is cheaper than contracts, is more flexible, and it is in the players' own interest to be seen to comply with agreements. It requires a judicious mix of mutual interest, shared ownership of specific investments and information, hostages and reputation, to achieve a balance of mutual dependence. There is no need for balance in every form separately, but for balance in the mix. Thus one-sided ownership of specific assets may be balanced by one-sided hostages going the other way, or by a rigorous reputation mechanism. The main problem of this form of governance is that it is not self-policing. Again there is a need for observation, measurement and monitoring. How does one measure and monitor degree of dependence, spillover, specificity of investments? For example, if a player claims that his investment in the relation is highly specific, and that he needs compensation for this, can he be believed, or is there a need to demand insight into his books to check that the investment is indeed not used for anyone else? Reputation works only if breach can be observed, and can be credibly communicated to potential future partners of the culprit. If the culprit can move out with unknown destination this may be impossible. The culprit may claim that the accusation is unjust and that there are ulterior motives to harm him. Self-interest in the form of agreements of secrecy, and the use of bilateral exchange of information as a hostage, makes sense only if spillover can be monitored. The breach of agreement to guard against spillover of knowledge cannot be observed if flows of knowledge cannot be observed. Such monitoring is more difficult to the extent that the knowledge involved is tacit. A second major problem is that the balance of interests, to prevent one-sided dependence, is difficult to ensure and maintain. It is sensitive to shifts in competence and external conditions. It is particularly vulnerable to the emergence on the scene of a more attractive partner for one of the players, who will then be tempted to defect and leave others with a gap in performance and worthless specific assets.

Relational contracting with loyalty as the basis for trust, in the strong sense of expectation that partners will not intentionally create damage even if they have the opportunity and the interest to do so, has several advantages. In contrast with obligational contracting it is cheap, flexible and self-policing, that is requires limited monitoring, since it is driven by internalized motivation. In contrast with relational contracting with incentives from self-interest it is less sensitive to contingencies. Trust may be already in place when a relation starts, on the basis of kinship, experience in previous contacts, reputation, shared values and norms of decent conduct. If not, then it will have to be developed in the unfolding of the relation. That indicates a limitation: if not already present, it cannot be effected instantaneously. The main problem concerning trust is: how far can it go? It should not be blind or unconditional: most people will break trust when the temptation is strong enough. Friendship and kinship can cause such blindness. In Chapter 3 I argued that trust can be conceptualized in terms of thresholds: people will not be opportunistic until temptation exceeds a certain threshold of resistance to temptation, and this threshold depends on values and norms, experience, character, kinship and friendship. Even so, trust matters. It has its advantages within these tolerance levels.

Network structure, and one's position in it, represent both a contingency and a set of instruments for governance. If network participants one is linked with, have links with one's (potential) competitors, there is a hazard of spillover, unless spillover constitutes no threat due to tacitness or speed of change. To guard against the risk, if it exists, one may limit information transfer, or attempt to control spillover by contracting, monitoring, hostage taking, or reputation. Conversely, one may need to be careful in establishing linkages with competitors of partners one already has strong linkages with. That might cause those partners to restrict information exchange. One can encourage openness by concessions of exclusiveness, but that reduces the variety of sources of learning. Next to spillover, contacts have implications for bargaining position. Having multiple partners in any given type of activity makes one less dependent on any of them. However, for this very reason it may yield a threat which withholds them from committing themselves to specific investments in a durable relation, which restricts the capital that can be derived from it. Also, it multiplies the costs of set-up and monitoring.

Intermediaries can perform useful services here, in yielding and controlling information flows, enabling 'trilateral governance' in lieu of elaborate contracts, building trust and implementing reputation mechanisms. In other words: here one designs structure in order to assist governance. One can mitigate relational risks by the use of a third party as a go-between (Nooteboom 1999a, b). This is discussed in the next section.

Roles of the Go-between

Chapter 3 indicated that, as several authors have analysed, there are innumerable agencies that act as guardians of trust (Shapiro 1987) and support, and form part of, institution-based trust (Zucker 1986). They monitor quality, control conformance to norms and standards of conduct, provide guarantees or insurance and provide intermediation or arbitration. Those are agencies that support or implement generalised, institution-based trust. Here, I extend the analysis with intermediaries that bolster or help to produce particularized, personalized trust, as a third party to a bilateral relationship. Admittedly, the boundary between these two kinds of intermediaries is not sharp. Nevertheless, the focus is different (particularized versus generalized trust).

One stream of literature on networks suggests that players who span 'structural holes' can gain advantage (Burt 1992). If individuals or communities A and B are connected only by C, then C can take advantage of his bridging position by accessing resources that others cannot access, and by playing off A and B against each other. In the context of information exchange, he can, for example, threaten to pass sensitive information that he has from A to B and vice versa, and can thereby extract advantage from both. As a result, the third party is maximally powerful and minimally constrained in his actions. The Latin term for this third party advantage is 'tertius gaudens'. Krackhardt (1999) pointed out that this principle goes back to Simmel (1950). However, Krackhardt shows that Simmel also indicated that under some conditions the third party is maximally constrained. This occurs when he bridges two different cliques, with dense and strong internal ties, with different values and norms, while his actions are observed by both. The third party then has to satisfy the rules or norms of both cliques (the intersection of norm sets). The key factor that determines whether the third party is minimally or maximally constrained is the degree to which the third party's actions are public, or at least known to both A and B. If not, then the situation described by Burt obtains, and he is minimally constrained. If his actions are public, he is maximally constrained.

I add the following consideration. So far, the assumption seems to have been that A and B are rivals or at the least stand in a substitutive relation: benefit for the one occurs at the expense of the other. If A and B are complementary, as in my studies of collaboration in learning and innovation, with complementary cognitive and other competencies, the logic is different. There, the go-between can obtain and supply advantage to both A and B by helping them to collaborate. Nevertheless, the earlier logic may still apply. The third party, acting as a go-between, may be tempted to exploit his bridging position by misleading and extorting A and B. To keep him from doing that, his actions should be public, or at least known to both A ad B, so that his reputation is at stake.

In collaborative relations, go-betweens can play beneficial roles by facilitating communication, reducing the need for specific investments in understanding, reducing risks of spillover, thus creating social capital rather than liability for the players he connects (Baker and Obstfeld 1999). One condition for this is that the third party is allowed to occupy an intermediary position only if breach of trust would destroy his reputation as an intermediary, and this would be costly for him.

There are several roles for intermediaries in the set-up and governance of inter-organizational relations, as discussed in Nooteboom (1999c). The first role is not related to governance so much as to help parties to learn from each other, and to achieve the mutual understanding needed for that. In terms of the theory of knowledge and learning set out in Chapter 1: the go-between may be needed to help partners to 'cross cognitive distance'. In the transfer of knowledge, there is not only a problem on the part of the sender of 'externalizing' tacit knowledge, or of dislodging knowledge from the tacit basis of underlying cognitive categories. There is also a problem for the receiver of interpreting the information, by embedding it in his more or less tacit cognitive categories. To the extent that the knowledge transferred has to replace existing tacit knowledge, there is the problem that existing tacit practice is taken for granted and is difficult to subject to criticism. Then, the tacit knowledge underlying practice may first have to be made explicit (Nooteboom 2000a). The go-between may have an important role to play here. Typically, in a small firm, where a greater proportion of knowledge is tacit, based on practice and stored in procedural memory, an outsider who comes with a proposal to change existing practice will be dismissed as not making sense and being 'impractical'. Only people who are trusted to be familiar with existing practice and the exigencies of that particular small firm may get the attention of the entrepreneur. This may be a colleague, or it might be a go-between who is known to be familiar with the firm and its practice.

A second role is related to the first one. It is to solve the 'revelation problem'. In the selling of information, there is Arrow's paradox of information: to judge the value of information one must already have it, but then there is nothing left to pay for. One solution is to offer licenses with only a small payment up front, and a subsequent payment in proportion to the proceeds the patent yields. However, this may not be easy to observe, for the purpose of control. An alternative is to let the go-between assess the value of the information. For this, the third party has to know both sides well enough to reliably inform them on the competence and intentions of each other, without surrendering much information on content.

A third role, connected to the second, is to control spillover, seeing to it that knowledge does not flow beyond where it is intended. This is relevant when one partner would not allow the other to come into the firm and monitor knowledge flow, because he would thereby have access to other sensitive information, creating a risk of reverse spillover, while the third party does not constitute such a risk.

A fourth role derives directly from transaction cost economics. Williamson (1985) indicated the possibility of engaging a third party as a go-between ('trilateral governance'). That was inspired by considerations of efficiency. It obtains when governance to control transaction costs is needed but the transactions involved are too small or infrequent to justify the often considerable costs of a 'bilateral' governance scheme. Then it is more efficient to make a simpler overall agreement and engage a third party for arbitration. That party must have the trust of both protagonists, in both his competence and his intention to judge effectively and fairly. There are more roles for the go-between, and they all have to do with trust in one way or another.

A fifth role is to act as a guardian of hostages. Without that, there may be a danger that the hostage keeper does not return the hostage even if the partner sticks to the agreement. The third party has an interest in maintaining symmetric trust and acceptance by both protagonists. He can be trusted more to sacrifice the hostage without hesitation if the giver does not stick to the agreement, and not to keep the hostage longer than agreed. This solution is antique, and was practised in the Middle Ages, in the exchange of hostages between kings (de Laat 1999), with an emperor as the third party.

Earlier, I suggested that often hostages are in the nature of information. Since information is non-exclusive, how can it be returned without the holder retaining it? One possibility is that the information is given in a sealed box (or its virtual equivalent, with computer technology), so that the hostage holder cannot actually access it. Here, the partner may actually keep the box, while the third party holds the key to its access. There are other forms of hostage. One is production machinery (possession is exclusive here). Another is people stationed at the partner, who may be poached, if the partner does not stick to the agreement. Here, the notion of a hostage comes closest to the traditional notion of a person held. Of course, staff cannot be held against their will, but they may be bought out. Another form is a minority participation, which may be sold off to a potential raider.

A sixth, and perhaps most crucial, role is to act as an intermediary in the building of trust. Trust relations are often entered with partners who are trusted partners of someone you trust (Sydow 1996). If X has competence as well as intentional trust in Y and Y has intentional trust in Z, then X may rationally give intentional trust in Z a chance. X needs to feel that Y is able to judge well and has no intention to lie about his judgment. This can speed up the building of trust between strangers, which might otherwise take too long. The intermediary can also perform valuable services in protecting trust when it is still fragile: to eliminate misunderstanding and allay suspicions when errors or mishaps are mistaken for opportunism. Intermediation in the first small and ginger steps of cooperation, to ensure that they are successful, can be very important in the building of a trust relation. As noted earlier, in Chapters 2 and 3, things may go wrong in a relation either because of mistakes or because of opportunism, but in practice they are difficult to distinguish because an opportunist will claim mistakes or mishaps as the cause of disappointing results. The intermediary may solve misunderstandings that turn mistakes into perceived indications of opportunism. This is particularly important in view of the dynamics of the build-up and breakdown of trust discussed in Chapter 3. There, I concluded that for this reason new relationships may have to start small, with low stakes that are raised as trust builds up. This may be needed especially when contracts are not feasible or desirable. The disadvantage of such a procedure is of course its slowness. In a competitive environment where speed to market is of increasing importance it may be too slow. Then, a go-between may provide help for a more speedy development.

A seventh role, related to the sixth, is to help in the timely and least destructive disentanglement of relations. A dilemma arises in ending a relation. If one wants to end a relation because a more attractive option has emerged, should one announce this attention at an early stage, or should one drop it on the partner at the last moment? In other words should one go for an adversarial or a collaborative mode of divorce (Nooteboom 1996,

1999a)? With the first, one offers the partner a way out with least damage: he/she stops making specific investments that would maintain his/her switching cost, one can help to find a new partner to minimize disruption. However, one also gives the partner time to obstruct one's departure. Collaborative divorce is viable if the partner can be expected to cut his/her losses and welcome the help to get out with minimal damage. There is a more subtle point attached to this. One may hesitate to criticize the partner even when it is part of voice, in the mutual honesty that can deepen trust, lest it should be interpreted as a signal of an intention to leave. This kind of sensitivity is most likely to arise in the case of asymmetric dependence. Here also, to eliminate misunderstanding, and to prevent acrimonious and mutually damaging battles of divorce, a go-between can offer valuable services.

An eighth role is to act as a lookout, a sieve, a channel and an amplifier in reputation mechanisms. As indicated earlier, for a reputation mechanism to work, infringement of agreements must be observable, its report must be credible, and it must reach potential future partners of the culprit. The go-between can help in all respects: to monitor infringement, to sift true reports from gossip, to connect with future potential partners of the culprit and bridge the distances involved. However, perhaps this goes beyond the micro level, particularistic perspective of this type of go-between.

Most of these roles are especially important in innovation. Here, exchange of knowledge is crucial, with corresponding risks of spillover, and specific investments are needed to set up mutual understanding and cooperation. There are corresponding risks of hold-up, while particularly in innovation the competencies and intentions of strangers are difficult to judge. Especially in innovation detailed contracts tend to have the adverse effect of a straitjacket, constraining the variety of actions and initiatives that innovation requires. Third party arbitration then yields a less constraining alternative, in trilateral governance and the development of trust instead of using detailed contracts to preclude opportunism.

Note that in all roles it is crucial that the go-between commands trust in both his competence and his intentions. He should be competent concerning the technologies involved, and concerning the relational skills required. He should be known to be impartial and incorruptible. He should have an interest to act scrupulously, with a view to his reputation as a go-between. There is a range of actors who could possibly play these roles, and not all roles have to be played by a single actor. Possible go-betweens are banks, consultants, interlocking directorates, and local government agencies, such as municipalities or development agencies, or subsidized technology transfer centres. Returning to the more suspicious view of go-betweens identified by Burt, we must recognize that they may occupy a position of power that can be used opportunistically. When the role is played by government agencies there is a risk of corruption. This yields the question, discussed earlier by Shapiro (1987) how go-betweens, in turn, can be subjected to control. This brings us to the second part of this chapter: the institutional conditions needed to support governance of relations. However, first some concluding comments must be made concerning the mutual relations between the different instruments for governance. In particular, how is trust related to the others, and how can it be combined?

Complements and Substitutes

There will rarely be exclusive use of only one of the instruments of governance. This raises the question where and how they complement each other, and when and how they may be in conflict. In particular, an important question is whether trust and contract are complements or substitutes. There is widespread appreciation of the fact that since contracts are generally incomplete, they must be supplemented with trust. On the other hand, trust as the only basis for collaboration is vulnerable. However, there has also been a widespread tendency in the literature to see them as substitutes, and I also fell for this temptation (see, for example, Macaulay 1963, Bradach and Eccles 1989, Parkhe 1993, Gulati 1995, Fukuyama 1995, Chiles and MacMackin 1996, Nooteboom 1996). The basic, in retrospect rather primitive, idea is that when there is trust there is no need for contract, and contract builds on and makes for suspicion, which destroys the basis for trust. This is not wrong so much as seriously incomplete.

Klein Woolthuis (1999) put the issue to an empirical test, in four case studies. She found that indeed contract and trust are at least as much complements as they are substitutes. Trust can and in fact does indeed operate as a substitute for detailed contracts, in so far as those are designed to foreclose opportunism. However, there may be detailed contracts for other reasons, notably to serve as an aid to memory, a record of conclusions how to technically coordinate complex processes. That can very well be complementary to trust. The reduction of uncertainty provided by clear agreements on procedures, tasks, authority and rewards can support trust by preventing misunderstandings and unjustified behaviour (see also Knights et al. 2001: 315). Also, trust may be needed as a precondition for a contract. Setting up a contract can itself be a costly affair, and constitutes a specific investment in its own right. One may require ex ante trust before taking on the risk involved in setting up such a contract. Next, a simple legal contract may be used more or less symbolically, to mark and celebrate what is in fact a psychological or relational contract. Finally, a contract has to be based on trust in the underlying institutions that support it, but that is a different matter, to be discussed in the second part of this chapter.

It should be noted also that, at least in the Netherlands, where the study took place, contracts are seldom actually enforced in front of a judge. In the study, one reason that emerged for this was that the plaintive expected to have to deal with his opponent again in future, and taking him to court would seriously jeopardize that. Among social scientists the actual use of legal sanctions is generally seen as incompatible with a trust relationship (Lane 2000: 13). However, if that constituted a general rule, the threat of litigation and thereby contracts would lose their credibility. There is also a more technical obstacle to full enforcement of contracts. Often contracts contain non-legally enforceable or even poorly specified intentions, promises, conditions and the like, which are supported by non-legal sanctions. Deakin and Wilkinson (2001: 150) note that 'Such arrangements may easily be misinterpreted by the courts, which do not have access to the specialized knowledge or assumptions shared by the parties'.

The study by Klein Woolthuis also illustrates some aspects of the dynamics of trust discussed in Chapter 3. In particular, it illustrates the cycle of trust development as described by Zand (1972) and Deutsch's (1973) 'crude law of social relations': 'The characteristic processes and effects elicited by a given type of social relationship (cooperative or competitive) tend also to elicit that type of social relationship'. Therefore I summarize some of her results.

> Two of the cases studied by Klein Woolthuis show how, as partners get to know each other and negotiate about goals and objectives, trust develops between them on the personal as well as on the company level. This increases their willingness to commit to the relationship since they have trust in the intentions and competencies of their partner. Their mutual trust leads to an atmosphere characterized by openness and a general willingness to listen to each other (compare this with Zand 1972, and the discussion of the process of trust, in Chapter 3). This in turn enables them to reach and formalize an agreement. Trust helps them to have an open discussion on goals and mutual commitments, but also on sensitive issues such as relationship termination or sharing costs in case things go wrong. Trust also makes it easier for parties to commit to their agreement by signing the contract. In a trusting atmosphere, the presence of (extensive) contracts might be interpreted as the embodiment of commitment and trust.
>
> On the other hand, other cases show that if partners fear each others' intentions, the opposite process is likely to occur. Contracts are more likely to be interpreted as safeguards against opportunism. In such a situation, partners show defensive behaviour and might not be willing to commit to a relationship before safeguards are installed to protect their interests. As a result, the contractual arrangements will likely focus on secrecy of information, protection of ownership, conflict resolution and relationship termination. Because of a lack of openness, it will be hard to arrive at detailed agreements on a practical level (for example a project-plan or management of the project). Incomplete or very general, poorly specified or unenforceable contracts may be the result.

The study shows that for the relation between trust and contract the process of collaboration plays a central role. Neither the mere presence or absence of contracts nor the extensiveness of the contract is the main issue. Instead, the focus should be on the aim and content of the contract, and the atmosphere in which it is set up. Contracts mostly have a mixture of purposes and meanings at the same time. Contracts may be envisaged as a reflection of the process of the negotiation and commitment stages that partners go through. The meaning of the contract mostly changes over time.

The idea that contract should be understood as both legal and social is not new. Earlier, I already referred to Macneil (1980: 1), who wrote: 'contract between totally isolated, utility maximizing individuals is not contract, but war'. Contracts should hence be interpreted as safeguards but also as the sedimentation of the formal and informal agreements between socially embedded actors.

If we consider the development of a relation as a process in which positive and negative behaviour can change the relationship atmosphere, as suggested by both Zand and Deutsch, the writing and signing of a contract should also be envisaged as a step in this development. Contracts can, just like trust, be seen as both cause and result of cooperation. Negotiating the contract can be seen as a process of getting to know and understand each other. Signing the contract can be seen as a sign of commitment. In an opportunistic atmosphere contract negotiations can resemble a battlefield where the most powerful partner dominates contract content and execution. In such a situation, contract often reflects the relative dependence between partners. Both the negotiation process and the signing of the contract will be interpreted by the dependent partner as negative behaviour and will decrease his trust in the more powerful partner. He may be on the lookout for evidence that confirms his fears of relational risk.

If a relationship starts in a trusting or neutral atmosphere, as a result of mutually positive behaviour (for example friendly negotiations, strong commitment, joint problem solving) the relationship shifts towards a more trusting atmosphere. This will be easier if the relationship started in a (rather) trusting atmosphere. If partners have previously had negative experiences with each other (or one has an opportunistic reputation), it will take disproportionately positive behaviour to break away from a distrusting atmosphere into a trusting one.

Unfortunately, it works much more easily the other way around, as expressed in the aphorism 'trust comes on foot but leaves on horseback'. If partners start in a trusting atmosphere and one (or more) of the partners shows negative behaviour (for example bad quality, late delivery, withholding information) trust will deteriorate. At first instance, trusting partners will give each other the benefit of the doubt and try to solve problems together. However, when doubts grow on the other's intentions, trust deteriorates very fast and is hard, if not impossible, to regain. This is where a go-between may serve an important role, as discussed previously, to prevent the initial slip of trust, possibly due to misunderstanding, before it develops into a landslide.

A particularly productive complementarity lies in the combination between trust and mutual dependence. Balanced, two-sided specific investments create dependence and the risk of hold-up on both sides of a bilateral relation. When well chosen, they also create mutual dependence, by creating unique value for the partner. Thus, one runs a risk of dependence (hold up due to specific investments) but also creates one for the partner (unique value). The causality of relational risk has many directions and loops (Nooteboom et al. 2000, De Jong and Nooteboom 2000). This is elaborated in Chapter 6, where I discuss several models of trust and relations. The attraction of managing relational risk by balance of mutual dependence is that it is productive: it does not hamper collaboration, as a detailed contract might, but accelerates it by adding more value. However, it is also vulnerable to change. The balance of dependence may be disrupted by a change of technology, the appearance of a new player in the field who is more attractive to one of the partners, a change in technology or in market conditions, or a difference between the partners in their rate of learning and ongoing development of competencies.

> The literature on inter-firm alliances is full of examples. A classical type of this is the alliance between an American firm who supplied the technology or design of a product, and a Japanese firm who supplies entry to the Japanese market. One of the examples was the alliance between Xerox and Fuji (Lorange and Roos 1992). After a while, the capability in technology and design had spilled over to the Japanese firm so that it became less dependent, while the American firm remained dependent on the Japanese firm, since entry to the Japanese market by foreigners remained as difficult as ever.

In view of this, balance of dependence may have to be supplemented by trust, in the sense of a give and take, in voice rather than exit. There, partners can rely on each other not to exit as soon as the balance of dependence is disturbed, but to try and redress the balance, by mutual investment or help. Of course, there is a limit to this. If in spite of joint efforts the imbalance of value continues and deepens, the relationship may have to be disentangled.

Conversely, trust will seldom operate on its own. It will have to be combined with sufficient mutual interest. As proposed in Chapter 3, trust will have its limits: in general, people can be expected to be loyal only within boundaries that depend on a range of factors, including the pressures for survival that they are subjected to. It may also be combined with a reputation mechanism. Remember that reputation may be fully self-interested, to maintain options for fruitful relations in the future, but may also have intrinsic value, from a preference for social acceptance or appreciation, as discussed in Chapters 2 and 3. As also discussed there, trust and being trusted may also have intrinsic value. Here, trust and reputation may be closely related, in social reciprocity and a dedication to voice.

4.2   INSTITUTIONAL CONDITIONS

This section considers the institutional conditions for trust and other instruments of governance. It analyses the locality of trust: to what extent and why are trust and governance spatially embedded, connected with location? This may contribute to the debate in geography concerning the role of location in 'Regional Innovation Systems' (RIS).

Institutional Structure and Variety

In Chapter 1 I proposed not to define institutions ontologically, with an inventory of institutional entities, but functionally: institutions enable, constrain and guide behaviour, and are (relatively) stable and not subject to free choice. What the relevant institutions are depends on the particular situation we are investigating. Legal systems are institutions for organizations, and organizations are institutions for the behaviour in them. This yields a hierarchy of institutions. There is a deep structure of more or less shared categories of perception, understanding and evaluation, as part of culture. Here the emphasis lies on the guidance of behaviour. In terms of the multiple causality of action used in this book, the emphasis lies on final and formal causality. There is also a surface structure of institutions, with laws, regulations, habits of commerce, labour unions, employers and industry associations, labour markets, financial markets, educational and scientific systems and the like. There the emphasis lies on enablers and constraints of action, or, in terms of the causality of action, on material and conditional causality.

Examples of underlying categories, in the deep structure, are: orientation towards individual self interest or to group values, to authoritarianism or consensus, to elitism or egalitarianism, to exit or voice, certainty or risk, planning or improvization, internal or external 'locus of control'. Such underlying categories are part of a more or less shared culture, with individual differences in susceptibility and loyalty to them. They vary to a

Table 4.2   Institutions for control of relational risk

Instrument	Underlying institutions
Integration	Organization (institutional arrangements)
Obligational contracting	Legal infrastructure for contracts: workable laws, competent lawyers, reliable, incorrupt judiciary and police (institutional surface structure)
Relational contracting with incentives from self-interest economic reciprocity	Clear ownership rights, communication infrastucture, reputation mechanisms (surface structure)
Relational contracting with loyalty as a basis for trust (in the strong sense), social reciprocity	Values and norms of conduct, standards of reciprocity, social (not purely individualistic) orientation, orientation towards voice (rather than exit), long-term orientation of relations (deep structure) and a market for corporate control that allows for that (surface structure)
Network structure	Legal and communication infrastructure enabling networks (surface structure)
Roles of a go-between	Availability of appropriate (competent, reliable) go-betweens, such as banks, professional associations, transfer agencies, municipalities, etc. (institutional arrangements)

greater or lesser extent between political groups, and political power determines whose categories are most reflected in surface structure. This distinction between deep and surface structure has the advantage of enabling us to reconcile change at the surface level with a more enduring deep structure.

For example, in the Netherlands there is a certain shift in corporate governance towards the Anglo-Saxon emphasis on shareholder value, but whatever comes out will reflect a more enduring deep structure of categories concerning the nature and purpose of organizations, their stakeholders and the Dutch need for deliberation and consensus.

Each of the instruments for governance discussed earlier requires its supporting institutions. These are indicated in Table 4.2. Trust in any of the instruments depends on trust in (or more precisely: reliance on) its underlying institutions.

Contractual sources of trustworthiness (or more accurately: reliability) require appropriate and effective institutions: laws of property and trade, reliable and competent lawyers, non-corrupt police and judiciary, and so on. These vary considerably between countries.

Clearly, values and norms of social conduct also vary greatly between countries, and may change in time, as has been emphasized by Fukuyama (1995), among many others. Fukuyama used the term 'spontaneous sociability'. This is enabled or constrained, muted or amplified, blocked or transmitted by a variety of 'intermediate communities distinct from the family or those deliberately established by governments' (Fukuyama 1995: 27). Such norms as well as the contractual sources are facilitated, mediated and arbitrated by a large variety of what Shapiro (1987) called the 'guardians of trust', as discussed in Chapter 3. Similarly, the importance and the functioning of kinship, friendship and routinization vary greatly across cultures. This variety of supporting institutions and their differences between countries, in different 'business systems' have also been demonstrated by other researchers (for example Zucker 1986, Hill 1990, Sako 1992, 1998, Hollingsworth and Boyer 1997, Whitley 1999).

These institutional differences yield differences in the viability and efficiency of different instruments for governance, and thereby yield different forms of inter-firm relations. In buyer–supplier relations, for example, differences were identified between Japan and the US by Cusumano and Fujimoto (1991), Helper (1990), Lamming (1993) and Kamath and Liker (1994), among others. Lane and Bachmann (1996) identified differences between Britain and Germany. Differences in the printed circuit board industry were identified between Britain and Japan by Sako (1994), in the machine tool industry between the US and Germany by Herrigel (1994). Lane (1997) identified differences in pattern and style of internationalization between British and German multinational enterprises.

Zucker (1986) and Fukuyama (1995) stated that in the US there has been a development from a prevailing sense of trust and community, based on norms of social behaviour and duty, towards a more individualistic and legalistic society. In other words: a decline of spontaneous sociability, although pockets of it still exist, in some communities. In terms of Table 3.1, this entails an upward shift from altruistic to egotistic sources of trustworthiness. Putnam (2000) adduced a number of statistics to illustrate this development. Fukuyama proposed that 'the French capacity for spontaneous sociability was effectively destroyed in the sixteenth and seventeenth centuries by a victorious centralising monarchy' (1995: 28). His analysis is not always correct, it seems. Fukuyama characterized all Chinese societies (in Taiwan, Hong Kong and Mainland China) as 'familialistic', because 'the essence of Chinese Confucianism is the elevation of family bonds above all other social loyalties' (1995: 29). However, here he overestimates the spread and depth of Confucianism across the large diversity of Chinese cultures and conditions, and neglects the importance of the more widespread social ties produced in army and school networks (Menkhoff 1992, Krug 2000).

The differences accord with the view that there are 'varieties of capital-ism', in different 'business systems', due to institutional differences between countries (Hollingsworth and Boyer 1997, Whitley 1999, Nooteboom 1999c, d). Hill (1990) argued that an institutional basis for trust yields lower transaction costs, and thereby produces a competitive advantage among nations, so that in time, in an evolutionary selection process, trust-based societies will prevail. This argument is the opposite of Williamson's, who argued that in markets trust would not survive. Against Hill's argument one can raise the objection that it seems to neglect the possible effects of the invasion of a trust-based society by opportunists. Will trust be robust under such invasion, or will the basis for trust unravel, as opportunists exploit trustors? To preclude that, one may have to erect barriers to entry, but this may provoke penalties imposed by the global economic community. And if trust can be maintained only at the cost of being barred from world markets, the trade-off is not so clear (Nooteboom 1999c).

In an earlier section, I identified several complications in the operation of different instruments for governance. Complete contingent contracts are generally impossible, depending on the uncertainty of relevant future con-tingencies. For small or infrequent transactions contracts may be too costly, and one may need to revert to the use of a third party to yield arbitration, in 'trilateral governance'. A reputation mechanism often requires a filter to sift out slander, and an amplifier and broadcaster of justified complaints. This may be the task of a third party. Hostages may not be returned to givers, in spite of their good behaviour, and it is a classic solution to have hostages kept by independent third parties. As discussed previously, these are just three roles for third parties out of several roles. The point here is that such third parties or go-betweens form an important element in the institu-tional structure that supports, or fails to support, trust. The roles identified here extend the roles of the 'intermediate communities' noted by Fukuyama and of the 'trust guardians' noted by Shapiro. The roles may be played by trade associations, professional bodies, banks, 'interlocking directorates' of firms, and so on. Here also, there is a wide variation between countries.

Generic Systems of Innovation[1]

The relation between institutions and economic performance has to be further unpacked. How, more precisely, does it work, in terms of the micro behaviour of firms and the people in them? I propose that an important part of the mechanism operates through instruments for governance. The

---

[1] This section is based on Nooteboom (2000b).

question therefore is how institutions affect economic performance through the effects they have on the availability of instruments for the governance of inter-firm relations. Here, I focus on innovative performance. Clearly, there is a large number of logically possible combinations between institutions, instruments of governance and performance. Any limited taxonomy of systems of innovation is likely to ignore possible combinations. However, not all combinations make sense. There is considerable systemic coherence between institutions themselves. A predilection for consensus decision making is difficult to reconcile with authoritarianism, elitism or an orientation to exit rather than voice. There is coherence between elements of governance themselves. An orientation towards highly detailed and strict legal governance of relations aimed at safeguards against opportunism is difficult to reconcile with an orientation towards trust, and it is difficult to reconcile with the unpredictability of contingencies involved in innovation. If there is no basis for trust in inter-firm relations, and inputs and outputs of efforts are difficult to observe, then for innovation one will probably need to integrate activities within a firm. Finally, as already indicated in this example, there is considerable systemic coherence between institutions, organizational form and mode of coordination. Such systemic constellations can have both positive and negative effects on performance.

Because of the complexities involved, there is an incentive to search for 'generic systems' of innovation. In view of systemic coherence this may not be a hopeless undertaking. There may indeed be more or less discrete, coherent alternative systems of innovation and governance. If we start with rough and general generic, coherent systems, we may then descend into further, more detailed systems, even if the generic systems are more stereotypes than realistic models of any existing system. Apart from the argument of method, to descend from the general to the specific, there is an argument of political debate. In fact, political debates take place in terms of stereotypes, and it would help if we can reconstruct them systematically and then deduce more detailed options for more sophisticated policy.

Stylized, stereotyped comparisons have been made, for example, between the US and Germany (Gelauff and den Broeder 1996). In this distinction one recognizes similarities to the distinction that has been made between continental European economies (in the 'Rhinelands') and the 'Anglo-Saxon' economies in the US and Britain (Albert 1993). In the stereotype of Germany vs. the US, the US is said to have a preference for the first three options of governance, in Table 4.1: evasion of specific investments to maintain independence, legal control if such investments are inevitable, integration under hierarchy if legal control is problematic. Germany is said to have a preference for a combination of the third, fourth and fifth options, taking for granted that specific investments are needed, with legal control

Table 4.3   Two generic systems of innovation

	System A Contractual, multiple	System B Relational, exclusive
Characteristic	Formal, extensive contracts	Limited, implicit contracts
	Multiple short relations	Lasting, more exclusive relations
Mode of conduct	Exit	Voice
Culture/institutions	Individualistic	Groups
	Large firms	Networks of firms
	Legalistic	Group ethic
Mediating variables		
specific investments	Low	High
switching costs	Low	High
value of the partner	Low	High
room for opportunism	Low	High
inclination to opport.	High	Low
Performance outcomes		
production costs	Low	Higher
transaction costs	Higher	Lower
product differentiation	Low	High
incremental innovation	Low	High
creative destruction	High	Low

Source: Nooteboom (1999e).

if it is feasible and not counterproductive for the purpose of innovation, mutual self-interest, commitment, trust and voice.

In Table 4.3 an abstraction is made from the specific US–Germany comparison, to arrive at two 'generic systems' A and B. Such abstraction is needed, because the two systems are stereotypes: the differences between the US and Germany are not in fact so clear-cut. There are aspects of the systems that point in other directions, there is considerable variety of structure between industries in those countries, and the situation has changed. In particular, differences between industries should be kept in mind. Differences in type of product, technology, knowledge (tacit, codified), type and intensity of competition, stage of development and the like constitute important contingencies that also affect the choice of instruments for governance. Important differences between products are whether they are goods or services, are aimed at consumers or at firms, and yield a possibility for judging quality prior to purchase. Important differences between technologies concern the extent and novelty of scientific content, effects of scale, sunk costs, and observability. Differences in competition concern the differentiability of products, the presence of entry barriers and monopolies. It is even possible that differences between industries are larger than those between countries. In going to two generic systems, I allow for the possibility that they apply to different industries within one country.

In system A the focus of buyers in their relations with suppliers is on low cost, achieved by bargaining under the threat of alternative partners, which in order to be credible requires abstention from switching costs due to specific investments. Legal contracting covers remaining risks of opportunism. The mode of conduct is exit as opposed to voice. When dissatisfied, rather than deliberating (voice) one exits from the relation: switches partners, calls in a loan, sells shares or part of a company, fires people, and so on. Absence of specific investments leads to absence of switching costs, which enables exit, but also leads to low quality in the sense of undifferentiated, standard products, to the extent that technology is inflexible. Lack of product differentiation entails a lower frequency and diversity of product innovation. Legal contracting is intended to leave little room for opportunism. There is high inclination towards opportunism, confirmed by mutual suspicion expressed in extensive legal contracting aimed at safeguards against opportunism and non-exclusive non-dedicated relations.

This is a caricature of US buyer–supplier relations, and it is no longer valid, at least in the auto industry, where the US has learnt from Japanese practice. However, the description aligns well with Walker's (1993) diagnosis of the British system of innovation as being weak in capabilities of coordination.

The performance of this system can be characterized as follows: low costs due to competitive bidding for standard components and products, low quality in the sense of undifferentiated products (if technology is inflexible), high transaction costs due to low trust and extensive legal contracting. Detailed contingent contracts are less feasible in turbulent environments of radical innovation, and if feasible would yield a straitjacket that frustrates the open-endedness required for collaboration in innovation. Low trust not only increases transaction costs, but also inhibits the information exchange required for such collaboration (out of fear for spillover). This limits collaboration to partners within the own firm, which yields the need to integrate contributing activities in the firm. But as argued above, this reduces cognitive distance and thereby reduces the variety and flexibility of sources of complementary competence and cognition.

This analysis is consistent with the diagnosis of the US system, discussed above, that there is too little diffusion and adoption of technology, at least in certain industries (Mowery and Rosenberg 1993).

The merits and limitations of system B are generally opposite to those of system A, and their systematic analysis is left to the reader. Its mode of conduct is voice: when dissatisfied, one announces this and tries to repair the relation by deliberation and renegotiation. As noted before, however, there will seldom be a complete absence of contracts, even in system B, but there they serve the purpose of a record of what was agreed, to prevent misunderstanding, to support coordination and enable division of labour. Contracts may also constitute what one might call a ritual of agreement. It is not the presence of contracts that counts but their content and purpose.

Next to its advantages system B has its disadvantages. Exclusiveness or small numbers of relations per activity has its function in reducing set-up costs of relations, reducing risks of hold-up due to specific investments. It thereby encourages such investments, and limits risks of spillover. And note that in linkages between firms there is more variety as a source of innovation than within firms. However, this variety may also be limited due to the exclusiveness of relations, which limits new entry into the network, and variety within the network may erode (and cognitive distance may become too small) when the linkages last too long.

A crucial issue now is this. It is suggested that due to the absence of durable network relations between firms, system A (the US) has more flexibility of configuration, deemed necessary for the Schumpeterian 'novel combinations' of radical innovation (Gelauff and den Broeder 1996). This is consistent with the prevailing view that the US is more entrepreneurial in the Schumpeterian sense. This can be due to either easy entry for newcomers or easy break-up of large firms, or both.

But note that in system A linkages that require specific investments are internalized, and what linkages are more flexible: between firms (system B) or within firms (system A)? System A can achieve the flexibility needed for radical innovation only if firm organization is flexible: firms can easily be broken up, labour relations are short term and susceptible to high turnover. Thus the superiority in radical innovation is not as evident as it seemed at first sight. The limitations of different types of innovation systems, and ways to eliminate or reduce them will be discussed in Chapter 5, which treats the limitations of trust.

There is a policy implication for continental European countries, particularly for the Netherlands, that seems to be on the forefront of following Anglo-Saxon systems of financial and corporate control, under the rallying cry of 'shareholder value'. Before we gravitate further towards that system we should be aware that we cannot adopt one part of the system (for example shareholder value in corporate governance) without the other (easy break-up of firms and short-term labour relations).

Regional Systems of Innovation

There is a large literature in geography, in studies of regional innovation systems (RIS), on the effects of locality and agglomeration on innovation (Krugman 1991, Maskell and Malmberg 1999). This goes back to Alfred Marshall's (1920) discussion of 'industrial districts'. I will not review the entire literature here, but the main points arising from it are that agglomeration yields advantages in a local accumulation of specialized labour skills and of specialized suppliers, and spillover of knowledge. A much debated question is to what extent location and distance still matter for collaboration in learning and innovation, in view of new opportunities from ICT for 'thick' communication at a distance. Will there be a 'death of distance'? An often heard argument against the death of distance is that local interaction remains needed for the transfer of tacit knowledge, because that requires on-line, real-time interaction, combining both auditory and visual perception, with demonstration, imitation and correction of skills. This is not so certain. Perhaps in due course broadband communication channels will offer economically viable on-line, real-time interaction with multiple media, by which interaction at a distance can mimic local interaction, yielding virtual presence. We already see how a surgeon in Amsterdam operates at a distance, through a robot, in Barcelona. For teams it is perhaps still more expensive and complicated to operate as a virtual team than taking a plane and meeting up, but this may be only a matter of time.

For an assessment of this issue, we should further unpack the notion of tacit knowledge. As I argued in Chapter 1, tacit and codified knowledge are not necessarily substitutes, with the one being transformed into the other, without residue. They are also complements. When knowledge is expressed, to be communicated to someone else, it is disengaged from a substrate of more or less tacit and context-specific knowledge, partly stored in procedural memory. The receiver has to re-embed the information, interpreting it on the basis of his more or less tacit categories of understanding, based on his practical experience and local specificities. In order for people to adequately share understanding of some message, they need to share a minimum of categories and experience. This may have to be built up in interaction, in a community of practice, where they establish an epistemic community. This is related to the view, discussed in Chapter 1, of an organization as a focusing device. Once such shared categories, or mental models, have been established, the team may disband and spread to different locations and send messages from a distance while maintaining a shared understanding. From this, my prediction is that people do not have to stay in the same place on an ongoing basis, but may stay together for a while and then interact at a distance, and reconvene from time to time to update and maintain their shared underlying cognitive categories. In this way, an epistemic community can be 'temporarily footloose'.

A more fundamental consideration is the following. If meanings are context-dependent, as I think is the case, then conversation away from a local context may fail to make local sense. Thus, the importance of periodic reconventions should not be underestimated.

The emphasis in the discussion of locality and agglomeration has been on economic factors of economies of scale, specialization and positive externalities, and in more modern forms on learning by interaction. However, the relation between learning and location may lie not so much on the side of competence as on the side of governance. Marshall already recognized that 'industrial atmosphere' plays a role in locality. Here, I explore that idea further on the basis of the preceding analysis.

As indicated in Table 4.2, instruments of governance depend on institutions on the surface level, such as legal infrastructure, and on a deep structure, with basic categories of perception, understanding and evaluation, which include standards of socially acceptable behaviour. To have trust in the wide sense of reliance, one needs to have trust in institutions that enable and constrain instruments for governance, including legal infrastructure, reputation mechanisms, go-betweens, and so on. For trust in the narrow, strong sense of expecting loyalty even in the face of opportunities and incentives for opportunism, or the 'give and take' of voice or reciprocity, one needs trust in underlying norms, motives and habits of conduct. All these may be more or less bound to location. They need not always be. A reputation mechanism may work at a distance. Norms of behaviour may be shared across large distances. Norms, habits and reputations may get established in virtual communities, at a distance. The use of the Internet will force the issue to some extent. Institutions specific to that medium will develop, to certify identity of agents, and the genuineness, origin and quality of information. The fact that in the past, without present means of communication, institutions were locally embedded does not imply that they will also be locally embedded with present extended means of communication.

Note that a reputation mechanism and norms of reciprocity entail a number of criteria. What is good behaviour? In some cultures being smart may be valued as good behaviour, and this may entail some amount of hard-headedness and opportunism. Is it acceptable, in negotiations, to threaten explicitly with exit (opt out, walk out, resign), or is this 'not done' and seen as a breach of trust? In some cultures there may be much attention to personal honour or honour of a family, in terms of loyalty to insiders and/or closure to outsiders. Social reciprocity entails more or less tacit norms concerning the time span in which a return favour is expected, and its size and type relative to the original gift. Does the return gift have to be of roughly equal size or not? Should it be of a similar kind, or on the contrary of a different one, to confirm that it is not a payment for services rendered? Does every gift have to be reciprocated singly or can one accumulate and give a large gift to reciprocate a series of small gifts? These features tend to develop locally, and since they are largely tacit they may be difficult to grasp and master from outside. However, it is not inconceivable that they could become more or less public, or could be accessed from outside via local agents. Furthermore, it is conceivable that they will newly develop across large distances, in Internet communities.

However, to the extent that instruments of governance or their underlying institutions are more particularistic or micro (see Table 3.1 in Chapter 3), embedded in specific relationships, rather than universalistic and valid anonymously across a wide range of relationships, they are more local or 'sticky'. This may apply when local intermediaries act as go-betweens, in the roles specified before. It may apply when there is spillover between different kinds of activities, in other words when reliability or trustworthiness in one unobservable activity is inferred from other observable activities, or when access to observed behaviour is mediated by gossip.

This is related to the earlier analysis of trust processes, in Chapter 3. There, I indicated that if we define trust as expectation that 'things will not go wrong', then for the build-up and maintenance of trust there is the complication that things may go wrong for so many reasons. It may be due to outside disturbances, accident, lack of competence, lack of dedication or opportunism. These have different implications for proper response and for the maintenance or breakdown of trust. The problem is that one often does not know which is at play. That was a reason for one of the roles of a go-between, to offer information and to prevent misunderstandings that can lead to an unwarranted breakdown of trust. Gossip matters here, as part of a reputation mechanism. One may infer trustworthiness in one area from observed behaviour in another. Earlier, in Chapter 3, I mentioned the example of inferring someone's trustworthiness from the way he is observed to treat his wife, or a waiter. This is related to the notion of 'relational signalling' (Lindenberg 2000, Wittek 2000). The point now is that go-betweens, gossip and spillover between activities have a local tie, to the extent that it is the location that connects these activities. A question is how one can select the right go-between, and how one can judge his competence and intentions if one comes from outside.

I now connect the governance and competence (especially cognitive) sides of collaboration. For both, people may have to establish a basis in local interaction, for developing shared cognitive categories and for establishing a basis for trust, and may then separate and interact at a distance, while reconvening now and then to maintain the shared basis for cognition and trust.

Local embeddedness may be desirable; yielding locally embedded social capital for the sake of efficient governance. However, it may also be undesirable, in tying activities down in a given location while for innovation and efficiency it would be better to spread them across different locations, to utilize opportunities for lower costs, specialization, scale and learning by exploring novel combinations (Nooteboom 2000a). This trade-off between the possible positive and negative sides of social ties will be discussed in Chapter 5.

Here, I note that the issue of cognitive distance arises in relation to RIS as it does in relation to firms, as discussed in Chapter 1. Here also, when relations in a RIS stabilize, and there are no outside linkages, cognitive distance reduces and there is not enough variety of cognition left to fuel ongoing innovation.

Communities

Within and between organizations, there are different types of groups, communities or meetings, corresponding with different stages in the development of collaborative relations. Some evidence for this is emerging from research at a consultancy firm by Irma Bogenrieder (2001). One type may serve simply for transactions of unproblematic codified knowledge; to be absorbed in cognitive structures that can be taken for granted. A second type may serve to explore potentially fruitful relations. The meeting is used not to actually develop collaboration but to explore its possibilities. Here, one may give only partial information, from fear of spillover, offering just enough to signal one's potential worth. One listens to others to find out who may have something worth while to offer. The meeting is used to assess trustworthiness concerning:

- competence: do others have useful, new and sufficiently comprehensible knowledge to offer, at the right cognitive distance
- commitment: will the potential partner refrain from shirking, and make an effort in collaboration, and will he/she be careful and accurate and make the required attempt to achieve mutual understanding
- benevolence: will he/she not be opportunistic, expropriating your knowledge, using it as a hostage, or exploiting your dependence resulting from specific investments in mutual understanding.

In this account, the motivation to contribute knowledge to a pool derives from self-interest: how can one usefully and reliably learn from others, for the sake of improving one's own project or competence. Firms may take measures to reward contributions more directly, by tying financial rewards to the extent of knowledge contributed to the pool, or to the extent that others use it.

> This was practised by Arthur Andersen consultancy. At first, consultants were rewarded for the amount of information contributed to a knowledge pool. Later, the reward was tied to the extent to which their colleagues used such knowledge. This is similar to the shift in the evaluation of academic research from the counting of publications (weighted by the prestige of the journal, as measured by its impact score) to the counting of citations.

The motivation to contribute knowledge may also be that it enhances personal prestige, which may further one's career, or may be valued for its own sake. It is also possible that people contribute knowledge not on the basis of economic or social reciprocity, but out of ethical considerations (it is part of the job or one's mission or one's responsibility to yield information without something in return) or personal loyalty and support.

After such an exploratory kind of meeting, on the basis of an initial assessment of trustworthiness of competence and intentions, one selects partners for more intensive collaboration, in a team or community of practice. This entails specific investments for crossing cognitive distance, to achieve sufficient common understanding, in the development of an epistemic community. Note that in order to function as a community of practice, that community has to be an epistemic community. Once that has been established, participants may collaborate and communicate at a distance.

> I propose that something like this happens when academics go to scientific conferences. This goes beyond the mere transfer of information, which could have been done by distributing papers via e-mail. One goes to explore who has something interesting to say, in a pool of people one may not all know, and who convene because of a shared interest. Having identified interesting potential partners, one assesses their trustworthiness in terms of competence, willingness and dedication to collaborate, and benevolence in not expropriating ideas and being willing to engage in voice. With such colleagues one may next convene for more intensive seminars, where one gets down to developing shared categories, crossing cognitive distance, building an epistemic community. This may next be followed up by teams jointly making innovative novel combinations, in the form of joint papers, in a community of practice.

The economic efficiency of this process lies in the alternation of meetings and dispersion. The meetings serve the need to develop shared tacit cognitive categories and to establish trust, and the dispersion guarantees the maintenance of cognitive distance, with participants tapping into a variety of localities where they operate daily, with different environments for learning, generating different insights.

5. Failures

Earlier chapters indicated that trust may fail. It has its errors and pathologies, in both lack and excess of trust. This is further discussed in the first part of this chapter. Pathologies of trust have implications for economic systems. Those are discussed in the second part. The question for this chapter is:

Question 9: Failures of trust
How can trust go wrong? What are its possible adverse effects? What are the limitations and boundaries of trust?

5.1 ERRORS OF TRUST

First I look at errors of trust on the level of individual people and organizations. A question before I start discussing pathologies is the following: from whose perspective is it a pathology? If people make themselves vulnerable by large trust, who is to judge that this is excessive? Of course, this is up to the individual. However, without committing oneself to full-fledged economic determinism, one can reasonably speak of what is risky from the perspective of the survival of the firm, depending on the intensity of competition. Blind, unconditional trust is excessive in the sense that it entails a large risk of economic and possibly also psychological damage, and a possible threat to survival of the firm. If for reasons of conviction or mission one goes ahead anyway, that is a respectable choice. However, as we shall see, excess of trust and suspicion may be due to psychological or organizational problems, which, when recognized, may be seen as undesirable and in need of remedy.

Pathologies and Errors

As claimed before, without any reliance there can be no activity. One may try to conduct relations on the basis of power, controlling behaviour by coercion, reward or economic reciprocity, and control of other people's knowledge, competence, material inputs or external conditions that affect their actions. That, however, produces lack of trust and alienation, depending on the degree, legitimacy and appropriateness of the controls imposed. As noted by Deutsch (1973: 88): 'Without the other's trust as an asset, power is essentially limited to the coercive and ecological (i.e. conditional) types, the types that require and consume most in the way of physical and economic resources'.

This is a way of repeating the claim, discussed in Chapter 4, that mistrust is uneconomic. However, the argument goes beyond that. The exercise of power itself requires reliance on its efficacy. Therefore, trust in the wide sense of 'reliance' is indispensable even for the use of power. Trust in the narrow, strong sense, defined in Chapter 2, is not easily reconciled with coercion. As discussed in Chapter 3, the trust process requires a surrender of a certain amount of control to the partner, and acceptance of a certain amount of control by him/her. If one has unlimited power, the most straightforward explanation of observed loyal behaviour is that it arises from self-interest: from coercion, survival, or gain. There is no scope for trust in the strong sense of believing that people will not be opportunistic even if they have the opportunity and incentive. The reason is that when they are subject to unlimited power such opportunity and incentive do not arise, so that there is never convincing evidence of such trustworthiness. Thus unlimited power builds or reconfirms suspicion, whereby it tends to become self-reinforcing and pathological. Earlier, I mentioned the example of Stalin.

Williamson (1993) was evidently correct when he noted that blind, in the sense of unconditional, trust is unwise and not likely to survive in markets. He was wrong in claiming that to be 'real' trust (that is trust in the strong sense discussed here), trust is necessarily blind and unconditional. In Chapters 2 and 3 I argued that this is not necessarily the case. Trustworthiness may be non-calculative and altruistic and yet not blind or unconditional, in two ways. One way is that it is based on tacit, routinized behaviour, sunk into subsidiary awareness, with exceptional events triggering a shift into focal awareness, for rational evaluation, in an assessment of causes and motives of other people's actions and the risks involved. A second way is that trust is always subject to some explicit or tacit limit of someone's perceived or inferred trustworthiness. This implies that one assesses the pressures of survival to which a partner is submitted, his ability to resist them, and the temptation of golden opportunities. Here, as well as in routinized behaviour, trust has a limit, beyond which awareness is triggered and mistrust may set in.

Trust is pathological in the sense of being blind or unconditional when it does not recognize such constraints. This may be so for a variety of reasons. Deutsch (1973) recognized several sources of excessive trust. One is naivety, ignorance, or cognitive immaturity: one sets no limits due to lack of awareness of risks. Here, experience of broken trust will teach awareness. Another reason is a feeling of omnipotence: overestimation of one's own power to control untrustworthy partners, with the feeling that one cannot be hurt by damage imposed by them. Another source is impulsiveness or nonchalance, which derives from the condition that one is careless or puts a large emphasis on the present benefits relative to later adverse effects. This is related to greed as a cause of disregarding relational risk. Other causes are despair (one has no alternative), masochism and an excessive drive towards social conformity, or an unconditional drive to virtue, 'turning the other cheek' when deceived, or becoming a martyr for some higher cause.

Deutsch (1973: 171) proposed that:

> [it is] to be expected that, wherever there is a pathology of trust or suspicion with regard to others, there is an accompanying pathology with regard to oneself. Pathological overtrust of others (gullibility) is usually accompanied by pathological undertrust of oneself and vice versa . . . the gullible person protects his image of his protector in order to feel protected . . . experiences non-fulfilment of trust as a confirmation of his helplessness and worthlessness . . . becomes depressed and self-pitying rather than angry . . . more compliant rather than less.

Perhaps we can be more precise in the analysis. What do we mean by excess of trust? About what form or object of trust are we talking here? Are we talking of trust in the broad sense of reliance, or in the strong sense? Is trust excessive when it goes beyond the available evidence of trustworthiness? My answer is negative, in view of the earlier argument that one can never be completely certain about future behaviour, because there is always radical uncertainty, so that trust always entails an unknown amount of risk, and can only serve as a default. In other words, trust always goes beyond the available evidence. When the evidence of trustworthiness is limited, for a given partner, and there is no reputation as a basis for trust, the default one takes is based on previous experience with other people. If on that basis trust is limited, one will start a relationship with low stakes, and raise them as evidence of trustworthiness accrues. How one infers trustworthiness from observed action was discussed in Chapter 3. Now we can identify one form of excessive trust as setting high stakes in the face of limited evidence of trustworthiness. As indicated, such excess is likely to be adapted on the basis of negative experience. A more extreme excess of trust would be to ignore evidence that would falsify previous assumptions of trustworthiness. As Deutsch (1973: 170) said:

The essential feature of nonpathological trust is that it is flexible and responsive to changing circumstances. Pathological trust or suspicion, on the other hand, is characterized by an inflexible, rigid, unaltering tendency to act in a trusting or suspicious manner irrespective of the situation or of the consequences of so acting. The pathology is reflected in the indiscriminacy and incorrigibility of the behaviour tendency.

Note that, as indicated in Chapter 3, adverse events that might be interpreted as evidence of lack of trustworthiness may be interpreted differently. It is part of trust, and the attitude of voice, not to jump to conclusions, and to grant benefit of the doubt. If benefit of the doubt and attempts to jointly sort out and, if possible, solve problems are successful they will deepen trust.

Deutsch's thesis that excess of trust can be due to lack of trust in the self can now be understood as follows. If one has no trust in one's competence to deal with the world, one may seek others to act as protectors. Why should one then ignore evidence that the protector is not trustworthy, as Deutsch claims that people would? This is evident when one has no other protectors to fall back on. Then one is gullible by despair: since one has no other option, one has to rely on this protector, and to avoid cognitive dissonance one may convince oneself that the evidence is not there or not valid. Also, by showing trusting behaviour one may ingratiate oneself to the person one is dependent on, and thereby placate him/her. By assumption, this trust is not justified. Things go wrong but one cannot afford to attribute this to wrongful action by the protector. Therefore it must be one's own fault. Therefore, what should be evidence of lack of the other's trustworthiness is transformed into evidence of one's own lack of trustworthiness. As a result: 'He becomes depressed and self-pitying rather than angry, contemptuous of himself rather than of the other, more compliant rather than less.' (Deutsch 1973: 174).

Could Deutsch also mean that the lack of self-trust refers to trust in the intentional sense: one suspects oneself of opportunism? This includes the possibility that one suspects one's own weakness of the will: one cannot resist opportunities to gain advantage at the expense of others. Would this yield excess trust in a protector? If one knows one is opportunistic oneself, would this not yield the expectation of opportunism from others? Or is the argument that one expects punishment for one's own inclinations towards opportunism, and therefore sees opportunistic actions by others not as opportunistic but as justified?

We also saw that lack of self-trust may yield excessive mistrust of someone else. This derives from the analysis of instruments of governance in Chapter 4. It runs as follows. Lack of self-trust leads one to underestimate the value and uniqueness of one's offering to the partner. Thereby one underestimates his/her dependence, and as a result overestimates one's own relative dependence. Thereby one perceives unilateral power dependence, which causes feelings of being threatened and as a result makes one overly sensitive to possibly suspicious behaviour of the partner. As discussed in Chapter 3, Klein Woolthuis (1999) found evidence for this in her empirical work.

Next to the rather psychoanalytical approach of Deutsch, relating to blatant pathologies of trust, there is more recent literature in social psychology that indicates many other, greater or lesser errors in interpretation of events and judgement of behaviour, which have implications for trust.[1]

Excess trust, in the sense of blindness or neglect of another's opportunism can have other causes than those indicated by Deutsch. People may incorrectly assign blame to themselves for several other reasons than lack of self-confidence or overconfidence. One is empathy: they can identify with the interests, needs and temptations of partners and thereby expand their tolerance level of trust. Another is to attain a sense of security from the idea that if one assigns blame to oneself one has more control over it. Yet another is belief in a just world: since one perceives the world as just, and this is a reassuring thought, when one encounters loss it must be one's own fault.

Errors can result from the decision heuristics discussed in Chapter 3, as described by Bazerman (1998). The availability heuristic entails a bias towards familiar experiences. Thus experience with trustworthiness may be blown up into an excess of trust. According to the anchoring and adjustment heuristic, early experiences in a relation may set the anchor, from which one adjusts too slowly. One may anchor on the status quo instead of substantial potential shifts of value. When events co-occur we tend to prematurely assign causality. Thus we may attribute trustworthiness (or the lack of it) on the basis of spurious characteristics, which we happened to observe in conjunction with the experience of (dis)trust, in the representativeness heuristic. We make errors by neglecting the sample size of experience: overestimating the probability of incidental occurrences, and underestimating those of frequent ones. We may succumb to the gambler's fallacy of being able to influence the chance of random phenomena. We may overestimate the correlation between subsequent phenomena and thereby neglect 'regression to the mean' of occurrences that are in fact independent. Trustworthiness is subject to many influences, and may not be constant. Tall people may beget small children. We may fall into the 'confirmation trap' of only selecting evidence that confirms our existing views.

---

[1] I owe a number of these insights to Gabriele Jacobs. Of course, any errors of interpretation are mine.

We may falsely attribute opportunism, or lack of it, on the basis of the 'hindsight of knowledge': we interpret actions in the light of knowledge that the partner could not have had at the time of his action. In competitive bidding for good partners we may experience the 'winners curse': paying more than is justified, in view of uncertainty concerning true value. In conflicts one may suffer from self-serving biases in judging one's own behaviour and too negative assessments of the behaviour of others.

As discussed in Chapter 3, relations may last too long due to the endowment effect, framing effects (loss versus gain frame), or a non-rational escalation of commitment by not cutting one's sunk costs. Now I add: the tendency to note only confirmatory evidence. However, their duration may be justified in view of growing empathy, mutual understanding and alignment of objectives. One may destroy fruitful relationships by defection as a result of inability to resist short-term temptations for the sake of long-term benefits.

I cannot presume to give a complete analysis here. I hope only to show that the social psychology of trust is important, and deserves much further attention.

Organizations

When we turn to organizations, one question is how an organization may affect trust relations between individual people, and how such relations can affect the organization. As discussed in Chapter 3, in organizations people have a range of options for including other people within the organization to deal with trust and its violation. One can retaliate or voice complaints directly to the antagonist, one can do this privately or in public, one can involve colleagues in gossip or coalitions, or one can go to one's boss and complain or demand action (Wittek 1999, Six 2001).

Above, I noted how pathologies of (mis)trust can arise from excess or shortage of self-confidence. In organizations such self-perception is subject to correction, but also to deepening, from interaction between people in the organization. Whether it is corrected or deepened depends on organizational culture and on the degree and kind of attention that management pays to it. In Chapter 3 I discussed how organizational culture affects these conditions.

From interpersonal interaction, pathologies can arise on the level of the organization. An atmosphere of gossip or intrigue with pathological mistrust can sway organizations. Conversely, a culture of trust and benevolence may become excessive and oppressive, turning the expression of criticism into a taboo. This obstructs creative conflict. It can yield suffocating, blinded 'group think'. As formulated by Bazerman (1998: 151):

Group think yields increasing cohesiveness, yielding shared illusions of invulnerability, collective rationalization, belief in the inherent morality of the group, stereotypes of out-groups, direct pressure on dissenters, individual self-censorship, illusion of unanimity, self-appointed mind guards. [All this can yield] incomplete surveys of alternatives and objectives, poor information search, selective bias in processing information, failures to examine risks of preferred choice, failure to work out contingency plans.

It can also block direct voice of complaints, thereby preventing fast and reliable direct solutions between partners in the conflict. Substantive disagreements that could have easily been resolved in voice may then become personalized and thereby much more difficult to resolve (Six 2001). This can lead to an accumulation of unresolved conflict, biasing perception towards evidence of incompetence or malevolence. It can lead to malicious gossip that perpetuates and deepens wrongful attributions and misunderstandings, and turns misperceptions into realities. Once established as part of organizational culture, an atmosphere of trust or mistrust can perpetuate itself in a process of socialization to which newcomers are subjected.

Before, I proposed that trustworthiness has limits, depending on pressures of survival and golden opportunities. This is affected by the competitive position of a firm, and by internal conditions concerning incentives, promotion and job security. To the extent that individual staff compete for promotion or jobs, interpersonal trust will in general be more difficult to build and maintain. Mistrust will then be enhanced when the firm is in trouble and jobs are at stake.

A further and perhaps more systematic analysis can perhaps be made on the basis of the cycle of trust building proposed by Zand (1972), as discussed in Chapter 3. There, trust building is based on the conveyance of appropriate information, mutuality of influence, encouragement of self-control, and avoidance of the abuse of the vulnerability of others. Each of these elements of the process can be enabled or frustrated by organizational structure, process or culture. One may not be allowed by one's organizational role to grant mutual influence or another's self-control, even if one would like to do so 'qua persona' (Smith Ring and van der Ven 1992, 1994). The conveyance of 'appropriate information' may be blocked by organizational procedures, instituted perhaps to control spillover of sensitive information. Allowance of mutuality and self-control may be against organizational culture. It may be interpreted as a sign of weakness that one cannot afford.

Let us move to trust on the organizational level: how an organization trusts another, and how it is trusted by it. As in individual trust, excesses of (mis)trust can arise for a number of reasons. As in the case of trust in people, the sources may be naivety, ignorance, or cognitive immaturity.

Firms may be too young and inexperienced to deal with trust properly. Here also there may be feelings of omnipotence, impulsiveness, nonchalance, or greed, with an overemphasis of the present relative to later adverse effects, and despair. Less likely on the firm level are masochism and an excessive drive towards social conformity, or an unconditional drive to virtue, 'turning the other cheek' when deceived, or becoming a martyr for some higher cause. Such pathologies may occur, however, when the firm is dominated by a strong, single leader, as can happen especially in smaller firms.

Here also, excessive trust may be based on excess of self-trust. Overconfidence may yield an underestimation of the power of others to cause harm. Lack of self-confidence may lead one to underestimate one's value to others, and thereby to overestimate one's risk of dependence, yielding an excessive tendency towards mistrust. The logic of Deutsch's argument that lack of self-confidence can also yield excessive trust also seems to apply, at least in part. Organizations also may be dependent on others to such an extent that one has no option of exit, and can only hope that the others will be benevolent, and try to obtain such benevolence by ingratiation or by blackmailing them with one's dependence. In a market economy, why should such others let themselves be blackmailed? One possibility might be that they are blackmailed by the loss of employment that harsh action would yield.

Considerable complications arise from the connections between trust in organizations and trust in the people working there, discussed in Chapter 3. One may have trust in an organization that is not supported by trustworthiness of employees and, conversely, trust in people that is not supported by their organization. Failures of trust by and in organizations doubtless form an important area for further research (see Six 2001).

5.2   INNOVATION SYSTEMS

Now I turn to the level of economic systems, and to the question how trust may have adverse effects there. First I turn to a recently emerging discussion of social capital and liability. Next, I extend the discussion of innovation systems that was started in Chapter 4.

Social Capital and Liability

Trust is generally seen as part of 'social capital'. Leenders and Gabbay (1999: 3) gave a useful definition of organizational social capital, as follows: 'The set of resources, tangible or virtual, that accrue to an organization through social structure, facilitating the attainment of goals.' Social capital entails access to resources in the general sense: markets, materials, components, finance, location, information, technology, capability, legitimization, credibility, reputation, and trust. Brass and Labianca (1999: 324) recall that Coleman (1988) proposed three forms of social capital: information from others, obligations and expectations, norms and sanctions. This is very congenial to the approach taken in this book, where I combine issues of competence, such as of knowledge and learning, with issues of governance. Trust is important for both of them, in its forms of both competence and intentional trust. Gargiulo and Benassi (1999: 299) summarize social capital as follows: 'networks facilitate access to information, resources and opportunities' and they 'help actors to co-ordinate critical task interdependencies and to overcome the dilemmas of collective action'. By the resolution of 'dilemmas of collective action', obligations, expectations, norms and sanctions reduce transaction costs and thereby favour exchange, collaboration and the utilization of complementary competencies. They may also enhance the intrinsic value of exchange, by making exchange less uncertain and threatening and therefore more agreeable. All this is just another way of saying what I said in Chapter 4, but now in terms of social capital.

While useful, the definition proposed by Leenders and Gabbay is incomplete. Social structure produces social capital or liability, but causality also runs in the other direction: social capital forms the basis for social structure. In fact, in a final chapter to the book they edited, Leenders and Gabbay (1999: 489–91) do recognize mutual causation between social capital and structure and between actors and social structure, which they called the 'problem of time and causality'. Social capital includes 'positional advantage' (Stoelhorst 1997) and this entails both the creation and utilization of networks. This is most obvious for obligations, expectations, norms and sanctions: they are based on networks and form the basis for networks. Trust is part of the basis for relations and is produced by relations. But reverse causality also applies to information and competence: they form one's attractiveness to others that motivates network relations.

The point here is this. While in the past attention in the literature was mostly focused on the positive aspects of social structure, more recently attention has also been given to the negative sides: the production not of social capital but of social liability (Leenders and Gabbay 1999, Gargiulo and Benassi 1999, Brass and Labianca 1999, Pennings and Lee 1999). Awareness is also growing that network conditions that are favourable under some conditions may be unfavourable under others, and vice versa. Then the question is not only how to develop networks but also how to change and to end them, and what the relevant contingencies are. Earlier analysis showed that there are several psychological mechanisms that may lead to relations that are too durable, as a result of an irrational escalation of commitment.

Obligations, derived from legal ties or ties of reciprocity, can create a basis for fruitful collaboration. They can also create an obstacle to change in general and to change of network configurations in particular. They yield stability, but the downside of that may be lack of flexibility. One may get stuck to partners that are falling behind. This is a liability especially for the goal of learning and innovation.

Also, to the extent that relations are durable, tight and exclusive, they can yield cognitive inbreeding: a convergence of cognition that eliminates the novelty and variety that are needed for innovation. Too much consensus can lead to groupthink that blocks the creativity offered by different views, and produces inertia. Network partners are particularly valuable to each other when they have different absorptive capacity (Cohen and Levinthal 1990), based on different experience in different markets and branches of technology. Then the building of mutual understanding in network relations is needed to use sources of knowledge that one could not utilize otherwise. To maintain such value of complementary absorptive capacity one needs to maintain differences in activities, markets and corporate culture. In terms of my earlier analysis, one needs to achieve and maintain optimal cognitive distance: sufficient proximity in understanding to communicate, but sufficient distance to generate the surprise of novelty.

This yields an argument in favour of alliances between more or less autonomous partners, with separate sources of experience and knowledge, rather than mergers/acquisitions, which entail a greater degree of integration of practice and understanding, within a single firm. This is not to say that alliances are always preferable. There are other considerations, and sometimes mergers/acquisitions are preferable. For a further discussion see Nooteboom (1999a). Within firms, there may be degrees of integration, allowing for considerable decentralization and autonomy of divisions, in the 'virtual firm'. On the other hand, networks between firms may also be more or less integrated, in 'industrial districts'. The cognitive liability of networks may now be formulated as follows: to the extent that networks are tight (more integrated), exclusive and durable, they may reduce learning potential.

Lack of learning and the lack of flexibility in network configuration are particularly serious under conditions of radical change that require frequent break-up of relations to cope with Schumpeterian novel combinations and creative destruction. This indicates one of several contingencies: for incremental innovation tight networks may have a net positive effect, while for radical innovation they may constitute a liability.

Networks that are exclusionary, harbouring little competition and

barring entry to potential competitors, will reduce the urge towards efficiency and innovation. This constitutes a liability when the network has to
compete with others in order to survive, or when there is a threat of government action to break the network up. This constitutes another contingency.
From this perspective the Japanese keiretsu are interesting: they yield
coherence for close collaborative ties within the network while there are
mutually competing keiretsu to ensure the stimulus of competition.

For high added value in relations one must exchange information even if
it is sensitive, in the sense of being close to core competence and competitive advantage. One needs to give information on one's capabilities to yield
value to the partner, and to help the partner to help oneself. The issue goes
beyond the mere exchange of information: it entails the pooled interdependence (Thompson 1967) of joint production of new knowledge and competence. Such interdependence arises, in particular, when complementary
knowledge and the new knowledge to be produced are largely tacit, requiring close interaction for the sake of understanding and for the matching of
knowledge. In these processes of information exchange and joint production of knowledge there is a risk of spillover. This is the risk that the partner
uses the knowledge he received to become a competitor, or that through
network linkages the knowledge leaks to existing competitors. The net
effect may be a decrease of knowledge or competence. In Chapter 4 I
argued that the spillover problem is often exaggerated. It is a real problem
only if it concerns knowledge that belongs to core competence, that can be
absorbed and effectively implemented by competitors before it is replaced
by new knowledge.

The possible disadvantages of networks came up in Chapter 4, in the discussion of regional innovation systems. There may be arguments why the
building of shared, tacit categories of cognition, in an epistemic community, and the building of trust require local interaction. However, this
entails a danger of entry barriers, exclusion of outsiders, and lack of
outside linkages, which limits the cognitive variety and distance needed for
ongoing innovation. There may be a solution, in an alternation between
local interaction, to establish shared cognition and trust, and dispersion, to
maintain cognitive distance and variety.

Innovation Systems: a Third Way?[2]

In Chapter 4 I compared different generic innovation systems 'A and B',
derived as stereotypes of Germany and the US. Table 5.1 repeats Table 4.3,
in which the differences are summarized. In Chapter 4 I noted that both

---

[2] This section and the following one is based on Nooteboom (2000b).

Table 5.1   Two generic systems of innovation

	System A Contractual, multiple	System B Relational, exclusive
Characteristic	Formal, extensive contracts	Limited, implicit contracts
	Multiple short relations	Lasting, more exclusive relations
Mode of conduct	Exit	Voice
Culture/institutions	Individualistic	Groups
	Large firms	Networks of firms
	Legalistic	Group ethic
Mediating variables		
specific investments	Low	High
switching costs	Low	High
value of the partner	Low	High
room for opportunism	Low	High
inclination to opport.	High	Low
Performance outcomes		
production costs	Low	Higher
transaction costs	Higher	Lower
product differentiation	Low	High
incremental innovation	Low	High
creative destruction	High	Low

Source: Nooteboom (1999d).

systems have their limitations and drawbacks. The limitations of system A (an ideal type derived from the US) are that in its orientation to the exit mode of relations transaction costs are higher, and economic relations (within and between forms) may be too short to allow for specific investments needed for innovation. Also, there is a larger degree of integration, by merger and acquisition, combined with a higher frequency of disintegration, which may preclude high levels of added value, in speciality products, and may provide an obstacle for incremental innovation and the diffusion of innovations.

On the other hand, the greater volatility of relations makes for greater flexibility and perhaps a greater potential for radical, Schumpeterian innovation by novel combinations. The disadvantage of system B (an ideal type derived from Germany) may be that the more or less durable networks between firms that it entails hinder radical innovation. I noted that:

Exclusiveness or small numbers of relations per activity has its function in reducing set-up costs of relations, reducing risks of hold-up due to specific investments. It thereby encourages such investments, and limits risks of spillover. And note that there is more variety as a source of innovation in linkages between firms than there is within firms. But this variety may also be limited due to the exclusiveness of relations, which limits new entry into the network, and variety within the network may erode (and cognitive distance may become too small) when the linkages last too long.

Here, I look at these differences between the two systems more closely, and see whether some 'third way' may be conceivable, which combines the advantages of both systems while avoiding their drawbacks.

Linkages between firms should be evaluated in comparison with all relevant alternatives. Not only the alternative of autonomous, unconnected firms, but also the alternative of integration by mergers and acquisition. Measures against inter-firm linkages may well result in further concentration and conglomeration, and from the perspective of both static and dynamic efficiency that may be worse than networks. This connects with an ongoing debate on the benefits of mergers and acquisitions. Policy tends to grant more room for them than for inter-firm linkages, but is that wise? Bleeke and Ernst (1991) showed that for firms with the same products in the same markets mergers and acquisitions yield the most success (from the perspective of the firms), and in other (vertical or lateral) linkages alliances do. Hagedoorn and Schakenraad (1994) found that 75 per cent of unrelated mergers and acquisitions failed.

The weight of this criticism of mergers and acquisitions increases when the resulting integrated firms cannot easily be broken up. There is not only a trade-off between, on the one hand, high quality plus efficient diffusion and incremental innovation (system B) and, on the other hand, radical innovation (system A). We should also be aware that easy break-up of firms needed for radical innovation in system A may have detrimental effects on the commitment of labour to firm-specific training and teamwork which may also be needed for radical innovation. The net effect on radical innovation is not obvious.

There is a further nuance to be taken into account. When the complementary knowledge from different sources needed for the novel combinations of radical innovation is explicit and thereby easily portable, then system A can yield the basis for radical innovation by novel combinations. If, on the other hand, complementary knowledge is tacit and embedded in people, teams, organizational structure or culture, it can be acquired only with close and durable relations, with specific investments in mutual understanding and close cooperation, and system B has the advantage. Now knowledge tends to be more tacit in the early stages of the cycle of discovery, so that system

B has an advantage in that stage, that is in the early stages of the emergence of radical innovation.

Finally, we need to return to the contingency of the flexibility of technology. When technology is flexible there is less need for specific investments in order to achieve differentiated products, and then system A has an advantage. This is important, because ICT has the effect of enabling flexible production of both services and goods, in particular flexible manufacturing systems, including computer-aided design and computer simulation for virtual instead of physical testing of prototypes. This yields the prediction that system A will be superior when this condition applies.

Summing up, on the crucial issue of comparative advantage in radical innovation the conclusion is as follows. System A has the advantage when even in early stages complementary knowledge is explicit and documented, production technology is flexible, required durability of employment, firm-specificity of knowledge and the need for building team work are low. System B has the advantage to the extent that the reverse applies: production technology is inflexible, knowledge is more difficult to codify, and is more firm- or relation-specific, so that durability of relations between and within firms is needed.

Clearly, we cannot freely engineer the more basic institutions, especially not the categories of thought that guide perception, interpretation and evaluation, such as conditions of trust and attitudes towards collaboration or rivalry, consensus or individualism, and exit or voice. Thus solutions need to be found that are consistent with the institutional environment that is given. While such deep structure of culture cannot easily be built, it can erode, and then becomes very difficult to rebuild, and therefore careful scrutiny of the merits of existing institutions is wise. Within institutional constraints, rather than trying to be like either of the two generic systems A or B, perhaps one should look for a 'third way' that is efficient in both the static and the dynamic sense, fits the national institutional set-up, and is systemically coherent and consistent. Could the advantages of both systems be achieved without the disadvantages? One way to look at this is to ask whether in system B more room can be made for less exclusive, multiple relations and sufficient flexibility of relations, while maintaining the depth and sufficient duration of relations. The latter are preserved to enable and protect specific investments for differentiated products, intensive cooperation and exchange of knowledge, with limited, implicit contracts and the building of trust.

As noted earlier (Chapter 4) the problem of spillover disappears in a world of radical speed of change in complex technologies and markets. If knowledge or competence is obsolete by the time that it reaches a competitor and can be embodied in products and brought to market by him, then the problem of spillover drops out. Then there no longer is any limit to the

Table 5.2   Third way

	System C Relational, multiple
Characteristic	Implicit, limited contracts Open, multiple relations
Mode of conduct	Voice
Culture/institutions	Networks Group ethic The 'go-between'
Intervening variables	
specific investments	High
switching costs	Middle
value partner	High
room for opportunism	High
inclination to opportunism	Low
Outcomes	
production costs	Low
transaction costs	Low
product differentiation	High
Incremental innovation	High
Creative destruction	High

Source: Nooteboom (1999e).

number of partners in cooperation. That offers more *possibilities* for multiple relations. And in such a world there is also a greater *need* of multiple relations: competition more and more becomes a race to the market with new products. To have any chance at winning the race one must limit oneself to core competencies, which implies cooperation with others. In that situation one needs more variety of sources for cooperation, rather than a few exclusive ones.

The 'third way' adopts from the relational system B its in-depth cooperation, with specific investments, differentiated products and intensive exchange of knowledge. However, it combines this with the greater flexibility and multiplicity of relations from the other system A. In short: whereas system A was characterized by 'contractual and multiple' relations, and system B by 'relational and exclusive', the third way would be characterized by 'relational and multiple' relations. Since the result remains close to system B it should perhaps be seen as a modification of that system rather than a radically different one. The goal then is as indicated in Table 5.2.

How is that goal realized? Multiplicity of relations entails multiplication of set-up costs of relations and of the costs of specific investments. The first problem may be mitigated by declining costs of contact between firms, due to the further development of ICT. That may be expected to further decrease the costs of setting up and entertaining a network linkage. The second problem becomes less if flexible technology is also a salient part of the new world, because, as discussed, products can then be differentiated without specific assets.

Suppose, however, that technology is not that flexible. In principle, in view of specific investments a relation need not last longer than needed to recoup those investments. As the theory of repeated games tells us, a danger may arise when one establishes beforehand when a relation is to be ended. It is precisely in the uncertainty about the end, and the possibility of an ongoing relation, that it may be in one's self-interest to refrain from opportunism. Yet these two principles can be reconciled. One can make firm agreements for a duration that does not exceed the time needed to recoup the investment, and yet keep the option open for renewed continuation if the relation fits the new conditions and yields attractive prospects. That gives more flexibility than now, in system B, for the re-configuration of relations when the gales of creative destruction gather. This is indicated in Table 5.2 by taking switching costs as of 'middle' height.

There still is the issue of the sources of trust. To the extent that initial trust is already in place, on the basis of well-developed and shared norms of conduct, as part of the institutional environment, there is no problem, except perhaps that it must then be protected against the invasion of opportunists. If trust is to be built up in each relation, in specific institutional arrangements, then the time needed to do that, and to recoup the specific investment that it constitutes, can pose a problem. The minimal duration of a relation then is determined by the longest of the following two: the time needed for recouping specific investments and the time needed for the building of trust and recouping the investment that it represents. If the latter is decisive, then a possible solution is that the source of trust is not sought within a given relation, but in a larger group of potential partners that can enter upon varying relations among each other. And that, it seems, is exactly the function of the Japanese enterprise groups (keiretsu). The advantage of such groups is that on the one hand there are trust and durable relations within the group, and on the other hand competition between the groups is maintained. This by itself does not imply that the Japanese system is ideal. The possibly excessive duration of relations and the relative exclusiveness of especially vertical buyer–supplier relations yield an obstacle to innovation, since they curtail the variety of contacts that is a source of innovation (Nooteboom 1998).

Along these lines, policy should seek to establish a reconciliation between cooperation (durable linkages) and competition in the sense of multiplicity of relations, a greater ease of entry and exit in networks. For this relations should be sufficiently durable but no more than needed to recover the specific investments needed for high quality of products and collaboration in innovation. A possible element of the 'third way' might be the use of a third party as a go-between, to mediate between would-be partners, as an engine of voice.

6. Figures

This chapter presents and discusses attempts to measure and model trust and to test theory about its conditions and effects. I focus on inter-firm relations. There has been much empirical research on those, and I will not attempt to give a survey. I focus on some methods and outcomes of own research. The question is:

Question 10: Testing and modelling trust
Can trust be empirically measured and tested? Can it be formalized and subjected to logical or mathematical analysis?

The first paragraph discusses empirical work, and the second paragraph discusses an attempt to model the build-up and breakdown of trust on the basis of an agent-based computational model. This chapter is more technical than the previous ones, and can be skipped by readers interested only in the conceptual and theoretical part of this book.

6.1 EMPIRICAL TESTS

The general question is how we can test the role of trust as one among different variables in the governance of relations. As in Chapter 4, I use the scheme for governance summarized in Table 4.1. The more specific question is what, if any, effect trust has on such relations, next to variables such as switching costs due to specific investments, and instruments such as contracts and incentives. I summarize three empirical studies of buyer–supplier relations, by Berger et al. (1995), Nooteboom et al. (1997) and De Jong and Nooteboom (2000).

An often heard complaint against transaction cost theory, or more generally the theory of governance of inter-firm relations, is that it is difficult to operationalize and test in empirical research. Variables such as asset specificity, transaction costs, innovation and trust are difficult or perhaps impossible to measure, or so the complaint goes. But there are methods to treat such variables as 'latent' ones, which can be seen as being 'spanned' or 'indicated' by 'indicators' that can be measured, often as judgement by people, on a five- or seven-point Likert scale. The methodology is based on factor analysis and is derived from psychographics. The indicators can then be combined into a joint variable, as an indirect measurement of the underlying latent variable.

In Chapter 1, I pleaded for an interpretative or hermeneutic approach, where we take into account that the effect of events or conditions on behaviour is not direct, but is mediated by the perceptions, interpretations and value judgements of people. Thus, the relevant variable often is what agents perceive and how they evaluate that. Therefore, many indicators of variables reflect perceptions or opinions.

In the empirical studies described below, most indicators were five-point Likert scales. They were chosen on the basis of their hypothesized relation to latent variables that resulted from the theoretical analysis. Confirmatory factor analysis was used to test the measurement hypotheses. Cronbach's alpha was used to determine overall construct reliability, with the cut-off point at the usual value of 0.7. Factor loadings were used to determine whether each item contributed significantly to the joint factor, with the cut-off point at the usual value of 0.3. When an item had a lower loading, it was dropped, and the analysis was repeated for the remaining items until a scale with reliable loadings emerged. The items were then added to yield a measure of the latent variable.

The dependent variable, or variable to be explained, was perceived dependence, or the perceived risks involved in such dependence. The explanatory variables were trust and other variables of governance such as specific investments as the cause of dependence, and contracts or incentives as alternative measures to control risk, next to trust.

A Study in the Photocopier Industry

In the first study, Berger et al. (1995) tested part of the causality of governance on the basis of a postal survey among 80 suppliers to Océ van der Grinten, a Dutch producer of copying machines (annual sales about 1.5 billion dollars, about 12 thousand employees). The response was 84 per cent.

The focus of the research was on the hypothesized effect of a number of variables on the perceived dependence of suppliers on the buyer. That perceived dependence was measured in two ways: the perceived one-sided dependence of the supplier on the buyer ('gross dependence'), and the degree to which the supplier perceived himself to be more dependent on the buyer than vice versa ('net dependence'). Among the explanatory variables, there were two trust variables: trust in the competence of the buyer and trust in his 'goodwill', which is synonymous to 'benevolence'.

*Table 6.1   Tests of effects on dependence perceived by suppliers,
photocopier industry*

	Net perceived dependence	Gross perceived dependence
Dependence buyer		–
Length of supply	–	
Trust in buyer's loyalty	–	– **
Competence trust in buyer		–
Specificity of assets	+ ***	+ ***
Extensiveness contract	–	–
Knowledge exchange	–	– **
Sales size supplier	– **	–
Supply to buyer as percent total sales	+	+ ***
Indirect supply	+ **	+ *
Bundling of supply	–	–

Notes:
   * indicates a significance >90%.
  ** indicates a significance >95%.
*** indicates a significance >99%.

Source: Berger et al. (1995).

The data allowed testing of the effects indicated in Table 6.1. The table
also shows whether the predicted effect on perceived dependence was positive or negative, and in how far the effect was statistically significant. The
measurement of the variables and the results are discussed below.

The variable 'specificity assets' is measured as the sum of different types
of specificity, entirely in line with transaction cost economics: location
specificity (measured by one indicator), physical asset specificity (two indicators), dedicated capacity (four indicators) and knowledge specificity (two
indicators). 'Extensiveness of contract' is measured as a sum of indicators
regarding conditions of supply, technical specifications and security stocks.
Trust in loyalty (lack of opportunism) is construed on the basis of six indicators. The remaining variables are more easily measured, and are all based
on a single indicator (direct measurement). When the theoretical effect,
hypothesized on the basis of the analyses of preceding chapters, is indeed
found this is indicated with one asterisk (*) when the statistical reliability
was more than 90 per cent, two asterisks if it was more than 95 per cent,
and three asterisks if it was more than 99 per cent.

The disconfirmation of hypotheses can be as interesting as confirmation,
or even more. It is interesting to find that the extensiveness of contracts had

no significant effect on perceived dependence, and this confirms earlier studies (Macaulay 1963). It confirms the suspicion that extensive contracts, in formal, legal governance can have only limited value: a closed contract is impossible anyway, it can limit the flexibility of operations and can even have a negative effect, in confirming and stimulating mutual suspicion. Of course this does not imply that there should be no contracts at all, but only that they should not always be extensive and aimed at controlling opportunism.

The strongest result is the positive effect of the transaction-specificity of assets, which confirms a central thesis of TCE. Of central importance here is the effect of trust in the partner's loyalty. It does have the expected negative effect on gross perceived dependence, but not on net dependence. This could make sense: net dependence would depend on the balance of loyalty. If the partner's loyalty is reciprocated by own benevolence, then the effect on net dependence (degree to which supplier is more dependent on buyer than vice versa) is not to be expected: the partner's dependence is reduced to the same extent as one's own. The expected effects of the share of supply in total sales (positive) and of total sales as a measure of the effect of the size of the supplier (negative) were also confirmed. The confirmation of the negative effect of information transfer from the buyer to the supplier is interesting. One theory behind this was that thereby the buyer makes himself more vulnerable, by weakening his bargaining position and by the risk of spillover to competitors (information as hostage), which reassures the supplier with respect to his own perceived dependence. An alternative interpretation goes back to the importance of openness to the building of trust, as proposed by Zand (1972), and discussed in Chapter 3. By offering information one surrenders control and thereby signals that one is trusting and is also to be trusted. Interesting also is the confirmation that supply to other suppliers of the same buyer ('indirect supply') increases supplier dependence. But the expected effect that a bundling of supply, as main supplier, would decrease dependence is not confirmed.

Summing up: effects from both transaction cost economics and its extensions were confirmed. In particular, trust was shown to have the expected effect on perceived dependence.

A Study in the Electrical/Electronic Components Industry

One of the shortcomings of the above study is that it concerns only one buyer, so that effects due to the buyer cannot be investigated. This is eliminated in the second study. There, Nooteboom et al. (1997) conducted a survey of ten companies supplying components and sub-assemblies to producers of electrical/electronic apparatus, with ten customer relations for each of the ten companies. The firms were visited by a member of the research team in the beginning of 1994. These visits took an average of three-and-a-half hours. During the visit, data pertaining to the relationships with ten of the firm's most important customers were collected. The questionnaire was based on one that was developed and tested in the previous study (Berger et al. 1995). Indicators that had proved to be of little value were omitted; some new indicators were added. The questionnaires were completed by the respondent, who was either the general manager or the sales manager of the firm, with the researcher clarifying questions when necessary. This minimized the risk of misunderstanding the questions and also guaranteed that there was no non-response, and hence no missing data. To maintain comparability between different customer relationships, the questionnaires were completed horizontally: a question was answered for all ten relationships before moving on to the next question. In this way, data were obtained with regard to 97 relationships.

Two dimensions of trust were hypothesized: habitualization and institutionalization. Habitualization is an operationalization of what in earlier chapters of this book was called 'routinization'. Recall that this played an important role, in Chapter 2, in refuting Williamson's claim that trust does not and should not go beyond calculative self-interest. Routinized behaviour is not calculative. By institutionalization was meant the emergence of common norms to regulate behaviour within a relationship. This is related to the notions of empathy, 'cognitive-based trust' and 'identification-based trust' discussed in previous chapters. The indicator variables (five-point Likert scales) are specified below. Cronbach's alpha for the constructs is also given (a).

HAB: Habitualization (a = 0.75)
- Because we have been doing business so long with this customer, all kinds of procedures have become self-evident
- Because we have been doing business for so long with this customer, we can understand each other well and quickly
- In our contacts with this customer we have never had the feeling of being misled

INST: Institutionalization (a = 0.73)
- In this relation, both sides are expected not to make demands that can seriously damage the interests of the other
- In this relation the strongest side is expected not to pursue its interest at all costs

HI: Habitualization/institutionalization (a = 0.77) = Habitualization + institutionalization + item:
- In this relation informal agreements have the same significance as formal contracts

The last item is kept apart from HAB and INST because it could with equal theoretical and empirical justification be added to either of them; in both cases Cronbach's alpha increases with ten percentage points. The resulting variables were included in an econometric model to explain perceived relational risk, with two dimensions: the probability that the relation goes wrong, and the penalty involved if it does. These were operationalized as follows:

SLE: Size of loss ego (a = 0.90)
–   Actually, we cannot afford a break with this customer
–   If the relation with this customer breaks, it will take us much effort to fill the gap in turnover
PLE: Probability of loss ego
–   The risk in this relation is sufficiently covered by contractual and non-contractual means

The trust variables competed for explanation with other, non-trust-related explanatory variables, as illustrated in Figure 6.1.

Factors that contribute to the (relative) value of the partner (competencies; VA) and to one's switching costs (SW) should determine the size of loss (SLE). This is what one would lose if the relationship breaks. Therefore, it is also the maximum to which one can be 'held-up' with the threat of breaking up the relationship. Factors that limit the room for opportunism (such as contractual, legal governance and monitoring; RO) and factors that limit incentives towards opportunism, to the extent that the partner is himself dependent (shared ownership of specific assets, guarantees, own interest in the relation, due to the value of the focal partner; VE), and propensity towards opportunism (on the basis of the trust-related variables habitualization and institutionalization; HI) should determine the probability of loss (PLE). This is the probability that loss due to a break-up of the relation or due to hold-up on the basis of threatening such a break-up does indeed occur.

One of the explanatory variables was 'continuity' of the relation (CON), which was expected to have a positive effect on the value of the partner (in view of the perspective of cooperation in the future), and hence on SLE, as well as on loyalty (due to habit formation, growth of familiarity and trust), and hence on PLE.

Note that the causal system is recursive: dependence of one side depends on dependence of the other side, because to the extent that someone is dependent he is less likely to exploit the dependence of his partner. That is why the value that the supplier thinks he has for the buyer was also included, with the hypothesis that it would have a negative effect on the

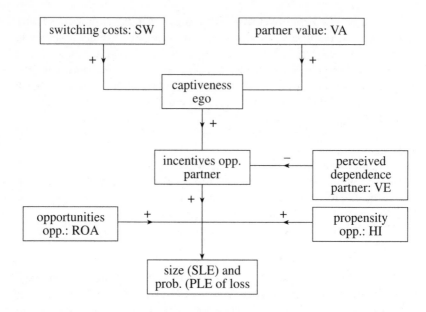

Figure 6.1   Determinants of size and probability of loss

Source: Nooteboom et al. (1997).

perceived probability that things go wrong due to the partner's opportunistic conduct.

Control variables were added to control for firm-specific attributes such
as firm size (measured by annual sales; SE) and risk- or uncertainty-
avoidance (UA). The latter was expected to have a positive effect on perceived probability of loss, with the idea that risk-averse firms take a
dimmer view of risks of dependence. The operationalization and measurement of the variables (ASE, VA, ROA, VE and UA) are specified in
Appendix 6.1.

The empirical results are specified in Table 6.2. It shows that indeed trust
has a significant effect on perceived probability of incurring a loss due to
opportunism, next to the effects of other variables that one would expect
from TCE. One disconfirmation of hypotheses was that instead of the
expected positive effect of uncertainty avoidance on probability of loss
there was a negative effect. But this can be interpreted very well: risk-averse
suppliers make sure they have low-risk partners. The second disconfirmation was that a high perceived value offered to the partner did not have the
expected negative effect on the perceived probability of loss. Our interpre-

Table 6.2   *Results from the study of the electrical/electronic components industry*

Explanatory variables	Size of loss (SLE)	Probability of loss (PLE)
Value partner (VA)		
% share turnover (%S)	0.52 (0.00) *** Y	0.02 (0.78) Y
Remaining value (RVA)	0.07 (0.42) N	−0.05 (0.60) Y
Switching costs	0.17 (0.03) ** Y	0.11 (0.21) Y
Restriction opport. partner (RO)	0.07 (0.36) Y	−0.34 (0.003) *** Y
Trust (HI)	−0.03 (0.75) Y	−0.22 (0.033) ** Y
Own value for partner (VE)	0.01 (0.87) Y	−0.005 (0.58) N
Continuity (CON)	0.306 (0.000) *** Y	−0.249 (0.019)** Y
Uncertainty avoidance (UA)	0.05 (0.48) Y	−0.201 (0.022) ** N
Firm size	0.01 (0.94) N	0.08 (0.43) Y
Adjusted R square	0.52	0.32

Notes:
Between brackets: significance level (T).
Confirmed hypotheses are indicated with Y; lack of confirmation is indicated with N.
 * indicates a significance > 90%.
 ** indicates a significance > 95%.
*** indicates a significance > 99%.

Source: Nooteboom et al. (1997).

tation of this is that firms are not sophisticated enough in their assessment of the situation: they did not take into account the motivations of the partner; did not ask the question what they would do if they stood in his shoes.

A Study in the Car Industry

De Jong and Nooteboom (2000) conducted an extensive secondary analysis of a large set of data on buyer–supplier relations in the US (665 observations), Japan (472) and Europe (268), collected by Mari Sako and Susan Helper. Sako (2000) used these data to investigate the effect of trust on performance. This large number of data allows for the use of the LISREL method, for estimating latent variables on the basis of indicators, as discussed above, and causal relations between them, including circular causality. This is important, because such circular causality is expected to play an important role in collaborative relationships. Variable A may affect variable B, but via a chain of other causalities B may also affect A. For example, making specific or dedicated investments makes one dependent, which yields a risk of hold-up. However, to the extent that they create unique value they also increase dependence of the partner, which reduces risk of hold-up; there may not be an increase in dependence relative to the partner.

The following variables were available:

'supplier's dedicated investments', defined as those specific investments in physical and/or human assets that are required to support the focal exchange and are of less worth elsewhere

'supplier's dependence', defined as the loss to the supplier due to a break of the relationship

'customer's dependence', defined as the loss to the customer due to a break in the relationship

'supplier's uncertainty avoidance', defined as the supplier's inclination to avoid risk of hold-up

'supplier's environmental uncertainty', defined as his inability to predict future contingencies affecting the relationship

'supplier's behavioural uncertainty', defined as inability to predict the customer's future behaviour and competencies

'supplier's value to the customer', defined as the competencies (including skills and capabilities) the supplier offers to the customer

'alternatives for the supplier', defined as alternative customers the supplier could fall back on

'customer's value to the supplier', defined as the customer's competencies (including skills and capabilities) the customer offers to the supplier

'alternatives to the customer', defined as alternative suppliers that the customer could fall back on

'habituation', defined as the establishment of habits, bonds, good communication and empathy

'customer's commitment', defined as the customer's efforts to maintain and continue the relationship, that is loyalty

'supplier's openness', defined as the amount of meaningful and timely information with which the supplier supplies the customer

'supplier's future perspectives', defined as the supplier's expected continuation of the relationship with the specific customer of the focal dyad

'past duration', defined as the length of the relationship

In the present context, the most salient variables are behavioural uncertainty (trust), customer commitment (loyalty) and uncertainty avoidance (trust behaviour). These variables are estimated with the following indicators.

Supplier's behavioural uncertainty BEHUNC:

SBU1 In the production of this product, how much certainty is there regarding the customer's production schedule 2 weeks ahead
Scale: 1 = fairly certain; 5 = completely unpredictable

SBU2 In the production of this product, how much certainty is there regarding the customer's production schedule 1 year ahead
Scale: 1 = fairly certain; 5 = completely unpredictable

SBU3 In the production of this product, how much certainty is there regarding the customer's final product specifications *before* job 1
Scale: 1 = fairly certain; 5 = completely unpredictable

SBU4 In the production of this product, how much certainty is there regarding the customer's final product specifications *after* job 1
Scale: 1 = fairly certain; 5 = completely unpredictable

SBU5 Given the chance, our customer might try to take unfair advantage of our business unit
Scale: 1 = strongly disagree; 5 = strongly agree

SBU6 We feel that our customer often uses the information we give to check up on us, rather than to solve problems
Scale: 1 = strongly agree; 5 = strongly disagree

SBU7 Please circle the number which best describes your belief that your customer will treat you fairly
Scale: 1 = customer always treats us fairly; 5 = can't depend on customer to treat us fairly.

The first four items clearly relate to competence trustworthiness, and the last three relate to benevolence trustworthiness. Interestingly, this is confirmed by the fact that in all the three regions (US, Japan, EU) a factor analysis on all seven items yields two factors, with the first four loading on the one factor, and the last three loading on the second. This is specified in Table 6.3. That confirms the distinction between those two dimensions of trust, proposed in Chapter 2.

Customer's Commitment CUSCOM:

CC1 How would your customer react if one of your competitors offered a lower price for a product of equal quality
Scale: 1 = switch to competitor as soon as technically feasible; 2 = switch at end of contract; 3 = reduce your market share; 5 = help you match your competitors' efforts

CC2 How would your customer react if your material suppliers raised their prices
Scale: 1 = reduce your business unit's market share or switch to another supplier at end of contract; 2 = hold you to your original price; 3 = allow

Table 6.3   Factor analysis on trust factors: factor loadings

	Factor 1 (benevolence)			Factor 2 (competence)		
Item no.	US	Japan	EU	US	Japan	EU
BU1	0.28	0.07	0.24	0.62	0.57	0.64
BU2	0.28	0.07	0.25	0.39	0.63	0.58
BU3	0.08	0.15	0.08	0.86	0.83	0.82
BU4	0.07	0.18	−0.06	0.86	0.82	0.82
BU5	0.87	0.75	0.84	0.13	0.28	0.10
BU6	0.72	0.73	0.70	0.15	−0.08	0.15
BU7	0.83	0.71	0.82	0.12	0.25	0.12
Alpha	0.77	0.60	0.72	0.70	0.71	0.71

Source: de Jong and Nooteboom (2000).

partial pass-through of your business unit's cost increases; 4 = allow full pass-through of your business unit's increases in out-of-pocket costs; 5 = provide significant help for your business unit to reduce costs

CC3 Suppose your business unit had an idea that would allow you to reduce your costs, but would require your customer to make a slight modification in its procedures. How would your customer react

Scale: 1 = customer does not welcome suggestions that would require modifications in its procedures; 2 = customer would adopt the suggestion, but would seek to capture most of the savings; 3 = customer would adopt the suggestion, but would seek to capture some of the savings; 5 = customer would eagerly solicit such suggestions

CC4 We can rely on our customer to help us in ways not required by our agreement with them

Scale: 1 = strongly disagree; 5 = strongly agree

Supplier's uncertainty avoidance SUPUNC:

SUA1 If our customer had given us less assurance of continued business for this product, we would definitely have invested less in plant, equipment and training which could be used to serve only this customer

Scale: 1 = strongly disagree; 5 = strongly agree

SUA2 If our customer had given us less assurance of continued business for this product, we would definitely have invested less in plant, equipment and training which could be used to serve either this customer or other customers

Scale: 1 = strongly disagree; 5 = strongly agree.

Table 6.4   Mean values of variables for the car industry

No.	Variable	US	Japan	EU
1	Supp. dedicated investments	14.2	5.9	16.1
2	Supp. dependence	10.5	11.3	10.7
3	Customer's dependence	8.1	8.2	8.4
4	Supp. uncertainty avoidance	0.4	1.1	0.4
5	Supp. environmental uncertainty	4.5	5.0	4.3
6	Supp. behavioural uncertainty	18.2	13.8	18.1
7	Supp. value	28.0	16.2	15.8
8	Alternatives for the supplier	4.1	4.6	5.9
9	Customer's value	11.3	12.7	11.2
10	Alternatives for the customer	8.1	6.1	5.8
11	Habituation	10.0	7.7	10.0
12	Customer's commitment	10.9	11.5	14.0
13	Supplier's openness	5.0	3.8	4.6
14	Supplier's future perspectives	7.7	24.9	17.7
15	Duration	5.1	6.2	5.3

Source: de Jong and Nooteboom (2000).

For the remaining variables, the items used are specified in Appendix 2. For all the variables, the averages found are specified in Table 6.4.

The literature on buyer–supplier relations suggests that such relations are quite different in Japan, compared with the US. In Japan, relations are supposed to be more durable and relation-oriented, with intensive collaboration and mutual investment, based on trust, while in the US relations are supposedly shorter, more transaction-oriented with less mutual investment and less trust. In Table 6.4 we do find differences between the US and Japan, but they are puzzling. As expected, we do find that in Japan suppliers experience less behavioural uncertainty and have higher future perspectives. However, dedicated investments are less than half the levels in the US and EU, customer commitment is not significantly higher, and suppliers are hardly more open. Perhaps the story about Japanese supplier relations is a myth, at least in part. An alternative is that the West has learned from the Japanese way and has imitated it, at least in part.

On the basis of theory developed in earlier research (Nooteboom 1999a), and partly discussed in Chapter 4 of this book, 25 hypotheses were specified concerning relations between these variables, as summarized in Table 6.5. The results for the US, Japan and EU are also included in Table 6.5, in terms of the coefficients (standardized correlation coefficients) of the causal paths and their significance levels. After testing the hypotheses,

Table 6.5 Hypotheses and results for the car industry

No.	Source of cause	Sign Target of cause	Results		
			US	Japan	EU
1	Supplier's dedicated investm.	+ Supp. dependence	0.26***	0.27***	0.25***
2	Supplier's future perspect.	+ Supp. dedicated investments	0.05*	0.09***	−0.04
3	Customer's value	+ " " "	0.10***	−0.01	0.01
4	Supplier's alternatives	− " " "	0.07**	0.14***	0.02
5	Supplier's dependence	+ Supp. uncertainty avoidance	0.15***	0.12**	0.10*
6	Supplier's environmental uncertainty	+ " " "	n.a.	n.a.	n.a.
7	Supplier's behavioural uncert.	+ " " "	0.15***	0.14***	0.11**
8	Supplier's uncert. avoidance	− Supp. dedicated investments	−0.23***	−0.48***	−0.40***
9	Supplier's dedicated investm.	+ Supp. value	0.27***	0.23***	0.17***
10	Supplier's openness	+ " "	0.15***	−0.04	−0.05
11	Customer's value	+ Supp. openness	0.19***	0.22***	0.20***
12	Supplier's value	+ Customer's dependence	0.22***	0.19***	0.11**
13	Customer's alternatives	− " "	−0.08**	−0.04	−0.13**
14	Customer's value	+ Supp. dependence	0.02	0.09**	−0.05
15	Supplier's alternatives	− " "	−0.01	−0.07**	−0.10**
16	Customer's dependence	+ Customer's commitment	0.11***	0.17***	0.09*
17	Customer's commitment	+ Cust. value	0.33***	0.20***	0.22***
18	"	+ Supp. future perspectives	0.18***	0.11***	0.14***
19	Duration	+ Habituation	0.12***	0.08**	0.09*
20	Habituation	+ Supp. future perspectives	0.16***	0.15***	0.22***
21	"	+ Cust. commitment	0.09**	0.07*	−0.01
22	"	− Supp. behavioural uncert.	n.a.	n.a.	n.a.

23	"	+ Supp. openness	0.21***	−0.04	0.09*
24	"	+ Supp. dependence	0.15***	0.10***	0.14***
25	"	+ Cust. dependence	0.25***	0.13***	0.19***
Inductive effects					
26	Customer's commitment	Supp. behavioural uncert.	−0.44***	−0.28***	−0.35***
27	Customer's dependence	Supp. dependence	0.27***	0.26***	0.16***
28	Supplier's environm. uncert.	Supp. behavioural uncert.	0.25***	0.40***	0.24***

Notes:
The coefficients are path coefficients, that is correlation coefficients.
 * indicates a significance > 90%.
 ** indicates a significance > 95%.
 *** indicates a significance > 99%.

Source: de Jong and Nooteboom (2000).

allowance was made for inductive links, that is additional causal links that the procedure offered as increasing the explanatory power of the model. Most of the hypotheses were confirmed.

Here, I focus on the relations that are salient in the context of the present book. Consistently across all three regions (US, Japan and the EU), we see that dedicated investments have a positive effect on supplier dependence (causal path 1), that behavioural uncertainty also has a positive effect on dependence (cause 7), that this dependence has a positive effect on uncertainty avoidance (cause 5), that is, causes the supplier to take measures against opportunism, and that this has a negative effect on dedicated investments (cause 8). This is yet another confirmation of that implication of transaction cost economics. This causal chain inhibits dedicated investments. However, there is another causal chain which stimulates it. Dedicated investments increase the value of the supplier (cause 9), which increases customer dependence (cause 12), which increases customer commitment (cause 16), which increases supplier's future perspectives (cause 18), and decreases supplier's behavioural uncertainty (cause 26), and the latter two effects have a positive effect on dedicated investments (cause 2, and cause 26 followed by cause 8). These causal loops can be more easily seen when we draw a causal map. Figure 6.2 gives such a map for the results for the US.

Relevant for the discussion of trust are also the following causal effects: habituation, which follows from the duration of the relationship (cause 19), has a positive effect on supplier's future perspectives (cause 20), customer's dependence (cause 25), customer's commitment (directly, by cause 21, and indirectly, through its effect on customer dependence, cause 24), and on supplier's openness (cause 23). Indirectly, then, this has a positive effect on dedicated investments and supplier's value. These causal chains confirm the idea that longer relations, engendering habituation, deepen commitment, mutual investment, value creation and dependence.

A striking result is that the causal structure seems similar for the US, Japan and the EU. While in Table 6.3 we saw a few differences in the average values of the variables, we see here that the underlying causal structure is very similar. In other words, while there are differences between the systems, they are subject to almost the same underlying causal structure. However, there are a few differences, and they may be significant, both statistically and theoretically. While most of the hypotheses are confirmed, there are exceptions, and they vary across the different regions.

One exception is that the expected negative effect of the supplier's alternatives on dedicated investments (causal effect 4) is contradicted by a positive effect that is significant in the US and Japan. The idea behind the original hypothesis was that when one has multiple relations one will be less

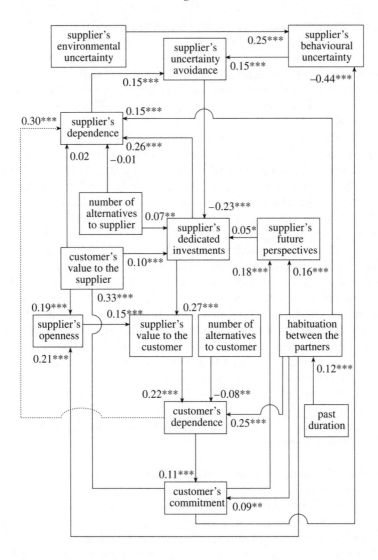

Notes:
   * indicates a significance >90%.
  ** indicates a significance >95%.
 *** indicates a significance >99%.

Source: De Jong and Nooteboom (2000).

Figure 6.2   Causal loops in long-term supply relationships in the US car industry

dedicated to one of them. A possible interpretation of the opposite effect is that when one has alternatives, one is less afraid of becoming dependent and therefore more willing to make dedicated investments. The evidence for a positive effect of customer's value on dedicated investments (cause 3) is limited (significant in the US but not in Japan and the EU). The expected positive effect of supplier's openness on his/her value (cause 10) is also significant only in the US. Customer's alternatives does not have the expected negative effect on customer dependence (cause 13) in Japan. Customer's value has the expected positive effect on supplier dependence (cause 14) only in Japan. The expected negative effect of supplier's alternatives on supplier's dependence (cause 15) is not significant in the US. The expected positive effect of habituation on customer's commitment (cause 21) is not significant in the EU. The expected positive effect of habituation on supplier's openness (cause 23) does not arise in Japan.

These differences are consistent with the following interpretation, offered by de Jong and Nooteboom (2000). In the US relations are less durable and less exclusive, that is more open to multiple relations, while in Japan they are more locked into the vertical business structures of the 'keiretsu'. This is consistent with the average values of the variables, presented in Table 6.3. In the US, duration is somewhat lower, and particularly future perspectives for the supplier, which measures the continuity of the relation that can be expected, is much lower in the US than in Japan, with the EU taking up an intermediate position. In the US customers on average have more alternatives than in Japan and the EU. For suppliers this difference does not appear.

When there is less variety of partner choice, as supposedly is the case in Japan, one would expect:

–   Fewer alternative partners, and hence less effect of that variable. We find that for customers, but not for suppliers.
–   Less effect of customer value on dedicated investments, since there is limited choice between more and less attractive customers, and dedicated investments are taken for granted. We find this.
–   Openness of suppliers is taken for granted and hence is not variable, and hence does not have an effect on supplier value, and does not depend on habituation. We find this.

Therefore, there is evidence for the thesis that in Japan vertical buyer–supplier structures are less flexible, being locked into keiretsu. This may be an example of social liability, as discussed in Chapter 5. Recall that in Japan the level of dedicated investments is lower and supplier uncertainty avoidance (measures against opportunism) is higher (see Table 6.3).

This may indicate that suppliers are locked in too much. That suspicion also arose from a game-theoretic analysis of Japanese buyer–supplier relations conducted by Nooteboom (1998, reported also in Nooteboom 1999a). That study indicated that in the Japanese system suppliers may be subject to one-sided dependence, and buyers are tempted to take advantage of that. That may explain what we find here: a lower level of dedicated investments, less openness, greater uncertainty avoidance. In terms of the comparative analysis of business systems conducted in Chapters 4 and 5, perhaps the US has found a 'third way' in buyer–supplier relations, in the car industry. This entails a combination of sufficient loyalty and continuity of relations to evoke dedicated investments to build value, while keeping relations from becoming too exclusive and rigid.

6.2   SIMULATING TRUST

This paragraph shows how the process of making and breaking trust can be modelled with computer simulation. Here, I make use of a PhD project of Tomas Klos (Klos 2000, Klos and Nooteboom 2001, Nooteboom et al. 2000). The model implements notions from previous chapters, such as: routinization as a basis for trust, societal norms as a source of trustworthiness, trust as a default, assessment of both profit and trustworthiness, a limit to trustworthiness and loyalty, and radical uncertainty in the evaluation of trustworthiness. I discuss the main design features of the model, to show how the notions from previous chapters can be operationalized. I indicate some of the results from experiments with the model.

Simulating Complexity of Interaction

When confronted with arguments against rationality, economists usually concede that assumptions of full rationality are counterfactual, and then resort to the argument of economic selection. We can proceed as if agents make rational, optimal choices, because selection by forces of competition will ensure that only the optimal survives (Alchian 1950, Friedman 1953). Williamson was no exception in this respect. He held that in due course, market forces will select inefficient forms of organization out. However, that argument of selection has been shown to be dubious, as was discussed in Chapter 1. In evolution it is not the best conceivable but the best that happens to be available that survives. Due to effects of scale a large firm that is inefficient for its size may win out over efficient small firms. Furthermore, entry barriers may hamper the selection efficiency of markets. Koopmans (1957) concluded long ago that if the assumption of efficient outcomes is based on an argument of evolutionary process, explicit modelling of that process should test its validity. Then, particularly in the study of inter-firm relations, we have to take into account the complexities and path-dependencies that may arise in the making and breaking of relations between multiple agents. That is what Klos (1999) aimed to do in developing his simulation model. As Coase (1998) recently admitted:

> [t]he analysis cannot be confined to what happens within a single firm. The costs of coordination within a firm and the level of transaction costs that it faces are affected by its ability to purchase inputs from other firms. Their ability to supply these inputs depends in part on their costs of coordination and the level of transaction costs that they face which are similarly affected by what these are in still other firms. What we are dealing with is a complex interrelated structure.

With his simulation model, Klos let the distribution of economic activity across different organizational agents emerge from processes of interaction between these agents, as they adapt decisions to experience. In other words, learning is included. The system may or may not settle down, and if it does the resulting equilibrium may or may not be transaction cost economic. In any case, '[i]t is the process of becoming rather than the never reached end points that we must study if we are to gain insight' (Holland 1992, p. 19). The methodology of artificial adaptive agents, in Agent Based Computational Economics (ACE), a method for studying Complex Adaptive Systems (CAS), seems just the right methodology to deal with this 'complex interrelated structure' of 'processes of interaction in which future decisions are adapted to past experiences' (Holland and Miller 1991).

The essence of this approach is that economic phenomena are studied as they emerge from actual (simulated) interactions between individual, boundedly rational, adaptive agents. They are not deduced from abstract models employing representative agents, auctioneers or anonymous, random matching, and so on. Rather, whether an interaction takes place between any two given agents is left for them to decide. What the agents subsequently do in that interaction is their own – possibly sub-optimal – decision, that they make on the basis of their locally available, incomplete information and as a result of their own (cognitively limited) processing of that information. Appropriate forms of reasoning are induction and abduction, rather than deduction as used in optimization models that are solved for 'never-reached end points'.

That methodology was used to model interactions between firms, in the making and breaking of relations on the basis of a boundedly rational, adaptive, mutual evaluation of transaction partners that takes into account both trust and (potential) profit. A system of buyer–supplier relations was modelled because that best illustrates transaction cost issues. The study focused on the role of trust and loyalty.

The modelling of trust incorporated the following features:

1. Trust is adaptive: it is based on experience with a (potential) partner's commitment to a relation, as exhibited by his/her past loyalty, that is lack of defection to more attractive alternatives.
2. Partner value goes beyond potential profit: trust is included, next to profit, in the determination of a (potential) partner's attractiveness. The weight attached to trust relative to expected profit is also adaptive: it depends on realized profits (α).
3. Trustworthiness, in the sense of commitment to a relation, is limited. There is a threshold of resistance to temptation below which the agent will not defect to a more attractive alternative (τ).
4. Trustworthiness also is adaptive: the threshold of defection is adjusted as a function of realized profits.

This approach allows us to experiment with the development of trust and trustworthiness, the role this plays in the making and breaking of relations, the resulting durability or volatility of relations and the outcome regarding efficiency, in terms of realized profits. These experiments are conducted under different conditions concerning costs and profits that are relevant for transaction cost analysis.

The choice and matching of partners is modelled as follows. Agents are assumed to have differential preferences for different potential partners. On the basis of preferences, buyers are assigned to suppliers or to themselves, respectively. When a buyer is assigned to himself this means that he 'makes rather than buys'. In other words: the 'make or buy decision' is endogenized. This process is generated by a so-called matching algorithm.

A matching algorithm produces a set of matches (a matching) on the basis of individual agents' preference rankings over other agents. Preferences are expressed in 'scores'. Each agent assigns a score to all agents it can possibly be matched to (a buyer can be matched with himself, to make rather than buy). The score is a function of (1) the profit the agent can potentially make as a result of the transaction and (2) his trust in the potential partner. A multiplicative specification of potential profit and trust is used, to express that they interact: the score must be zero if either trust or potential profit is zero. The product of potential profitability and trust interpreted as a probability of realization would constitute expected profit. Note, however, my objections, discussed in Chapter 2, against treating trust as a probability. In order to allow agents to attach varying weights to profitability versus trust, instead of simple multiplication of the two a Cobb–Douglas functional form is used:

$$\text{score}_{ij} = \text{profitability}_{ij}^{\alpha_i} \cdot \text{trust}_{ij}^{1-\alpha_i} \tag{6.1}$$

where: score_{ij} is the score i assigns to j, $\text{profitability}_{ij}$ is the profit i can potentially make 'through' j, trust_{ij} is i's trust in j and $\alpha_i \in [0, 1]$ is the importance i attaches to profitability relative to trust, that is the 'profit-elasticity' of the scores that i assigns; i may adapt the value of α_i from each timestep to the next. Later sections describe how profitability and trust are determined, and how adaptation takes place.

Besides a preference ranking, each agent maintains a 'minimum tolerance level' that determines which partners are acceptable. Each agent also has a maximum number of matches it can be involved in at any one time (a quotum).

The matching algorithm proceeds as follows. Buyers may have one or more suppliers and suppliers may have one or more buyers; each buyer i has an offer quotum o_i and each supplier j has an acceptance quotum a_j. Before the matching, all buyers and suppliers establish a strict preference ranking over all their alternatives. The algorithm then proceeds in a finite number of steps, as follows.

1.   In the first step, each buyer sends a maximum of o_i requests to its most preferred, acceptable suppliers. The algorithm structurally favours the agents that send the requests; it is plausible that buyers do this. Because the buyers typically have different preference rankings, the various suppliers will receive different numbers of requests.

2.   The suppliers first reject all requests received from unacceptable buyers.[1] Then, each supplier 'provisionally accepts' a maximum of a_j requests from its most preferred acceptable buyers and rejects the rest (if any).

3.   Each buyer that was rejected in any step fills its quotum o_i in the next step by sending requests to (o_i minus the number of outstanding, provisionally accepted, requests) next- most-preferred, acceptable suppliers that it has not yet sent a request to.

4.   Each supplier again rejects requests received from unacceptable buyers and provisionally accepts the requests from up to a maximum of a_j most preferred, acceptable buyers from among newly received and previously provisionally accepted requests and rejects the rest. As long as

---

[1]   It is assumed that all buyers are acceptable to the suppliers; suppliers do not, like the buyers, have any alternative, so they will rather supply to any buyer than remain single.

one or more buyers have been rejected, the algorithms goes back to step 3. The algorithm stops if no buyer sends a request that is rejected. All provisionally accepted requests are then definitely accepted.

A buyer's potential to generate profits for a supplier is a function of the buyer's position on the final market – where he is a seller – as expressed in the degree of product differentiation. A supplier's potential to generate profits for a buyer is determined by the supplier's efficiency in producing for the buyer. The model allows for varying degrees of product differentiation. As indicated before, a more differentiated product yields a higher profit margin. This is expressed in a buyer-specific variable d_i (in the interval [0, 1]) that determines the profit the buyer will make when selling his products. Different values for d_i are investigated to see how they affect the choices that agents make.

Production, whether conducted by a supplier or by the buyer himself, requires investments in assets. One unit of asset is normally required to produce one product, but increasing efficiency may decrease this amount. Assuming the production technology is more or less rigid (differentiated products require specialized assets), a connection is assumed between the differentiation of a buyer's product and the specificity of the assets required to produce it. To the extent that assets are specific, they entail switching costs. On the other hand, if products are not differentiated, investments to produce the product for one buyer can easily be switched to producing the product for other buyers. The simplest way to model this relation is to assume that asset specificity is equal to product differentiation, that is the proportion of the asset that is specific to a buyer is equal to the extent to which that buyer's product is differentiated. If a buyer produces for himself, it makes no sense to distinguish between buyer-specific and non-specific assets.[2] A buyer's minimum acceptance level of suppliers is the score that the buyer would attach to himself. Since it is plausible that he completely trusts himself, trust is set at its maximum of 1, and the role of trust in the score is disregarded: $\alpha = 1$.

If a supplier produces for one or more buyers, then his investments are split into two categories: buyer-specific and non-specific – that is general purpose – assets. As explained above, the percentage of investment that is specific to that buyer is the same as the extent to which that buyer's product is differentiated. The supplier adds the remaining general purpose investment for each buyer over all the buyers he is matched to. The corresponding volume of production is subject to economy of scale. The utilization of

---

[2] Remember that overlap between both sides of the market is not allowed, which takes away the possibility for buyers to produce for themselves as well as for their competitors.

specific assets is subject to experience effects: uninterrupted use for the buyer involved yields learning by doing.

The way profits are made, then, is that suppliers may reduce costs by generating efficiencies for buyers, while buyers may increase returns by selling more differentiated products. It is assumed that the profit that is made resulting from both partners' contributions is shared equally between the buyer and the supplier involved.

The simulation proceeds in a sequence of time steps, called a 'run'. Each simulation experiment may be replicated several times (multiple runs), to reduce the influence of draws from random distributions on the results. At the beginning of a simulation starting values are set for certain model parameters. The user is prompted to supply the number of buyers and suppliers, as well as the number of runs, and the number of timesteps in each run. The program's random number generator is seeded and finally, the agents are instantiated and given a number for identification. At the start of each run, each of the agents is initialized. For example, the agents' profits (from the previous run) are re-set to zero and the agents' trust in other agents is re-set. The simulation is described in more detail in Klos (1999).

In each timestep, before matching takes place, each agent calculates scores and ranks potential partners accordingly. Random draws are used to settle the ranking of alternatives with equal scores. To calculate scores each agent chooses a value for α: the elasticity of the score with respect to potential profit. Potential profitability depends on profit margin, related to the degree of product differentiation, economies of scale and economies of experience. As discussed before, suppliers enjoy scale economies in the total of general purpose assets used in the production for multiple buyers. Furthermore, as a supply relation lasts, the supplier accumulates experience and efficiency at using specific assets in the production for a particular buyer. Suppliers' scale efficiency is inferred from the outcome of the previous timestep. Only after the matching does it become clear to how many and which buyers each supplier is actually matched, and what the real extent of his scale efficiency is. Expectations of the supplier's position on each buyer-specific experience curve, on the other hand, will already be accurate before the matching – assuming, of course, that the relation makes it through the matching.

After the calculation of scores the matching algorithm is applied. The outcome is determined by the agents' preference rankings over acceptable alternatives. After the matching, suppliers that are matched to a buyer produce for their buyer(s), while buyers that are 'self-matched' (not matched to a supplier) produce for themselves. Assets that suppliers invest in for the production for a certain buyer are specific to that buyer to the extent that the buyer's product is differentiated. The remainder of the assets is 'general purpose'. After production, all buyers sell their products on the final-goods market. Net revenue is determined by the profit rate, which depends on the degree of product differentiation, and costs, depending on efficiency of scale and experience. Net profits are equally divided between buyer and supplier. The events in this latter part of each timestep – that is, after the matching – may lead the agents to adapt their preference rankings, used as input for the matching algorithm in the next timestep. In particular, they adapt their values of α and τ, as discussed in the previous section. A relation is broken if, during the matching, a buyer does not send any more requests to the supplier or he/she does, but the supplier rejects them. Across timesteps realized profits are accumulated for all buyers and suppliers, and all the relevant parameters are tracked.

Adaptive Trust

The model focuses exclusively on benevolence trust, which pertains to the risk that a partner will defect and thereby cause switching costs. Therefore, as noted before, in the score that a buyer attaches to himself, for in-house production as an alternative to engaging a supplier, we assume maximum trust. It is assumed that trust increases with the duration of a relation, for two reasons. First, as a relation lasts longer, one starts to take the partner's behaviour for granted, and to assume the same behaviour (that is commitment, rather than breaking the relation) for the future. This models the notion of routinization discussed in earlier chapters, and what was called habituation in the study by Nooteboom et al. (1997), discussed above. Second, as discussed in Chapter 3, prolonged interaction without defection is expected to yield indentification-based trust, as a result of converging cognitive categories, or a reduction of cognitive distance. Like effects of scale and experience, this is subject to decreasing returns to scale, and we use the same basic functional form employed before. A base level of trust was added. This reflects basic norms of behaviour yielding ex ante expected trustworthiness as an institutional feature of a society. It may be interpreted as the expected percentage of non-opportunistic people, or as some standard of elementary decency that is assumed to prevail. On top of that basic level of trust one can develop partner-specific trust on the basis of experience in dealings with him.

For each agent, trust starts out at a certain starting value that is set exogenously, and is adapted to experience with the loyalty of partners. If an agent i, involved in a relation with an agent j, 'breaks' their relation, then j's trust in i decreases. In effect, j's trust drops by a percentage of the distance between the current level and the base-line level of trust; it stays there until the next time j and i are matched, after which it starts to increase again for as long as the relation lasts without interruption.

The other side of the coin is, of course, one's own trustworthiness. This is modelled as a threshold τ for defection. One defects only if the advantage over one's current partner exceeds that threshold. In other words, in the matching algorithm the threshold is added to the score for the current partner.

An agent is adaptive if 'the actions of the agent in its environment can be assigned a value (performance, utility, payoff, fitness, or the like); and the agent behaves in such a way as to improve this value over time' (Holland and Miller 1991: 365). The adaptive character of the artificial agents in the present model refers to the possibility for the agents to change the values they use for α (weight attached to profit relative to trust) and τ (threshold of loyalty) from each timestep to the next. To each value of α and τ, each agent assigns a strength, which is its selection probability.[3] This expresses the agent's confidence in the success of using that particular value; the various strengths always add up to a constant C. At the beginning of each timestep each agent chooses a value for α and τ. The choice between the different possible values is probabilistic – a simple roulette wheel selection – with each value's selection probability equal to its relative strength, that is its strength divided by C. The strength of the value that was chosen at the start of a particular timestep is updated at the end of that timestep, on the basis of the agent's performance during that timestep, in terms of realized profit.[4] As an output of the simulation, each agent i's weighted average value is calculated. This indicates where i's emphasis lies: because the value with the highest strength pulls the weighted average in its direction, the emphasis lies on low values if the weighted average is low and vice versa.

In early experiments with the model, Klos and Nooteboom (2001) varied the degree to which investment in any given buyer–supplier relation is specific, and hypotheses were tested concerning the effects on the 'make or buy' decision. The hypothesis, taken directly from TCE, was that more product differentiation will favour 'make' over 'buy'. The model reproduced that outcome. One of the core objections to transaction cost economics was that it neglects problems that may obstruct the achievement of optimal outcomes. The effect was investigated on outcomes in terms of cumulative profit, to see to what extent optimal profits are indeed realized, and how this varies across runs of the model. Lack of optimal outcomes and a

---

[3] This form of adaptation is called reinforcement learning. A classifier system is used to implement it. See Arthur (1991, 1993), Kirman and Vriend (2000) and Lane (1993) for discussions and other applications in economic models; good general introductions to classifier systems are Booker et al. (1989), Goldberg (1989) and Holland et al. (1986).

[4] This works as follows: the agent adds the profit obtained during timestep t to the strength of the value that was used for α or τ. Then, all strengths are renormalized to sum to C again (see Arthur 1993 for a discussion of this learning mechanism).

variety of outcomes would form an illustration of unpredictability and path-dependence in the formation of relations among multiple agents. Indeed, the simulations illustrate that optimal results are seldom achieved. Interestingly, optimal results are approached more closely when products are more differentiated and, correspondingly, assets are more specific. The reason for this is that then buyers go for more 'make' rather than 'buy', and then they are less subject to the uncertainties involved in which suppliers they will wind up with, and at what profit. This adds an insight that transaction cost economics was unable to give. Next to the classic advantage of 'make' over 'buy', for the control of hold-up risk, there now appears the additional advantage that then one is less subject to the unpredictabilities and path-dependencies in relations that make it difficult to achieve optimal results.

Nooteboom et al. (2000) focused on trust. Experiments were conducted concerning the development of trust and trustworthiness. A cynic would expect that trust does not pay, and if he is right, we would expect a more or less uniform decline of both loyalty and the weight attached to trust. The counter hypothesis is that to the extent that the advantages of durable 'buy' relations are higher, trust and trustworthiness, in terms of commitment to an ongoing relationship in spite of more attractive alternatives, matter more. We would expect that adaptive agents then evolve to relatively high levels of trustworthiness, less frequent switching, higher perceived commitment and hence trust, and a high weight attached to trust in the evaluation of partners.

Buyers adapt the value they use for α and τ. As explained before, the weighted averages of α and τ for each agent indicate the emphasis they put on other agents' profitability vs. their trust in those other agents and on their own loyalty. The agents' learning can be represented as an adaptive walk across the fitness landscape on the multi-dimensional problem space that is defined by α and τ.

Three different types of trajectory were found. One trajectory was a decrease of both loyalty and weight attached to trust (increasing α, decreasing τ), a second an increase in weight attached to trust (decreasing α), with little change in loyalty, and the third entails a decreasing weight attached to trust and increasing loyalty. So, both strategies of trust and loyalty and a strategy of opportunism can be learned to yield improved performance. This can make sense as follows: opportunistic agents engage in ongoing switching to seek out profitable partners, thereby relinquishing the advantage of learning by doing in ongoing relations, but gaining from the hunt for short-term advantage, and perhaps gaining more benefits from economy of scale. Trust-oriented agents go for learning by doing in more durable relations.

The process is accompanied with progressively higher levels of performance (profit), because realized profit drives the learning process. The system
can be thought of as annealing over time, leading to a state in which all
agents are attuned to one another. The extent to which such a state is robust
under entry of other types of agents is the subject of future work. The model
is still new and limited. It allows for many further experiments and extensions. One type of experiment is to create different sub-populations, of trust-
oriented and of opportunistic agents, and see how their interaction develops.
Do partners with trust strategies team up, excluding opportunists who are
then left to deal with each other? Does it occur that opportunists prey on
trust-oriented agents who have no options left for switching? Is it ever viable
to be a loyal 'sucker'? An extension of the model would be to allow for new
entry. That would allow us to investigate the robustness of evolved loyalty
and trust under entry of opportunists. Does prevailing trust then break
down, or do entrants adapt by learning to be loyal? Does the population
perhaps split up in loyalists and opportunists? This would help us to investigate the proposal by Hill (1990) that loyalist societies have competitive
advantage, due to reduced transaction costs and more fruitful collaborative
relations. That may be the case only if such a society closes itself off from
new entry by possible opportunists. Under what conditions does existing
trust unravel under such entry? Another option is to build in a reputation
mechanism. Currently, trust is based on personal, direct experience with
potential partners. A reputation mechanism would entail that such experience is shared with others. This is likely to have significant effects on the
development of trust and loyalty.

APPENDIX 6.1   MEASUREMENTS IN THE STUDY OF THE ELECTRICAL/ELECTRONIC COMPONENTS INDUSTRY

The specification of variables in the empirical study by Nooteboom et al. (1997)
which were not yet given in the main text is given below. Here, α refers to Cronbach's
alpha.

Value partner
%S: percentage of total sales to the buyer, as a cardinal measure of value alter
RVA: remaining indicators of value alter ($a = 0.70$)
−   Because we supply to this customer we are able to build up technological know-
    how that is also useful for other customers
−   Because we supply to this customer we obtain market knowledge that would
    otherwise be difficult to access
−   Our firm is involved in an early stage in the development of new components for
    this customer ('early supplier involvement')
−   This customer involves us in the testing of components and/or in prototyping

Switching costs
DA: dedicated assets (a = 0.83)
– Our firm employs significantly more people than if we did not supply to this customer
– Our firm must have people with specific expertise in house to be able to supply to this customer
– Our firm has had to create extra capacity to supply to this customer
– We had to make investments to satisfy the specific supply conditions of this customer (for example for 'just-in-time')
PAS: physical asset specificity (a = 0.70)
– For our production for this customer highly specific machines, apparatus or instruments are needed
– Most of the machines, apparatus or instruments needed for the production for this customer can also be used for other customers, if necessary
KAS: knowledge specificity (a = 0.68)
– We have had to invest much time in acquiring the procedures desired for this customer (for example in the area of logistics and quality control)
– Much specific technological know-how is required to effectively supply to this customer
– Much knowledge of the internal organization of this customer is required for effective cooperation
LS: location specificity
– The location of our firm plays an important role in the relation with this customer
SW: switching costs ego = ASE asset specificity ego (a = 0.84) = dedicated assets + physical asset specificity + knowledge specificity + location specificity

Room for opportunism
LO: legal ordering (a = 0.79)
– The contract with this customer is as complete as possible
– The contract forms the core of our relation with this customer
– In this relation it is not so important to have a good contract
PO: private ordering (a = 0.71)
– The customer shares in the payment for specific machines and apparatus that we must make for the production for him
– The customer shares in the payment for the investments in specific tools and/or measurement apparatus that we must make for the production for him
– Guarantees are given for minimal custom over an agreed period of time
– We give guarantees for supply for an agreed period of time
RO: restriction of room for opportunism (a = 0.79) = legal ordering + private ordering

Incentives for opportunism
VE: value ego (a = 0.76)
– Our supply performance to this customer cannot be assessed on its merit if one looks only at the price
– This customer is aware that our supply performance cannot be assessed on its merit if one looks only at price
– Our supply to this customer is clearly custom made
– We provide an important source of information on new technologies for this customer

–   Our firm is involved in an early stage in the development of new components for this customer ('early supplier involvement')
–   This customer involves us in the testing of components and/or in prototyping
GR: growth (a = 0.68)
–   The relation between our firm and this customer has continually improved in the course of time
–   Our supply to this customer has increased strongly in the course of time
FP: future perspective (a = 0.67)
–   In this relation it is assumed that contracts will in general be renewed
–   For the foreseeable future we do not expect a break with this customer
–   We see the relation with this customer as a long-term relation, in which one must invest, and in which both sides are willing to make concessions if it is really needed
CON: continuity (a = 0.78) = growth + future perspective.

APPENDIX 6.2   MEASUREMENTS IN THE STUDY OF THE CAR INDUSTRY

Supplier's dedicated investments SUPINV
   Please estimate the total amount of your business unit's investment in equipment to make this product over the last four years.

Supplier's dependence SUPDEP
SD1 If you were to stop getting these orders from this customer, approximately how much of your investment for this product in plant, equipment and training would you be unlikely to find alternative uses for and have to write off?
   Scale: 1 = 10% or less; 2 = 11–33%; 3 = 34–66%; 4 = 67–89%; 5 = 90–100%.
SD2 Please estimate the technical complexity involved in manufacturing the product in 1992.
   Scale: 1 = fairly simple; 5 = highly complex.
SD3 Please check the appropriate range for the average piece price of the product in 1992.
   Scale: for the United States 1 = <\$1; 2 = \$1–10; 3 = \$11–50; 4 = \$51–100; 5 = >\$100.
SD4 Does your business unit have any of the following?
   A marketing office near your customer; a design office near your customer; a facility near your customer to consolidate shipments of your parts for 'Just-in-Time' (JIT) delivery; an engineer resident at your customer's facility.
   Scale: one point for each.

Customer's Dependence CUSDEP
CD1 Please estimate the number of months it would take your customer to replace your business unit with another supplier. Consider the time required to locate, qualify, train, make investments, test and develop a working relationship with another firm. Please exclude legal considerations such as the existence of long-term contracts.
   Scale: 1 = 0; 2 = 1–3; 3 = 4–12; 4 = 13–24; 5 = 25–48; 6 = >48.
CD2 What percent of your business unit's sales ends up as original equipment for cars or light trucks?
   Scale: 1 = 0–10; 2 = 11–25; 3 = 26–40; 4 = 41–65; 5 = 66–80; 6 = 81–100.

Supplier's environmental uncertainty SUPENV

SEU1 In the production of this product, how much certainty is there regarding your production costs over 4 years.
Scale: 1 = fairly certain; 5 = completely unpredictable.

SEU2 In the production of this product, how much certainty is there regarding the production technology for this product over 4 years.
Scale: 1 = fairly certain; 5 = completely unpredictable.

Supplier's value to the customer SUPVAL

SV1 For design engineering. Currently, how would you rate your business unit's skills at making modifications to products or processes? Please compare yourself to other firms in your industry throughout the world.
Scale: 1 = significantly below average; 5 = significantly above average.

SV2 For making incremental process improvements. Currently, how would you rate your business unit's skills at making modifications to products or processes? Please compare yourself to other firms in your industry throughout the world.
Scale: 1 = significantly below average; 5 = significantly above average.

SV3 For implementing entirely new processes. Currently, how would you rate your business unit's skills at making modifications to products or processes? Please compare yourself to other firms in your industry throughout the world.
Scale: 1 = significantly below average; 5 = significantly above average.

SV4 Of the metal cutting machines currently in use at the plant which makes this product, about what percent are CNC?
Scale: 1 = 0%; 2 = 1–25%; 3 = 26–50%; 4 = 51–75%; 5 = 76–100%.

SV5 Of the other machines currently in use at the plant which make this product, about what percent have PLC?
Scale: 1 = 0%; 2 = 1–25%; 3 = 26–50%; 4 = 51–75%; 5 = 76–100%.

SV6 About how many robots (programmable machines with at least three axes of movement) are in use at the plant?
Scale: 1 = 0; 2 = 1–2; 3 = 3–5; 4 = 6–10; 5 = >10.

SV7 Approximately what percent of the contacts with your customer regarding this product were for 'your business unit providing technical assistance to customer'?
Scale: 1 = 0–19; 2 = 20–39; 3 = 40–59; 4 = 60–79; 5 = 80–100.

SV8 Which range best describes your business unit's R&D as a percent of sales?
Scale: 1 = 0%; 2 = 0.1–1%; 3 = 1.1–2%; 4 = 2.1–4%; 5 = >4%.

SV9 Please check the descriptions which apply to the product development process for your company's product.
Scale: 1 = customer took entire responsibility; 2 = customer provided majority of engineering hours; your business unit provided the rest; 3 = customer and your business unit contributed equally to the design; 4 = your business unit provided majority of engineering hours; 5 = your business unit took entire responsibility.

Alternatives to the supplier SUPALT.
Please indicate the number of automakers of each nationality of ownership to whom you supply this product from this plant. Scale: the number of firms.

Customer's value to the supplier CUSVAL

CV1 Over the last four years, what sorts of technical assistance have you received from your customer?

Provided personnel who visited your site to aid in implementing improved procedures for zero or a nominal charge; for a fee; did not provide. Arranged for training of your personnel at their site for zero or a nominal charge; for a fee; did not
provide. Provided personnel who worked two weeks or more on your shop floor
to improve your processes for zero or a nominal charge; for a fee; did not provide.
Scale: one point for each.

CV2 Approximately what percent of the contacts with your customer regarding
this product were for 'customer providing technical assistance to your business
unit'?
Scale: $1 = 0$; $2 = 1-10$; $3 = 11-20$; $4 = 21-30$; $5 = 31-100$.

CV3 The advice our customer gives us is not always helpful.
Scale: $1 =$ strongly agree; $5 =$ strongly disagree.

CV4 In dealing with this customer, we have learned much that will help us with
other customers.
Scale: $1 =$ strongly disagree; $5 =$ strongly agree.

Alternatives to the customer CUSALT

Please indicate the appropriate number of other firms supplying the same
product to same automaker or other firms potentially able to supply similar
product (without major investment).
Scale: the number of firms.

Habituation HABIT

HAB1 For face to face contact. In each year, approximately how often did someone
from your business unit have a substantive discussion with your customer?
(Please include discussions about issues such as design changes and quality problems, but exclude routine delivery notifications and contacts by resident engineers).
Scale: $1 =$ every 6 months or less often; $2 =$ monthly; $3 =$ weekly; $4 =$ daily; $5 =$
more than once a day.

HAB2 For phone contact. In each year, approximately how often did someone
from your business unit have a substantive discussion with your customer?
(Please include discussions about issues such as design changes and quality problems, but exclude routine delivery notifications and contacts by resident engineers).
Scale: $1 =$ every 6 months or less often; $2 =$ monthly; $3 =$ weekly; $4 =$ daily; $5 =$
more than once a day.

HAB3 For fax contact. In each year, approximately how often did someone
from your business unit have a substantive discussion with your customer?
(Please include discussions about issues such as design changes and quality
problems, but exclude routine delivery notifications and contacts by resident
engineers).
Scale: $1 =$ every 6 months or less often; $2 =$ monthly; $3 =$ weekly; $4 =$ daily; $5 =$
more than once a day.

Supplier's openness SUPOPN

What types of information does your business unit provide to your customer
about the process you use to make the product you listed above?
Detailed breakdown of process steps; cost of each process step; financial information not publicly available; production scheduling information; type of equip-

ment used; your sources of supply; detailed information regarding materials you use.
Scale: one point for each.

Supplier's future perspectives SUPFUT
For how long do you think there is a high probability that your business unit will be supplying this or a similar item to your customer (in years)?
Scale: the number of years.
Past duration of the relationship PAST
Approximately how long has your firm sold products in this product line to this customer (in years)?
Scale: the number of years.

7. Summary and conclusions

This chapter summarizes the answers to the questions specified in Chapter 1, and reviews directions for further research. The ten questions from Chapter 1 are repeated below, in Table 7.1.

7.1   TRUST, PROBABILITY AND CALCULATION

This concerns questions four and five from Table 7.1. In much literature, trust has been rendered as a subjective probability. In Chapter 2, I argued that trust in people (behavioural trust) cannot entail certainty and cannot be treated and calculated as a probability. The reason is the presence in human behaviour of radical uncertainty (unlike laws of nature): the set of future options for behaviour, for one's partner and for oneself, is open; the range of options is indeterminate. As Shackle indicated long ago, under such conditions one cannot employ the notion of probability in any usual sense (satisfying the axioms of probability theory). Next to uncertainty about future options of choice, there is uncertainty concerning preferences, which are also subject to unforeseeable change. I propose that even if prediction were possible, it would be unethical to claim full knowledge about other people's future options and preferences for action, since that would rob them of their autonomy of choice.

As a result, trust in behaviour can never yield certainty, and cannot be completely calculative. It always remains a wager to a greater or lesser extent. That does not deny that there may be better and worse reasons for trust. There may be good reasons on the basis of available evidence from one's own experience or that of others (by reputation). Trust is often calculative, not in the literal sense of calculating probabilities, but in the sense of a rational evaluation of the evidence for trustworthiness. On the basis of observed or reputed behaviour one may make inferences about trustworthiness. This involves a logic of inference and attribution, about which more will be said later.

This is not to say that trust is always calculative to some extent, or can ever be completely calculative. Trust can never be completely calculative because at some point calculation in the sense of critical reflection must stop, not to

Table 7.1   Questions

Questions	Chapters
1: Value of trust What are the value dimensions of trust: intrinsic and extrinsic value, self- and other oriented value, and how are they related?	2: Forms, and 3: Foundations
2: Economic function of trust What is the extrinsic, economic value of trust? How does it work? What are the effects? What are the institutional conditions?	4: Functions
3: Failures of trust How can trust go wrong? What are its possible adverse effects? What are the limitations and boundaries of trust?	5: Failures
4: Trust and probability If trust entails risk, how is this to be understood? Can trust be modelled as a subjective probability? Can trust go together with certainty?	2: Forms
5: Calculative and non-calculative trust How calculative or rational is trust? When it is not calculative, does this necessarily lead to blind, unconditional trust? If not, why not, and how does this work? Can calculative and non-calculative trust be combined? How?	2: Forms
6: Objects and aspects of trust What can we have trust in? Things, people, institutions, organizations? What are the aspects of trust: competence, intentions, and what else?	2: Forms
7: The sources of trustworthiness On what is trustworthiness of people based? Coercion, self-interest, ethics, friendship, routinization? Does it go beyond self-interest? If it does, can it survive in markets?	2: Forms 3: Foundations
8: The mental basis of trust On what is trust based, and how: knowledge, experience, analysis, emotions, habits, faith?	3: Foundations
9: The process of trust How does the mental basis of trust develop in processes of interaction, and how does it shape that process? How does the mutual shaping work of trust, process and trustworthiness?	3: Foundations
10: Testing and modelling trust Can trust be empirically measured and tested? Can it be formalized and subjected to logical or mathematical analysis?	6: Figures

get bogged down in an infinite regress of questioning the reliability of the terms in which one assesses reliability. At some point, one has to take terms or basic assumptions for granted. Trust can be non-calculative for other reasons. First, as indicated in the discussion of uncertainty, whatever good reasons one has, one can never claim to know all relevant future conditions. Trust is a default: we entertain or reject trust on the basis of the best available evidence. When we trust, we assume trustworthiness until evidence to the contrary appears.

I propose that there are limits to trustworthiness, which one is wise to take into account, beyond which people are unable to resist opportunities or pressures for opportunism. There is an upper limit, with drastic events that the partner is unable to cope with, or temptation or pressure that he cannot resist. There is also a lower limit of small imperfections that he cannot control, or pilferage he thinks will not be noticed. These limits vary with trustees and for a given trustee will vary across trustors and situational conditions. One such condition is the pressure of survival. Firms in industries with intense competition will have a lower limit to loyalty than firms in a monopoly situation. One also has one's own limit of trustworthiness, though one may not know it. Limits to trustworthiness are subject to adaptation. One may learn to become more or less loyal. Chapter 6 discussed an attempt to model a threshold of loyalty in a simulation model that was designed to reproduce the process of building up and breaking down trust.

Trust can be based on routinized behaviour, where the awareness of other people's opportunities for opportunism, and one's own, is dropped, and subsides into subsidiary awareness. One does not continually scout for opportunities for opportunism for oneself, and one is not on the lookout for signs of opportunism from a partner. The rational basis for this is that 'things' have consistently been going 'all right' in the past, and scarce capacity for attention and rational evaluation is spent on other things. Chapter 6 discussed empirical studies that attempted to measure trust and routinization (or 'habituation') as one of its antecedents.

Such routinized trust does not necessarily yield blind in the sense of unconditional trust. There tend to be tolerance levels of trust. These are related to the limits of trustworthiness, indicated above, in two ways. First, the tolerance level entails a sensitivity to conditions that exceed the perceived or assumed limits of a partner's trustworthiness. When such a condition is perceived, one is called to caution: a situation is perceived to arise that may put the partner's competence or loyalty under strain. Second, the tolerance levels entail sensitivity to events or acts that may constitute evidence against assumed trustworthiness, indicating that the limit of a partner's trustworthiness is lower than one thought. When such events or acts are perceived, trust is recalled from subsidiary into focal awareness, and is subjected to critical scrutiny. This may yield a narrowing of one's perceived limits of the partner's trustworthiness. In case of small errors or deviations one may not be able to observe them, or one may prefer to ignore them. Tolerance levels may be largely or partly tacit. They may be underdeveloped and they are subject to learning on the basis of experience. As Herbert Simon indicated long ago, emotions play a role to break out of routinized behaviour and jolt awareness from subsidiary to focal. Anxiety or indignation help to trigger awareness of possible disloyalty. Wisdom then requires that one does not jump to conclusions and tries to coolly assess the evidence, not to attribute malevolence too hastily. Third parties, acting as go-betweens, may help to exert such self-control.

The objection has been raised that with these notions of limits of trustworthiness and tolerance levels of trust the notion of trust is devalued and becomes entirely calculative and self-interested. This objection is not valid, for three reasons. First, within the limits of trust, trust does operate as a default. In other words, within those limits one assumes trustworthiness and refrains from questioning it and demanding safeguards of behaviour. Second, trustworthiness can go beyond self-interest, as will be discussed later. Third, trustworthiness and trust can be non-calculative, as in routinized behaviour, where opportunism is neither sought for oneself nor suspected from others. The fact that this is subject to limits does not deny that within those limits it is real and important.

Non-calculative trustworthiness and trust can take other forms than routinized behaviour. They can be based on values and norms of behaviour, or on feelings of empathy or friendship. This may influence the limits of trustworthiness indicated above, and the tolerance levels of trust. Then, trust can still be adaptive and subject to learning from experience. The foundations of trustworthiness and trust will be summarized in more detail later.

Trust can go even further, to become non-adaptive and rigid, and blind in the sense of unconditional. Then we arrive at the pathology of trust, to be discussed later.

7.2 FORMS OF TRUST

This concerns question 6 from Table 7.1. There are different forms of trust, with different meanings and different objects. One central question is whether trust goes beyond self-interest. Trustworthiness may be purely based on self-interest, in two ways. First, one may stick to an agreement because one is forced to do so, one has no alternatives, that is there are no *opportunities for opportunism*. Second, it may be in one's material interest to stick to the agreement, that is there are no *incentives for opportunism*. This is not what people ordinarily mean by trust. In Chapter 2, I proposed to use the term 'reliance' rather than trust when trustworthiness includes motives of self-interest. 'Real' trust, or trust in the strong sense, goes beyond self-interest. It entails loyalty to an agreement or to a partner, even if there are both opportunities and incentives for opportunism. As in most discourse on trust, I will often use the term 'trust' in a loose sense, leaving aside whether I mean reliance or real trust. When it matters, I will state the intended meaning more precisely.

Real, altruistic trust need not be blind or unconditional. As argued in the previous section, trust, including trust in the strong sense, is likely to have its limits. One will not and should not expect even the greatest of friends to remain loyal under threat of survival, and it is wise to take into account that people may not be able to resist a golden opportunity to defect. Thus, it is wise to assume limits to trustworthiness. Within those limits one can trust.

There are many objects of trust, that is things one can have trust in. One can have trust in things, people, higher powers, forces of nature, institutions and organizations. Trust in powers that one cannot avoid or influence is called confidence rather than trust. This applies to higher powers such as god or institutions. To trust is to expect that 'things will not go wrong', or to neglect the possibility of things going wrong. This neglect may be due to routinized behaviour, naivety or cognitive or psychological defects. Behavioural trust has as many objects as there are causes of action.

Trust in people, behavioural trust, is the most complicated form because there are so many causes of action, which may each fail. Chapter 2 gave a systematic analysis of the different forms of behavioural trust on the basis of a theory of action, for which I adopted a theory of multiple causality from Aristotle. This yields a taxonomy of objects of behavioural trust that is repeated in Table 7.2.

Expectations of behaviour can be broken due to faults on the part of the actor and due to faults in other causes of action. Faults of the actor can be lack of requisite competence, or lack in intentions, that is motivation and goals. I propose two kinds. A weak form is lack of care or commitment to act scrupulously, with effort and attention. This includes shirking. A strong form is opportunism, that is lack of benevolence, which entails theft, expropriation and extortion, or the threat of them. Other causes of action that may fail are the requisite means for action and outside enabling conditions. The latter may fail in the form of unforeseeable disturbances or accidents. In organizations, enabling conditions include the working conditions for the people in it. That includes rules, procedures, incentives and cultural features that guide behaviour, such as role models or 'exemplars' of behaviour.

A major problem is that when something does go wrong, one does not

Table 7.2 Elements of behavioural trust

Form of trust	Object of trust	Type of cause (Aristotle)
Behavioural trust	An actor	Efficient cause
Material trust	Means, inputs	Material cause
Competence trust	Ability, skills, knowledge, to use technology, methods, language, etc.	Formal cause
Intentional trust dedication trust benevolence trust (or goodwill trust)	Aims, intentions Dedication/care benevolence, goodwill, lack of opportunism	Final cause
Conditional trust	Outside enablers, constraints	Conditional cause
Exemplar trust	Role models	Exemplary cause
Informational trust honesty trust	Information Truthfulness	All causes

know which of these possible causes fails. The most serious threat is perhaps that of opportunism. But precisely when a partner is opportunistic he will hide it and claim accident as the cause of failure, or if that is not credible, a temporary lapse of competence. In view of this uncertainty another object of trust arises: the truth of information or the truthfulness or honesty of a partner. Can one believe a partner's explanation of events or his behaviour? As in the case of intentions, we have a weak and a strong form. The weak form of dishonesty entails that information is withheld or given too late. The strong form entails lying and misinformation.

One can have behavioural trust also in organizations, with the expectation that in our dealings with them they will not fail us. One form of this is competence trust in the organization's technology, organizational structure and procedure, yielding an overall, collective ability of an organization to perform. Other forms are material trust in the supply of raw materials, components, labour, and so on, intentional trust in codes and standards of business ethics, honesty trust in the truth of reporting and public statements, and conditional trust in the effects of the institutional environment and competition. Trust in organizations is based on corporate image and reputation, and on one's own dealings with them. Of course, an organization itself does not have an intention, but it has interests and can try to regulate the intentions of its workers to serve those interests. One's trust in an individual may be based on one's trust in the organization he belongs to. Trust in an organization can be based on trust in the people in it. In a later section I expand on the foundations of organizational trust.

Institutions also can be the object of trust, but here we approach confidence rather than trust, to the extent that we generally cannot choose the institutions under which we live, and it is difficult to dodge their influence. In Chapter 1, I defined institutions as enabling, constraining or guiding action, while one cannot freely choose or change them.

7.3   FOUNDATIONS

This concerns questions 7, 8 and 9 from Table 7.1. In Chapter 3, I proposed that trustworthiness has a number of different sources. The source may be universalistic ('macro'), applying to everyone in a culture or community, or particularistic ('micro'), applying to a specific relation. It can be egoistic, oriented only to self-interest, or it can be altruistic, going beyond self-interest. A self-interested macro source is legal coercion. Self-interested micro sources are the material interests one has in a relation: one depends on the value that the partner offers, the partner holds a hostage, or one needs to be seen to act decently in order to preserve a good reputation. Altruistic macro sources are shared values and norms of behaviour. Altruistic micro sources are friendship, empathy, routinization or other bonding that may arise in a specific relationship. With strangers our starting point is 'thin' generalized trust based on general norms, and in a personalized relationship this may develop into 'thick' trust.

There are connections between egoistic and altruistic sources, in that people may be altruistic because they enjoy it for itself, or because they enjoy the social recognition that the following of norms may give. However, they may also have internalized those norms, and the underlying values, to such an extent that they would follow them even without any recognition by others. Social reciprocity is a mix of altruism and egoism; of norm-following and self-interest. It has been characterized as 'short-term altruism for long-term self-interest'. For a gift, one will in general expect something more or less commensurate in return, sooner or later, though one cannot demand it, and one must also not be seen to give the gift with such expectation in mind. The expectation of something in return may be weak or even absent, and then reciprocity can turn into pure altruism. For reasons discussed in the previous sections, altruism need not be unconditional, and can yet be genuine, within limits.

The possible combinations of altruism and self-interest do not reduce my theory to the economist's assumption of calculative self-interest. First, as indicated before, routine behaviour is not calculative. Within the tolerance limits of trust there is no calculation. Second, loyalty may not include any self-interest. Third, even if it does, and there are mixed motives, there is a conflict between them: one is at odds with oneself what to do. One is subjected to opportunistic temptation, which one may try to resist, and to which one may yet succumb. There is no clear, consistent objective function to maximize.

When we turn to the design of relations, some mix of sources of trustworthiness (more precisely: reliability) will be in operation. No universally best mix, regardless of specific conditions, can be specified. Often, trust based on friendship or kinship will not suffice as a basis for cooperation. It may not be sufficiently robust under extremes of temptation. Conversely, material self-interest and coercion are seldom sufficient as a basis for cooperation: one needs trust on the basis of non-egotistic sources to the extent that one cannot fully control the partner's conduct by threat, and to make such fragile basis for cooperation more resilient.

Resilience arises from what Hirschman called voice. In exit, one walks out when dissatisfied, avoiding argument. That is, one quits from one's job, fires people, sells shares or part of a firm. In voice, the first response is not to walk out, but to seek amends. One reports one's dissatisfaction, asks for an explanation, welcomes criticism and asks for and offers help to 'work things out' together by solving problems, repairing shortcomings and eliminating misunderstandings.

Empathy is crucial for this. That entails sympathetic perceptiveness and imagination: the ability to see and respect the other's goals, to imagine and regret the effects of one's own faults for the other, and to make an effort to prevent them. Empathy also enables one to see when the limits of the other's trustworthiness are or will be exceeded, due to the pressures and temptations he is subjected to, and to have a reasonable guess where the limits lie, and on what conditions they depend, as discussed earlier. Therefore, empathy provides the basis for both trustworthiness and trust, as well as the basis for the limits of both. The same perceptiveness that leads one to assess the damage one may cause to others leads one to assess conditions where the other may cause damage.

As noted above, we can have trust in organizations, which is related to trust in the people in them. When we base organizational trust on trust in its people, and when we base trust in the people on trust in the organization, we need to carefully take into account the position and role of those people in the organization. Are their competencies and intentions supported and backed up by the organization? Are the interests and the culture of the organization properly endorsed and implemented by the people? If the basis for one's trust in an employee is friendship or empathy that has built up in the course of the relationship with him, is this in line with the interest of his firm, and with the norms of conduct that form part of the firm's culture? If not, to what extent can he back up his promises nevertheless, and is there a risk that he will be forced to renege on his promises when found out? Conversely, if one's trust in the organization is based on the fact that its interests demand loyalty to an agreement, can one rely on the people implementing them? Suppose there is personal animosity between you and them. Could they sabotage the agreement and get away with it?

Trustworthiness of organizations depends on their conditions and safeguards of survival. Such safeguards depend on industry conditions, such as the effectiveness and importance of reputation mechanisms, and the intensity of price competition. For example, in order to survive, the organization may have to guard its reputation for quality, protecting its brand names. Clearly, a firm that is under great pressure to make all the profit it can get and to cut costs where it can, as a matter of sheer survival, can afford less benevolence at the sacrifice of profit, than a firm that is not under such pressure. This yields differences especially between industries. In Chapter 3, I mentioned the example of the car industry, especially in a situation of excess capacity, in comparison with a firm that has a state-protected monopoly in the exploration and production of natural gas.

Summing up, in dealing with organizations one has to consider the basis for reliance both on the people one is dealing with and on the organization. What mix of foundations of reliance is there on the different levels, of people and organization, and how consistent are they, that is to what extent do they support or compensate for each other? Structure of ownership and control, organizational culture and procedures for guiding, supporting and controlling people in their organizational roles have a crucial mediating role here, and become part of the basis for organizational trust.

Chapter 3 also discussed modes of trust 'production', that is the ways in which one can infer trustworthiness from observed or reputed behaviour, and ways to enhance the development of trust. As proposed by Zucker, to some extent sources of trustworthiness can be inferred from the availability and effectiveness of institutions (such as laws and judiciary, professional standards), and personal characteristics of various kinds (such as membership of family or of professional, cultural or religious associations, or educational achievements). However, Zucker also recognized that much is derived as 'process based trust' in interactions in specific relations. Earlier, I pointed out that when things go wrong, this may be due to a variety of causes, some of which cannot be blamed on the partner. Conversely, as recognized by Deutsch, when results from interaction are favourable, one can infer trustworthiness, in the strong sense of trust, only when the outcome was due to conscious effort of the partner, he had to make a sacrifice for it and does not masochistically enjoy sacrifice. Power can have an adverse effect on one's trust. If one is very powerful, one tends to harbour more suspicion that people subjected to one's power are trustworthy only because they have no choice. Thus power can breed suspicion, and absolute power can yield rampant paranoia.

Chapter 3 also discussed the dynamics of trust: how it develops, deepens or breaks down. When the expectation of trust is not fulfilled, this does not necessarily yield a breach of trust. Remember that trust can have as many objects as there are causes of action. One may observe that external conditions rather than a partner's behaviour were the cause of disappointing outcomes. It is possible that this cannot be seen, but is claimed by the partner as an explanation. Will the trustor accept the explanation, or will he see it as an excuse for something else: for lack of dedication or competence, or worse, a sign of opportunism? Will he, perhaps, turn a blind eye to the mishap, negate evidence of incompetence or opportunism out of cognitive dissonance or blind trust? Or will he give the partner the benefit of the doubt, but remain alert to future mishaps and their possible causes? Or will he jump to a conclusion of opportunism? Which is the case will depend on a number of things: the sources of previous trust or suspicion, the history of the relationship, the psychological make-up and the personal experience of the trustor, external social and economic conditions (for example intensity of price competition).

Broken expectations may be evidence of learning, and are then to be appreciated. The main purpose of the relation may be to learn, that is to obtain new insights from the partner, or to jointly produce new knowledge. This view is underpinned by my theory of cognition, summarized in Chapter 1. If our cognition is indeed based on categories that we construct in interaction with our environment, then our knowledge is not objective, and our only hope for correcting our errors is to reap the benefit of different insights from others, with different categories based on different experience. The tension of disagreement then is an essential part of the process.

The joint solution of conflict can enhance and deepen trust, in several ways. One way is that it yields learning, as just indicated, which confirms the value of the relation and increases mutual commitment. Another way is that the fact that problems are solved in itself reduces perceived risk in the relation. The conflict yielded a test of the strength of mutual benevolence and the dedication to 'work things out', in a mutual 'give and take'. The fact that the relation survived the test strengthens trust in the strength and resilience of benevolence and dedication. This is how the process of ongoing and successful relations, with solutions of conflicts, can deepen trust.

The positive effect of the solution of conflicts carries force especially because the reverse is so often observed, that under adverse conditions a relation breaks down in mutual recrimination and suspicion. This can easily arise especially when the stakes are high at the beginning of a relation between strangers. As indicated, when things do not go all right, this may be due to accident, lack of dedication, lack of competence or opportunism. If in fact the cause is opportunism, this will not be admitted. Knowing this, one may suspect opportunism even when it is denied, or for the suspicious especially when it is strongly denied. In this delicate stage of a beginning relation with high stakes of dependence, a third party may play a useful role in eliminating such incipient misunderstandings and attributions of fault before suspicion becomes so large, and evokes such hostile reactions from the unjustly accused partner, that it escalates beyond repair.

All this is connected with the idea of trust as a default, discussed before, and the notions of limits of trustworthiness and tolerance levels of trust. In interaction, one may have developed an explicit or implicit assessment of the partner's trustworthiness, and a tolerance level for deviant behaviour. A positive cycle of reciprocation can raise the limit of trustworthiness and widen the tolerance level. Deviant behaviour, on the other hand, triggers awareness and possibly the beginning of suspicion. It may narrow tolerance and reduce the inferred limit of trustworthiness. Events that previously were given the benefit of the doubt, or were even not noticed, may now be scrutinized for evidence of untrustworthiness. As a result, deviant behaviour is sooner perceived, and a spiral of suspicion may be set in motion. Again, intermediaries may play an important role here, to stop such a dynamic from gaining momentum.

In view of this potential self-reinforcing dynamic of trust and suspicion, honesty and trust in honesty are crucial. Honesty here is openness: giving appropriate and truthful information. Dishonesty is the withholding or distortion of appropriate information. Honesty and trust reinforce each other, as suspicion and dishonesty do. Honesty serves to deal with deviant phenomena without narrowing tolerance levels and without reducing perceived limits of trustworthiness. They may even widen both, and thereby deepen trust.

When there is no intentional trust (that is trust in dedication and benevolence), one is afraid to be honest, lest the partner will misuse information for opportunistic purposes or to relax the level of his dedication. If there is lack of trust in dedication, one may think praise will cause slack. If there is lack of trust in benevolence, one may think that information on one's needs, opportunities and their limits, or competencies will be used opportunistically in power play, such as bargaining, reduction of one's options for choice, or treating sensitive information as a hostage (blackmail).

However, there is also a subtle reason for dishonesty that is benevolent. One may withhold criticism out of fear of (further) reducing a partner's self-confidence. When the other side perceives that he is receiving neither trust nor information, he is likely to reciprocate with dishonesty. One elementary lesson is the following. When a disaster is foreseen, one is tempted to keep it secret. This should be resisted. Here is a chance to win trust by announcing the problem before it becomes manifest, asking for help and engaging in a joint effort to redress or mitigate the disaster.

A special problem here lies in the situation where collaboration has to develop between partners who are unequal in their dependence on each other. The most dependent partner may be suspicious because of the one-sided risk he runs, whereby he starts the relation on the basis of mistrust or apprehension, and is on the lookout for signs of opportunistic exploitation of his dependence. His perceived limits of trustworthiness and his tolerance levels are narrow. This is a special case of a more general phenomenon that lack of self-confidence engenders mistrust, which breeds reciprocal mistrust. Earlier, I identified a benevolent reason for dishonesty, not to reduce a partner's self-confidence or expose his weakness. Here, it becomes clear that this can be in one's self-interest, not to make the partner more apprehensive, defensive and suspicious.

With his 'crude law of social relations', Deutsch suggested that there is circular causation between characteristics of participants and the results of interaction: effects elicited by a given type of social relationship (cooperative or competitive) tend also to elicit that type of social relationship. If this is true, then one must be very careful how to start a relationship, because it may be difficult to get out of the initial mode of interaction. This yields a lesson for the development of collaboration, including the preparation of an alliance or merger. Often, in the initial situation of bargaining, games are played in the manoeuvring for position that set the relation going in a mode of rivalry, which may then be difficult to turn around to cooperation, in the stage of implementation. Perhaps, there is another role for a third party here: to guide negotiations prior to collaboration.

Suppose two strangers need to rely on each other, with large dependence and much at stake, and there is no basis for trust from earlier experience, reputation, advice from a third party, kinship, or apparent values and norms of behaviour. Then they may be tempted to make a safeguard in the form of an extensive contract to limit 'opportunities for opportunism'. The relation starts in an atmosphere of mistrust and rivalry, which may be difficult to turn around into one that allows for the building and deepening of trust. The lesson from this is that a good way to start a relation between such strangers is to take small steps that are likely to yield positive results soon, with limited risk, so an extensive contract against opportunism is not needed, and a basis for trust may soon be built.

Process-based trust can move through several stages. For people who are not acquainted ex ante, at the beginning of the process calculativeness may prevail. This depends on the strength of 'thin', generalized trust. When it is weak, the relation may nevertheless be hazarded in view of potential gains or needs. One will be forced to build trust when there is strong mutual dependence. The greater the gain or urgency, the more risk one may be willing to take. Partners are given the benefit of the doubt, within certain margins of risk left by incomplete contracts, accepted on the basis of some heuristic that takes into account prevailing ethics, customs, experience, urgency and the intrinsic value attached to trust. Perceived limits of trustworthiness and tolerance levels of trust may initially be quite narrow. As the relation begins to generate value, trust in both competence and intention may deepen due to perception and understanding of the sources of both. Next, bonds of friendship and identification with each others' interests may develop to deepen trust further, and routinization may weaken the awareness of risk. Perceived limits of trustworthiness and tolerance widen. Here, a process of sharing experience plays a crucial role.

Zand proposed a cycle in which trust engenders openness, yielding information which provides a basis for the exertion and acceptance of mutual influence, which yields the willingness to demand less and accept more control from the partner, which further engenders trust. In other words, the provision of information based on trust promotes responsiveness to trust, which may already be latent but requires a trigger of information that has the dual function of demonstrating trust and reducing the risk of trust reciprocation. This can set a positive dynamic of trust going. Here, we see a positive relation between trust and information: A trusts B and therefore gives information (even if B could use that to the detriment of A), which makes B trust A and give information in return. The analysis seems to come close to the notion of voice, as opposed to exit.

7.4   FUNCTIONS

This concerns questions 1 and 2 from Table 7.1. Trust is indispensable and pervasive for several reasons. Trust-based behaviour has intrinsic value. It is often seen as preferable even if it yields less profit. It often yields greater efficiency because governance only by contract and self-interest may be costly or infeasible due to uncertainty. Governance on the basis of coercion or self-interest always has to be supplemented by trust, because future contingencies and motives are never completely known, and language cannot yield certainty of meaning, so that contracts and self-interest always leave a gap of uncertainty. While the extent of this uncertainty depends on states of the world, the fact of its existence does not: to a greater or lesser extent it is always there. At that point, where the gap of uncertainty yawns, we must surrender to trust or die from inaction. At that point trust is blind, in the sense that it is based on tacit assumption, not rational evaluation, let alone calculation, or even affect of love or friendship, or revisable routines. However, this blindness does not mean that trust is unconditional. There is a limit, where trust ends and conditions begin. The functioning of trust in the economy, in combination with various instruments of governance, depending on conditions, was analysed in Chapter 4.

Trust enables relations, in economies and organizations, and reduces transaction costs by reducing relational risk. Such reduction of relational risk is the purpose of 'governance'. Trust does not operate on its own, but in varying combinations with other instruments of governance, such as contracts, mutual dependence, hostages, reputation mechanisms, intermediaries, and structure of networks.

In my analysis of inter-organizational relations, I included learning: the utilization of complementary sources of knowledge between actors, and the joint production of new knowledge. A central feature in this is the management of cognitive distance. This notion was discussed in Chapter 1. In order to achieve a common purpose, one needs a sufficient cognitive alignment, of perceptions, interpretations, evaluations and goals, that is limited cognitive distance. The 'tightness' of the focus depends on the need for efficient exploitation of existing competencies relative to the need for exploration of new ones. This depends on the industry, the need and rate of innovation and the place of a firm in the industry. This yields the notion of a firm as a focusing device. However, such focus or cognitive proximity yields a risk of myopia, and one needs complementary cognitive competence in outside relations, at sufficient cognitive distance. This distance has to be sufficiently large to yield novel insights, but not too large to preclude mutual understanding.

There are two kinds of relational risk: risks of dependence ('hold-up') and risk of loss of knowledge ('spillover'). The risk of dependence or hold-up is taken from transaction cost economics. In spite of the fundamental objections to that theory, discussed in Chapter 1, here the theory is still very useful. When one is unilaterally dependent on a partner, he may be tempted to take opportunistic advantage of that and extort a greater share of added value. Can we trust the partner not to do this? On what could such trust be based? Dependence arises especially from switching costs: switching from the present partner to another. Such costs arise, in particular, from investments which are specific for the partner or the relationship, cannot be recouped and have to be made anew in another relationship. Such investments have to be made up front, as part of an agreement, and once they are made one is 'locked in'.

To the classic cases of specific investments, I add specific investments in crossing cognitive distance: in building appropriate absorptive capacity and capacity to make oneself understood to the partner. This may have a large specific component, particularly when the knowledge involved is tacit. Tacitness of knowledge tends to arise especially in early stages of innovation, where one has hit upon new ways of doing things without knowing why or even how, precisely, this works. I also add the building of process trust as a specific investment. By definition the process of interaction on which the building of trust is based, as discussed in Chapter 3, is specific to the relationship.

The mutual exchange of information, to achieve understanding and to utilize complementary cognitive competencies, also creates a second type of risk: the risk of 'spillover' to competitors of core competence, which can jeopardize competitive position. Of course, the whole point of utilizing complementary sources of knowledge is to create and utilize knowledge flows between partners. This may even occur between competitors, to jointly produce new technology or to set technological standards in order to conquer markets. There is a danger of being too protective of knowledge, of myopically attaching too much weight to appropriability, while neglecting the dynamic of new knowledge creation in a network of firms, and the development of communicative and learning capacity. Spillover is not a real threat when the knowledge involved is not part of one's core competence and competitive advantage, or when competitors would not be able to grasp or implement the knowledge, or when by the time they are able to do so the knowledge has shifted.

When the problem of spillover does arise, it entails issues of trust. To what extent are partners, or other members of one's network, motivated not to steal competitive advantage. To what extent are they competent and committed to guard against accidental spillover to the partner's competitors. Information and knowledge can play the role of 'hostages'. They yield the recipient power: he may threaten to divulge it to your competitors. He may use this, for example, to keep you away from contacts with his competitors. Conversely, the information you receive from a partner may limit access to other parties that are potential competitors to the focal partner.

In Chapter 4, I focused on the governance of problems related to intentional trust, that is intentions to perform to the best of one's ability and to honour agreements. This includes trust in benevolence (absence of opportunism) and in commitment or care. I do this in terms of risk control: the control of the two risks of hold-up and spillover indicated before.

To mitigate risks of dependence one may eliminate the cause of dependence, or exert direct control on possible opportunistic actions, or reduce 'opportunities for opportunism', associated with scope for action left in contracts and the monitoring of compliance, or reduce 'inclinations to utilize such opportunities'. The latter can be based on incentives of self-interest or on loyalty.

This yields the following instruments for governance. One solution of course is to prevent the risk from arising: do not engage in specific investments that give rise to the risk of hold-up, do not give information that may constitute a threat of spillover. I call this 'evasion'. If one does accept specific investments and information exchange, one may control risk by direct control of actions, by choosing integration under a 'hierarchy' as the form of governance. Alternatively, one may relinquish such centralized control, and try to settle risks of transactions between autonomous parties. One way to do this is to reduce 'opportunities for opportunism', with obligational contracting as the form of governance, by means of formal, legal contracts and the monitoring needed to enforce them. However, as indicated already in transaction cost economics, complete contingent contracting is impossible due to uncertainty. If opportunities for opportunism cannot be eliminated, one can aim to reduce inclinations to utilize such opportunities by reducing the incentives to do so, in the governance form of relational contracting. For this one may use some judicious mixture of symmetric mutual dependence, shared ownership, hostages and reputation mechanisms. This is relational contracting on the basis of self-interest. Perhaps relational contracting can also be interpreted to include social rather than only economic reciprocity. However that may be, what I add here is governance beyond self-interest, on the basis of trust, in the narrow, strong sense of 'real' trust. Here one reduces inclinations to utilize opportunities for opportunism on the basis of some degree of loyalty, which may be based on ethics, empathy, kinship or habituation/routinization.

Risks of hold-up and spillover depend on one's position in a network of relations, and one may therefore control those risks by selecting an appropriate position in such a network, or designing the network around one's position. This strategy does not seem to fit in any of the existing forms of governance (integration, obligational and relational contracting). Perhaps it constitutes a fourth form of governance, which we might call 'positional governance'. However, perhaps one can argue that it is a special form of relational contracting. Finally, one can also make good use of intermediaries, or third parties or go-betweens. The instruments for risk control are repeated in Table 7.3.

In Chapter 4, I identified eight roles for a go-between. The first was not related to governance but helps partners to cross cognitive distance. The second was to help solve the 'revelation problem': to assess the value of information in exchange before it is actually exchanged. The third was to help control spillover: to see to it that acquired knowledge is not used to

Table 7.3   Instruments for control of relational risk

Instrument	Description
Evasion	Don't yield sensitive information and don't engage in specific investments
Integration	Unified administrative control, i.e. by merger or acquisition
Obligational contracting	Contracts to control hold-up, and patenting to control spillover
Relational contracting with incentives from self-interest economic reciprocity	Use of mutual dependence, ownership of assets or information, hostages, reputation mechanisms
Relational contracting with loyalty as a basis for trust (in the strong sense), social reciprocity	Based on values and norms of conduct, personal bonds, routinization
Network structure	One's position, in terms of density, centrality, spanning holes
Roles of a go-between	Trilateral governance, solving the revelation problem, monitoring, hostage keeping, sieve and amplifier of reputation

compete, and that it does not spill over to competitors. The fourth is to act as a guardian of hostages. The fifth is taken from transaction cost economics: trilateral governance, to replace costly contracting when that would not be worth the effort due to small volume or frequency of transactions. The sixth, and perhaps most crucial role, is to act as an intermediary in the building of trust. The seventh is to help in the timely and least destructive ending of relations. The eighth is to act as a lookout, a sieve, a channel and an amplifier in reputation mechanisms.

Most of these roles are especially important in innovation. There, exchange of knowledge is crucial, with corresponding risks of spillover, and specific investments need to be made to set up mutual understanding and cooperation. There are corresponding risks of hold-up, while especially in innovation the competencies and intentions of strangers are difficult to judge. Especially in innovation detailed contracts tend to have an adverse effect of a straitjacket, constraining the variety of actions and initiatives that innovation requires. Third party arbitration then yields a less constraining alternative, in trilateral governance and the development of trust instead of using detailed contracts to preclude opportunism.

Note that in all roles it is crucial that the go-between command trust in both his competence and his intentions. He should be competent concerning the technologies involved, and concerning the relational skills required. He should be known to be impartial and incorruptible. He should have an interest to act scrupulously, with a view to his reputation as a go-between. There is a range of actors who could possibly play these roles, and not all roles have to be played by a single actor. Possible go-betweens are banks, consultants, interlocking directorates, and local government agencies, such as municipalities or development agencies, or subsidized technology transfer centres.

There will rarely be exclusive use of only one of the instruments of governance. This raises the question where and how they complement each other, and when and how they may be in conflict. Empirical research has shown that contract and trust are at least as much complements as they are substitutes. Trust can and in fact does indeed operate as a substitute for detailed contracts, in so far as those are designed to foreclose opportunism. However, there may be detailed contracts for other reasons, notably to act as an aid to memory, a record of conclusions how to technically coordinate complex processes. That can very well be complementary to trust. Trust may be needed as a precondition for a contract. Setting up a contract can itself be a costly affair, and constitutes a specific investment in its own right. One may require ex ante trust before taking on the risk involved in setting up such a contract. When this is not in place, one may start a relationship in small steps to build up sufficient trust and then consolidate the relation in a contract. A simple legal contract may be used more or less symbolically, to mark and celebrate what is in fact a psychological or relational contract. Finally, a contract has to be based on trust in the underlying institutions that support it, but that is a different matter.

A particularly productive complementarity lies in the combination between trust and mutual dependence. Balanced, two-sided specific investments create dependence and the risk of hold-up on both sides of a bilateral relation. When well chosen, they also create mutual dependence, by creating unique value for the partner. Thus, one runs a risk of dependence (hold-up due to specific investments) but also creates one for the partner (unique value). The causality of relational risk has many directions and loops, as was demonstrated in the discussion of empirical research in Chapter 6. The attraction of managing relational risk by balance of mutual dependence is that it is productive: it does not hamper collaboration, as a detailed contract might, but accelerates it by adding more value. However, it is also vulnerable to change. The balance of dependence may be disrupted by a change of technology, the appearance of a new player in the field who is attractive to one of the partners, a change in technology or in market conditions, or a difference between the partners in their rates of learning and ongoing development of competencies. In view of this, balance of dependence may have to be supplemented by trust, in mutual give and take, in voice rather than exit. There, partners can rely on each other not to exit as soon as the balance of dependence is disturbed, but to try and redress the balance, by mutual investment or help. Of course, there is a limit to this. If in spite of joint efforts the imbalance of value continues and deepens, the relationship may have to be disentangled.

Chapter 4 also analysed the institutional conditions for trust and other instruments of governance. Contractual sources of trustworthiness (or more accurately: reliability) require appropriate and effective institutions: appropriate laws of property and trade, reliable and competent lawyers, non-corrupt police and judiciary, and so on. These vary considerably between countries. Clearly, values and norms of social conduct also vary greatly between countries, and may change in time, though slowly. Third parties or go-betweens form an important element in the institutional structure that supports, or fails to support, trust.

Based on earlier publications, Chapter 4 gave an analysis of different generic systems of innovation, in terms of such institutional differences, the basis they offer for governance of inter-firm relations, and the effects on innovative performance. The analysis yielded two such systems. In one, firms are more autonomous, engaged in ad-hoc, largely contractual relations, engage in mergers and acquisitions and divestments, and are generally oriented to exit. The other system is orientated towards more or less durable inter-firm relations and networks, based on voice. The first system exhibits more flexibility, and therefore more potential for radical Schumpeterian creative destruction and novel combinations. The second is better in incremental innovation and the diffusion of innovations. However, some doubt was raised on this. Radical innovations also may require more or less durable relations, to recoup the specific investments involved in mutual investment in training, crossing cognitive distance and building trust.

Chapter 4 also analysed the locality of trust: to what extent and why are trust and governance spatially embedded, tied to location? I argued that intensive local interaction may be needed to develop a basis for mutual understanding or absorptive capacity, on the basis of shared tacit categories of cognition, in an epistemic community. However, having built that, the members can disband and communicate at a distance, with regular meetings to maintain and develop their shared basis for cognition and communication. I suggested that arguments for shared locality may lie more on the side of governance than on the side of competence. To the extent that trust is needed or advantageous, the development of thick trust in relations requires on-line visual cues from observed activities and body language. For the moment, the inclusion of such on-line, real-time visual information is not yet technically and commercially feasible for use on a large scale. In future it no doubt will be. However, there may be other reasons for periods of shared locality. One is that to make inferences of trustworthiness one may need to observe other, tangential actions of partners, or to tap into the local gossip that is part of reputation systems. This relates to the process dynamics of trust discussed in the previous section. Here also, web-based reputation mechanisms will no doubt develop, but the question is to what extent they have sufficient scope and richness. A second reason is that to employ mechanisms of reciprocity one needs to know what the established rules are concerning the timing and type of reciprocal gifts or services. One may find this out from a local agent, but it may also be necessary to have experience from local presence.

However, as for cognitive competence, this local basis for governance may be temporary: one may spend some time locally to develop and maintain the basis for governance, and then utilize it from a distance. In other words, while shared locality may remain important, it might be maintained off and on, in an alternation of meetings and dispersion. The meetings serve the need to develop shared tacit cognitive categories and to establish trust, and the dispersion guarantees the maintenance of cognitive distance, with participants tapping into a variety of localities where they operate daily, with different environments for learning, generating different insights.

7.5 FAILURES

This concerns question 3 from Table 7.1. Chapter 5 recognized pathologies of trust and mistrust on the micro level of people and organizations, and on the macro level of economic systems.

Trust becomes pathological not when it is blind in the sense that it assumes trustworthiness in the absence of complete evidence, because it must inevitably do that. Trust and mistrust become pathological when they become blind in the sense of being unconditional, that is when they disallow or persistently ignore or negate evidence that would contradict them. There is asymmetry here between trust and mistrust. Pathological mistrust will keep one from entering into relations, which robs one of the opportunity of favourable experience. When relations are inevitable, pathological mistrust leads one to ignore or negate evidence of trustworthiness. This is particularly easy for the powerful, because for them it stands to reason that people cooperate only because they have no alternative or because it is in their interest. Trustworthiness in the strong sense does not get a chance to prove itself.

Pathological trust invites disaster, but ignores or negates it. This may be due to cognitive defects: one is not able to adequately interpret the evidence. It can also be due to both excess and shortage of self-confidence. Excess self-confidence can lead one to underestimate potential or actual damage. However, this is subject to learning: persistent damage is likely to correct excess self-confidence. Lack of self-confidence, or more generally lack of perceived options, can make perceived dependence on others inevitable, and one may then have confidence in them out of despair. Evidence of untrustworthiness is hard to admit, because one has no choice but to submit to it. We recognize this in religious faith: one cannot avoid God and hence one has confidence in him no matter what happens. Punishment is seen as just, cleansing, or as a test.

Pathologies can also arise on the level of organizations. An atmosphere of gossip or intrigue, with pathological mistrust can sway organizations. Conversely, a culture of trust and benevolence may become excessive and oppressive, turning the expression of criticism into a taboo. This obstructs creative conflict. It also blocks direct voice of complaints, thereby prevents fast and reliable direct solutions between partners in the conflict. This can lead to an accumulation of unresolved conflict, biasing perception towards evidence of incompetence or malevolence. It can lead to malicious gossip that perpetuates and deepens wrongful attributions and misunderstandings, and turns misperceptions into realities. As discussed earlier, trust building is based on the conveyance of appropriate information, mutuality of influence, encouragement of self-control and avoidance of the abuse of the vulnerability of others. Each of these elements of the process can be enabled or frustrated by organizational structure, process or culture. Once established as part of organizational culture, an atmosphere of trust or mistrust can perpetuate itself in the process of socialization to which newcomers are subjected.

Between organizations, excesses of (mis)trust can also arise for a number of reasons. As in the case of trust in people, they may be due to defects of information and understanding. In organizations also there may be feelings of omnipotence, impulsiveness, nonchalance, or greed, with an overemphasis of the present relative to later adverse effects, and despair. Less likely on the firm level are masochism and an excessive drive towards social conformity, or an unconditional drive to virtue, 'turning the other cheek' when deceived, or becoming a martyr for some higher cause. In organizations also, excessive trust may be based on excess of self-trust. Overconfidence may yield an underestimation of the power of others to cause harm. Lack of self-confidence may lead one to underestimate one's value to others, and thereby to overestimate one's risk of dependence, yielding an excessive tendency towards mistrust. Organizations also may be dependent on others to such an extent that one has no option of exit, and can only hope that the others will be benevolent, and pretend that they are.

On the macro level, trust and social capital can be counterproductive. Obligations, derived from legal ties or ties of reciprocity, can create an obstacle to change in general and to change of network configurations in particular. They yield stability, but the downside of that may be lack of flexibility. One may get stuck to partners that are falling behind. This is a liability especially for the goal of learning and innovation. To the extent that relations are durable, tight and exclusive, they can yield cognitive inbreeding: a convergence of cognition that eliminates the novelty and variety that are needed for innovation. Too much consensus can lead to 'group think' that blocks the creativity offered by different views, and produces inertia. It can also breed prejudice, discrimination and paranoia.

Lack of learning and the lack of flexibility in network configuration are particularly serious under conditions of radical change that require frequent break-up of relations to cope with Schumpeterian 'novel combinations' and 'creative destruction'. This indicates one of several contingencies: for incremental innovation tight networks may have a net positive effect, while for radical innovation they may constitute a liability. Networks that are exclusionary, harbouring little competition and barring entry to potential competitors, will reduce the urge towards efficiency and innovation.

Earlier, I compared two 'generic systems' of innovation. A network type of system with more or less durable and more or less exclusive relations can be strong in incremental innovation and radical innovation that requires the development of epistemic communities as a basis for new knowledge and technology. A disintegrated, volatile structure with ad-hoc, short-term relations that are easily broken up is strong in its flexibility of novel combinations, needed for radical innovation. Chapter 5 considered the possibility of a 'third way', in which relations are no more durable than needed for innovation, and demand no exclusiveness. The latter is feasible when the speed of change is so fast that spillover is no longer an issue.

7.6   FIGURES AND FURTHER RESEARCH

This concerns question 10 from Table 7.1. Chapter 6 offered a survey of research in which attempts were made to measure and model trust, its antecedents and its effects. In empirical research, factor analytic methods were used to measure the latent variables associated with trust, its determinants, and its effects, on the basis of indicators that were measured in surveys on the basis of Likert scales. Econometric models were used to test hypotheses about the determinants of trust and the effects of trust on relational risk. Techniques were also used (LISREL) that allow for circular causality, to investigate different causal loops. One such loop is that while on the one hand specific investments make for dependence, and hence a risk of hold-up, which inhibits such investments, on the other hand they can make the partner dependent, whereby his incentives to opportunism are reduced, which stimulates such investment. Most of the hypotheses derived from the analysis of preceding chapters, as discussed above, were confirmed. The methodology was used to derive the causal structures underlying buyer–supplier relations in the US, Japan and the EU. The results indicate a high degree of similarity in underlying causality. A shortcoming of this research is that it attempts to infer time-based effects on the basis of cross-section studies. To proceed further, research is needed of panels of relations that develop in time.

Chapter 6 also reported on an attempt to model the process of the production and breakdown of trust by means of simulation (using agent-based computational methods). This was used, in particular, to model the notion of a limit of trustworthiness and a weight attached to trust which are both adaptive in the light of experience. A central purpose was to investigate under what conditions trust can survive when realized profit is the condition for survival and the goal of learning. Analyses are under way. The model is open to much further improvement, both in the process of learning that it models and in the features of governance that it incorporates.

Much more process analysis is needed on the micro level of people and their interactions within and between organizations, to test and further develop insights in the process dynamics of trust. This needs to include considerations from social psychology and social dynamics of interaction. In this book I have tried to incorporate such elements, but there is much scope for developing further insights. While trust in inter-firm relations has received much attention in empirical research, much less effort in empirical work has been spent on intra-organizational trust (compare Grey and Garsten 2001). This yields an important priority for further research.

References

Albert, M. (1993), *Capitalism against Capitalism* (translated from the French), London: Whurr Publishers.

Alchian, A. (1950), 'Uncertainty, evolution and economic theory', *The Journal of Political Economy*, **43**/1: 211–21.

Archer, M.S. (1995), *Realist Social Theory: The Morphogenetic Approach*, Cambridge: Cambridge University Press.

——(1974), *The Limits of Organization*, New York: W.W. Norton.

Arthur, W. Brian (1991), 'Designing economic agents that act like human agents: A behavioral approach to bounded rationality', *American Economic Review*, **81**/2: 353–9.

——(1993), 'On designing economic agents that behave like human agents', *Journal of Evolutionary Economics*: **3**/1: 1–22.

Axelrod, R. (1984), *The Evolution of Cooperation*, New York: Basic Books.

Bachmann, R. (2000), 'Conclusion: Trust – Conceptual Aspects of a Complex Phenomenon', in C. Lane and R. Bachmann (eds), *Trust Within and Between Organizations*, Oxford: Oxford University Press, paperback edition.

Baker, W.E. and D. Obstfeld (1999), 'Social capital by design: Structures, strategies, and institutional context', in R. Leenders and S.M. Gabbay (eds), *Corporate Social Capital and Liability*, Dordrecht: Kluwer, pp. 88–105.

Barkow, J., L. Cosmides and J. Tooby (1992), *The Adapted Mind: Evolutionary Psychology and the Generation of Culture*, Oxford: Oxford University Press.

Bazerman, M. (1998), *Judgement in Managerial Decision Making*, New York: Wiley.

Berger, J., N.G. Noorderhaven and B. Nooteboom (1995), 'The determinants of supplier dependence: An empirical study', in J. Groenewegen, C. Pitelis and S.E. Sjöstrand (eds), *On Economic Institutions; Theory and Applications*, Aldershot: Edward Elgar: 195–212.

Blau, P.M. (1964), *Exchange and Power in Social Life*, New York: Wiley.

Bleeke, J. and D. Ernst (1991), 'The way to win in cross-border alliances', *Harvard Business Review*, November/December: 127–35.

Bogenrieder, I. (2001), 'Not only communities of practice: An exploration of structural forms of learning in groups', Working Paper, Rotterdam School of Management, Erasmus University Rotterdam: ERS-2001-23-Org.

Booker, L.B., D.E. Goldberg and J.H. Holland (1989), 'Classifier systems and genetic algorithms', *Artificial Intelligence*, **40**: 235–82.

Bradach, J.L. and R.G. Eccles (1989), 'Markets versus hierarchies: From ideal types to plural forms', in W.R. Scott (ed.), *Annual Review of Sociology*, **15**: 97–118.

Brass, D.J. and G. Labianca (1999), 'Social capital, social liabilities, and social resources management', in R. Th. A.J. Leenders and S.M. Gabbay (eds), *Corporate Social Capital and Liability*, Dordrecht: Kluwer: 323–40.

Brown, J.S. and P. Duguid (1996), 'Organizational learning and communities of practice', in M.D. Cohen, and L.S. Sproull (eds), *Organizational Learning*, London: Sage, 58–82. First printed in 1991 *Organization Science*, **2**/1.

Buckley, P.J. and M. Casson (1988), 'A theory of cooperation in international business', in Contractor and Lorange (eds), *Cooperative Strategies in International Business*, Lexington Books.

Burt, R.S. (1992), *Structural Holes: The Social Structure of Competition*, Cambridge, MA: Harvard University Press.

Butler, R. (2001), 'Review of Lane and Bachmann (1998)', *Organization Studies*, **22**/2: 367–9.

Campbell, D. and D. Harris (1993), 'Flexibility in long-term contractual relationships: The role of cooperation', *Journal of Law and Society*, **20**/2: 263–323.

Casson, M. (1991), *The Economics of Business Culture*, Oxford: Clarendon Press.

——(1995), *The Organization of International Business: Studies in the Economics of Trust*, Aldershot: Edward Elgar.

Chesbrough, H.W. and D.J. Teece (1996), 'When is virtual virtuous? Organizing for innovation', *Harvard Business Review*, Jan.–Feb.: 65–73.

Child, J. (2001), 'Trust and international strategic alliances', in Lane and Bachmann (eds), *Trust Within and Between Organizations*, Oxford: Oxford University Press: 241–72.

Chiles, T.H. and J.F. McMackin (1996), 'Integrating variable risk preferences, trust and transacton cost economics', *Academy of Management Review*, **21**/7: 73–99.

Choo, C.W. (1998), *The Knowing Organization*, Oxford: Oxford University Press.

Coase, R. (1937), 'The nature of the firm', *Economica*, N.S. **4**: 386–405.

——(1998), 'The new institutional economics', *American Economic Review* **88**/2: 72–74.

Cohen, M.D. and D.A. Levinthal (1990), 'Absorptive capacity: A new perspective on learning and innovation', *Administrative Science Quarterly*, **35**: 128–52.

——and P. Bacdayan (1996), 'Organizational routines are stored as procedural memory', in M.D. Cohen and L.S. Sproull (eds). *Organizational Learning*, London: Sage: 403–30; first printed in *Organization Science*, **5**/4, in 1994.

Coleman J.S. (1988), 'Social capital in the creation of human capital', *American Journal of Sociology*, **94** (special supplement): 95–120.

Cosmides, L. and J. Tooby (1992), 'Cognitive adaptations for social exchange', in H. Barkow, L. Cosmides and J. Tooby, *The Adapted Mind*, Oxford: Oxford University Press: 163–228.

Cusumano, M.A. and T. Fujimoto (1991), 'Supplier relations and management: A survey of Japanese, Japanese-Transplant and U.S. auto plants', *Strategic Management Journal*, **12**: 563–88.

Damasio, A.R. (1995), *Descartes' Error: Emotion, Reason and the Human Brain*, London: Picador.

Das, T.K. and B.S. Teng (1998), 'Between trust and control: Developing confidence in partner cooperation in alliances', *Academy of Management Review*, **23**/3: 491–512.

——(2001), 'Trust, control and risk in strategic alliances: An integrated framework', *Organization Studies*, **22**/2: 251–84.

Dasgupta P. (1988), 'Trust as a commodity', in D. Gambetta (ed.), *Trust; Making and Breaking of Cooperative Relations*, Oxford: Blackwell: 49–72.

Deakin, S. and F. Wilkinson (2001), 'Contract law and the economics of interorganizational trust', *Organization Studies*, **22**/2: 146–72.

Deutsch, M. (1962), *Cooperation and Trust: Some Theoretical Notes*, in M.R. Jones (ed.), Nebraska Symposium on Motivation, Lincoln, Nebraska: University of Nebraska Press: 275–319.

——(1973), *The Resolution of Conflict: Constructive and Destructive Processes*, New Haven: Yale University Press.

Dore, R. (1983), 'Goodwill and the spirit of market capitalism', *British Journal of Sociology*, **34**: 459–82.

Durkheim, Emile (1933), *The Division of Labour in Society*, New York: Macmillan.

Frank, R.H. (1988), *Passions Within Reason, the Strategic Role of the Emotions*, New York: W.W. Norton.

Friedman, M. (1953), 'The methodology of positive economics', in *Essays in Positive Economics*, Chicago, IL: The University of Chicago Press: 1–43.

Fukuyama, F. (1995), *Trust, the Social Virtues and the Creation of Prosperity*, New York: Free Press.

Gabbay, S. and R. Leenders (eds) (1999), *Corporate Social Capital*, Dordrecht: Kluwer,

Gambetta, D. (1988), 'Can we trust trust?', in D. Gambetta (ed.), *Trust; Making and Breaking of Cooperative Relations*, Oxford: Blackwell: 213–37.

Garfinkel, H. (1967), *Studies in Ethnomethodology*, Cambridge: Polity Press.

Gargiulo, M. and M. Benassi (1999), 'The dark side of social capital', in R.Th.A.J. Leenders and S.M. Gabbay, *Corporate Social Capital and Liability*, Dordrecht: Kluwer: 298–322.

Gelauff, G.M.M. and C. den Broeder (1996), *Governance of Stakeholder Relationships, The German and Dutch Experience.*, Research Memorandum 127, Central Planning Bureau, The Hague.

Giddens, A. (1984), *The Constitution of Society*, Cambridge: Polity Press.

Gioia, D.A. and P.P. Poole (1984), 'Scripts in organizational behaviour', *Academy of Management Review*, **9**/3: 449–59.

Goldberg, David E. (1989), *Genetic Algorithms in Search, Optimization and Machine Learning,* Reading, MA: Addison-Wesley.

Granovetter, M.S. (1985), 'Economic action and social structure: A theory of embeddedness', *American Journal of Sociology*, **91**: 481–510.

Granstrand, O., P. Patel and K. Pavitt (1997), 'Multi-technology corporations: Why they have distributed rather than distinctive core competencies', *California Management Review*, **39**/4, 8–25.

Grey, C. and C. Garsten (2001), 'Trust, control and post-bureaucracy', *Organization Studies*, **22**/2: 229–50.

Gulati, R. (1995), 'Does familiarity breed trust? The implications of repeated ties for contractual choice in alliances', *Academy of Management Journal*, **30**/1: 85–112.

Hagedoorn, J.and J. Schakenraad (1994), 'The effect of strategic technology alliances on company performance', *Strategic Management Journal*, **15**: 291–309.

Heide, J.B. and A.S. Miner (1992), 'The shadow of the future: Effects of anticipated interaction and frequency of contact on buyer–seller cooperation', *Academy of Management Journal*, **35**: 265–91.

Helper, S.(1990), 'Comparative supplier relations in the US and Japanese auto industries: An Exit/Voice approach', *Business and Economic History*, **19**: 1–10.

Hendriks-Jansen, H. (1996), *Catching Ourselves in the Act: Situated Activity, Interactive Emergence, Evolution and Human Thought*, Cambridge, MA: MIT Press.

Herrigel, G. (1994), 'Industry as a form of order', in J.R. Holligsworth, P.C. Schmitter and W. Streeck (eds), *Governing Capitalist Economies*, Oxford: Oxford University Press: 97–28.

Hill, C.W.L. (1990), 'Cooperation, opportunism and the invisible hand: Implications for transaction cost theory', *Academy of Management Review*, **15**/3: 500–513.

Hirschman, A.O. (1970), *Exit, Voice and Loyalty: Responses to Decline in Firms, Organisations and States*, Cambridge, MA: Harvard University Press

Holland, John H. (1992), 'Complex adaptive systems', *Daedalus*, **121**/1: 17–30.

——and John H. Miller (1991), 'Artificial adaptive agents in economic theory', *American Economic Review*, **81**/2: 365–70.

——, Keith J. Holyoak, Richard E. Nisbett and Paul R. Thagard (1986), *Induction: Processes of Inference, Learning, and Discovery*, Cambridge, MA: The MIT Press.

Hollingsworth, R. and R. Boyer (eds) (1997), *Contemporary Capitalism: The Embeddedness of Institutions*, Cambridge: Cambridge University Press.

Jarillo, J.C. (1988), 'On strategic networks', *Strategic Management Journal*, **9**: 31–41.

Johnson-Laird, P.N. (1983), *Mental Models*, Cambridge: Cambridge University Press

Jong, G. de and B. Nooteboom (2000), *The Causal Structure of Long-term Supply Relationships*, Dordrecht: Kluwer.

Kamath, R.R. and J.K. Liker (1994), 'A second look at Japanese product development', *Harvard Business Review*, November–December: 154–70.

Kirman, A.P. and N.J. Vriend (2000), 'Evolving market structure: An ACE model of price dispersion and loyalty', *Journal of Economic Dynamics and Control*, **25**.

Klein Woolthuis, R. (1999), 'Sleeping with the enemy: trust, dependence and contracts in inter-organisational relationships', Doctoral dissertation, Twente University, P.O. Box 217, 7500 AE Enschede, the Netherlands.

——, B. Hillebrand and B. Nooteboom, 'Trust and formal control in inter-organizational relations', unpublished paper, Rotterdam School of Management, Erasmus University Rotterdam.

Klos, Tomas B. (1999), 'Decentralized interaction and co-adaptation in the repeated prisoner's dilemma', *Computational and Mathematical Organization Theory*, **5**/2: 147–65.

——(2000), 'Agent-based computational transaction cost economics', doctoral dissertation, Groningen University, the Netherlands.

——and B. Nooteboom (2001), 'Agent-based computational transaction cost economics', *Journal of Economic Dynamics and Control*, **25**: 503–26.

Knight, F. (1921), *Risk, Uncertainty and Profit*, Boston: Houghton Mifflin.

Knights, D., F. Noble, T. Vurdubakis and H. Willmott (2001), 'Chasing shadows: Social control, virtuality and the production of trust, *Organization Studies*, **22**/2: 311–36.

Kohnstamm, R. (1998), in a column in NRC/Handelsblad.

Koopmans, Tj.C. (1957), *Three Essays on the State of Economic Science*, New York: McGraw Hill.

Krackhardt, D. (1999), 'The ties that torture: Simmelian tie analysis in organizations', *Research in the Sociology of Organizations*, **16**: 183–210.

Krug, B. (2000), 'The process of China's market transition' (Comment), *Journal of Institutional and Theoretical Economics*, **156**/1: 175–79.

Krugman, P.R. (1991), *Geography and Trade*, Cambridge, Mass.: The MIT Press.

Laat, P.B. de (1999), 'Dangerous liaisons: Sharing knowledge within R&D alliances', in A. Grandori (ed.), *Interfirm Networks, Organization and Industrial Competitiveness*, London: Routledge: 208–36.

Lakoff, G. and M. Johnson (1980), *Metaphors we Live By*, Chicago: University of Chicago Press.

——(1999), *Philosophy in the Flesh*, New York: Basic Books.

Lamming, R. (1993), *Beyond Partnership*, New York: Prentice Hall.

Lane, C. (1997), 'International networks in a changing global environment', paper EGOS conference, Budapest, July 1997.

——(2000 paperback edition, first edition 1998), *Trust Within and Between Organizations*, Oxford: Oxford University Press.

——and R. Bachmann (1996), 'The social constitution of trust: Supplier relations in Britain and Germany', *Organization Studies*, **17**: 365–213.

Lane, D.A. (1993), 'Artificial worlds and economics, part II', *Journal of Evolutionary Economics*, 3/3: 177–97.

Langlois, R.N. and P.L. Robertson (1995), *Firms, Markets and Economic Change*, London: Routledge.

Larson, A. (1992), 'Network dyads in entrepreneurial settings: A study of the governance of exchange relationships', *Administrative Science Quarterly*, **37**: 76–104.

Lawson, T. (1997), *Economics and Reality*, London: Routledge.

Lazaric, N. and E. Lorenz (1998), 'The learning dynamics of trust, reputation and confidence', in N. Lazaric and E. Lorenz (eds), *Trust and Economic Learning*, Cheltenham, UK: Edward Elgar: 1–22.

Leenders, R.Th.A.J. and S.M. Gabbay (1999), 'Corporate social capital: The structure of advantage and disadvantage', in R.Th.A.J. Leenders and S.M. Gabbay, *Corporate Social Capital and Liability*, Dordrecht: Kluwer: 1–14.

Lewicki, R.J. and B.B. Bunker (1996), 'Developing and maintaining trust in work relationships', in R.M. Kramer and T.R. Tyler (eds), *Trust in*

Organizations: Frontiers of Theory and Research, Thousand Oaks: Sage Publications: 114–39.

Lindenberg, S. (2000), 'It takes both trust and lack of mistrust: The workings of cooperation and relational signalling in contractual relationships', *Journal of Management and Governance*, **4**: 11–33.

Lissoni, F. (2001), 'Knowledge codification and the geography of innovation: The case of the Brescia mechanical cluster', paper for the workshop on 'The influence of cooperation, networks and institutions on Regional Innovation Systems', Max Planck Institute Jena, 8–10 February.

Lorange, P. and J. Roos (1992), *Strategic Alliances*, Cambridge: Blackwell.

Lounamaa, P.H. and J.G. March (1987), 'Adaptive coordination of a learning team', *Management Science*, **33**, 107–23.

Luhmann, N. (1979), *Trust and Power*, Chichester: Wiley.

——(1988), 'Familiarity, confidence, trust', in D. Gambetta (ed.), *Trust; Making and Breaking of Cooperative Relations*, Oxford: Blackwell: 94–108.

Macaulay, S. (1963), 'Non-contractual relations in business: A preliminary study', *American Sociological Review*, **28**: 55–67.

Macneil, I. (1980), *The New Social Contract: An Enquiry into Modern Contractual Relations*, London: Yale University Press.

Maguire, S., N. Philips and C. Hardy (2001), 'When "silence = death", keep talking: Trust, control and the discursive construction of identity in the Canadian HIV/AIDS treatment domain', *Organization Studies*, **22**/2: 285–310.

March, J. (1991), 'Exploration and exploitation in organizational learning', *Organization Science*, **2**/1.

March J. and H.A. Simon (1958), *Organizations*, New York: Wiley.

Marshall, A. (1920, 8th edition), *Principles of Economics*, London: Macmillan.

Maskell, P. and A. Malmberg (1999), 'Localised learning and industrial competitiveness', *Cambridge Journal of Economics*, **23**: 167–85.

Mayer, R.C., J.H. Davis and F.D. Schoorman (1995), 'An integrative model of organizational trust', *Academy of Management Review*, **20**: 709–34.

McAllister, D.J. (1995), 'Affect- and cognition-based trust as foundations for interpersonal cooperation in organizations', *Academy of Management Journal*, **38**/1: 24–59.

Menkhoff, Th. (1992), 'Yinyong or how to trust trust. Chinese non-contractual business relations and social structure', *Internationales Asienforum*, **23**: 262–88.

Merleau-Ponty, M. (1964), *Le Visible et l'Invisible*, Paris: Gallimard.

Milgrom, P. and J. Roberts (1992), Economics, Organization and Management, Englewood Cliffs: Prentice Hall.

Minsky, M. (1975), 'A framework for representing knowledge', in P.H. Winston (ed.), *The Psychology of Computer Vision*, New York: McGraw-Hill.

Mintzberg, H. (1983), *Structure in Fives: Designing Effective Organizations*, Englewood Cliffs, NJ: Prentice–Hall.

Mowery, D.C. and R.N. Rosenberg (1993), 'The US national system of innovation', in R.R. Nelson (ed.), *National Systems of Innovation*, Oxford: Oxford University Press: 29–75.

Murakami, Y. and T.P. Rohlen (1992), 'Social-exchange aspects of the Japanese political economy: Culture, efficiency and change', in S. Kumon and H. Rosorsky (eds), *The Political Economy of Japan, vol. 3, Cultural and Social Dynamics*, Stanford, California: Stanford University Press: 63–105.

Nelson, R.R. and S. Winter (1982), *An Evolutionary Theory of Economic Change,* Cambridge: Cambridge University Press.

Nelson, R.R. and B.N. Sampat (2000), 'Making sense of institutions as a factor shaping economic performance', *Journal of Economic Behaviour and Organisation*, (forthcoming).

Nonaka, I. and H. Takeuchi (1995), *The Knowledge-Creating Company*, Oxford: Oxford University Press.

Noorderhaven, N.G. (2001), 'Exploring boundaries in international management research: A hermeneutical approach', EGOS conference, 5–7 July, Lyon.

Nooteboom, B. (1992), 'Towards a dynamic theory of transactions', *Journal of Evolutionary Economics*, **2**: 281–99.

——(1993), 'Firm size effects on transaction costs', *Small Business Economics*, **5**: 283–95.

——(1996), 'Trust, opportunism and governance: A process and control model', *Organization Studies*, **17**/6: 985–1010.

——(1998), 'Cost, quality and learning based governance of buyer-supplier relations', in M.G. Colombo (ed.), *The Changing Boundaries of the Firm*, London: Routledge: 187–208.

——(1999a), *Inter-Firm Alliances, Analysis and Design*, London: Routledge.

——(1999b), 'Roles of the go-between', in S.M. Gabbay and R. Leenders (eds), *Corporate Social Capital*, Deventer: Kluwer: 341–55.

——(1999c), 'Trust as a governance device', in M.C. Casson and A. Godley (eds), *Cultural Factors in Economic Growth*, Springer: 44–68.

——(1999d), 'Innovation and inter-firm linkages: new implications for policy', *Research Policy*, **28**: 793–8–5.

——(1999e), 'Voice and exit-based forms of corporate control: Anglo-American, European, and Japanese', *Journal of Economic Issues*, **33**/4: 845–60.

——(1999f), 'Innovation, learning and industrial organization', *Cambridge Journal of Economics*, **23**/2: 127–50.

——(2000a), *Learning and Innovation in Organizations and Economies*, Oxford: Oxford University Press.

——(2000b), 'Institutions and forms of coordination in innovation systems', *Organization Studies*, **21**/5: 915–39.

——(2001), 'Problems and solutions in knowledge transfer', paper for the conference on 'The influence of cooperation, networks and institutions on regional innovation systems', Max Planck Institute, Jena, 8–10 February.

——, J. Berger and N.G. Noorderhaven (1997), 'Effects of trust and governance on relational risk', *Academy of Management Journal*, **40**/2: 308–38.

——, T.B. Klos and R.J.J.M. Jorna (2000), 'Adaptive trust and cooperation: An agent-based simulation approach', Paper for the ISNIE conference, Tuebingen, 22–24 September.

North, D.C. (1990), *Institutions, Institutional Change and Economic Performance*, Cambridge: Cambridge University Press.

——and R. Thomas (1973), *The Rise of the New World: A New Economic History*, Cambridge: Cambridge University Press.

Pagden, A. (1988), 'The destruction of trust and its economic consequences in the case of eighteenth-century Naples', in D. Gambetta (ed.), *Trust, the Making and Breaking of Cooperative Relations*, Oxford: Blackwell: 127–41.

Parkhe, A. (1993), 'Strategic alliance structuring: A game theoretic and transaction cost examination of inter-firm cooperation', *Academy of Management Journal*, **36**: 794–829.

Parsons, T. (1951), *The Social System*, London: Routledge and Kegan Paul.

Pennings, J.M. and K. Lee (1999), 'A relational resource perspective on social capital', in R.Th.A.J. Leenders and S.M. Gabbay, *Corporate Social Capital and Liability*, Dordrecht: Kluwer: 43–67.

Pettit, Ph. (1995a), 'The cunning of trust', *Philosophy and Public Affairs*, **14**/3: 202–25.

——(1995b), 'The virtual reality of homo economicus', *The Monist*, **78**/3: 308–29.

Polanyi, M. (1962), *Personal Knowledge*, London: Routledge.

Powell, W.W. (1990), 'Neither market nor hierarchy: Network forms of organization', in B.M. Staw and L.L. Cummings (eds), *Research in Organizational Behavior 12*, Greenwich, Conn: 295–336.

Putnam, R.D. (2000), *Bowling Alone; the Collapse and Revival of American Community*, New York: Simon and Schuster.

Quine, W. (1960), *Word and Object*, New York: Wiley.

Reed M.I. (2001), 'Organization, trust and control: A realist analysis', *Organization Studies*, **22**/2: 201–28.

Rosch, E. (1977), 'Human categorization', in N. Warren (ed.), *Advances in Cross-cultural Psychology*, vol.1, New York: Academic Press.

Sako, M. (1992), *Prices, Quality, and Trust: Inter-firm Relations in Britain and Japan*, Cambridge: Cambridge University Press.

——(1994), 'Neither markets nor hierarchies; A comparative study of the printed circuit board industry in Britain and Japan', in J.R. Hollingsworth, P.C. Schmitter and W. Streeck (eds), *Governing Capitalist Economies*, Oxford: Oxford University Press: 17–42.

——(1998), 'The information requirements of trust in supplier relations: Evidence from Japan, Europe and the United States', in N. Lazaric and E. Lorenz (eds), *Trust and Economic Learning*, Cheltenham,UK: Edward Elgar: 23–47.

——(2000), 'Does trust improve business performance?', in C. Lane and R. Bachmann (eds), *Trust Within and Between Organizations*, Oxford: Oxford University Press: 88–117.

Schein, E.H. (1985), *Organizational Culture and Leadership*, San Francisco: Jossey-Bass

Shackle, G. (1961), *Decision, Order and Time in Human Affairs*, Cambridge: Cambridge University Press.

Shank, R. and R. Abelson (1977), *Scripts, Plans, Goals and Understanding*, Hillsdale: Lawrence Erlbaum.

Shapiro, S.P. (1987), 'The social control of impersonal trust', *American Journal of Sociology*, **93**: 623–58.

Simmel, G. (1950), 'Individual and society', in K.H. Wolff (ed.), *The Sociology of George Simmel*, New York: Free Press.

——(1978), *The Philosophy of Money*, London: Rouledge and Kegan Paul.

Simon, H.A. (1983), *Reason in Human Affairs* Oxford: Basil Blackwell.

Six, F. (2001), 'The dynamics of trust and trouble', Paper seminar on 'Trust and trouble in organisations', Erasmus University Rotterdam, 4–5 May.

Smircich, L. (1983), 'Organization as shared meaning', in L.R. Pondy, P.J. Frost, G. Morgan and T.C. Dandridge (eds), *Organizational Symbolism*, Greenwich, Conn: JAI Press, 55–65.

Smith, Adam (1982) (originally published in 1759), *The Theory of Moral Sentiments*, Indianapolis: Liberty Classics.

Smith-Doerr, L., J.O. Owen-Smith, K.W. Kogut and W.W. Powell (1999), 'Networks and knowledge production: Collaboration and patenting in biotechnology', in R.Th.A.J. Leenders and S.M. Gabbay, *Corporate Social Capital and Liability*, Dordrecht: Kluwer,

Smith Ring, P. and A. van de Ven (1992), 'Structuring cooperative relationships between organizations', *Strategic Management Journal*, **13**: 483–98.

——(1994), 'Developmental processes of cooperative interorganizational relationships', *Academy of Management Review*, **19**/1: 90–118.

Spender, J.C. (1989), *Industry Recipes*, Oxford: Basil Blackwell.

Stoelhorst, J.W. (1997), 'In search of a dynamic theory of the firm', doctoral dissertation, Twente University, the Netherlands.

Sydow, J. (1996), 'Understanding the constitution of inter-organizational trust', paper SASE conference, University of Geneva, 12–14 July.

——(2000), 'Understanding the constitution of interorganizational trust', in C. Lane and R. Bachmann, *Trust In and Between Organizations*, Oxford University Press: 31–63.

Teece, D.J. (1986), 'Profiting from technological innovation: implications for integration, collaboration, licensing and public policy', *Research Policy*, **15**: 285–305.

Telser, L.G. (1980), 'A theory of self-enforcing agreements', *Journal of Business*, **53**: 27–44.

Thompson, J.D. (1967), *Organizations in Action*, New York: McGraw-Hill.

Tooby, J. and L. Cosmides (1992), 'The psychological foundations of culture', in J.H. Barkow, L. Cosmides and J. Tooby, *The Adapted Mind*, Oxford: Oxford University Press: 19–136.

Vandevelde, A. (2000), 'Reciprocity and trust as social capital' (in Flemish), in A. Vandevelde (ed.), *Over Vertrouwen en Bedrijf*, Leuven: Acco: 13–26.

Verhezen, P. (2000), 'Omkoping of gift? Vertrouwen en vrijgevigheid', in A. Vandevelde (ed.), *Over Vertrouwen en Bedrijf*, Leuven: Acco: 133–42.

Walker, W. (1993), 'National innovation systems: Britain', in R.R. Nelson (ed.) *National Innovation Systems*, Oxford: Oxford University Press, pp. 158–91.

Weick, K.F. (1979), *The Social Psychology of Organizing*, Reading, MA: Addison-Wesley.

——(1995), *Sensemaking in Organisations*, Thousand Oaks, CA: Sage.

Weigelt, K. and C. Camerer (1988), 'Reputation and corporate strategy: A review of recent theory and applications', *Strategic Management Journal*, **9**: 443–54.

Whitley, R. (1999), *Divergent Capitalisms: The Social Structuring and Change of Business Systems*, Oxford: Oxford University Press.

Williams, B. (1988), 'Formal structures and social reality', in D. Gambetta (ed.), *Trust: Making and Breaking of Cooperative Relations*, Oxford: Blackwell: 3–13.

Williamson, O.E. (1975), *Markets and Hierarchies*, New York: The Free Press.

——(1985), *The Economic Institutions of Capitalism: Firms Markets, Relational Contracting*, New York: The Free Press.

——(1991), 'Comparative economic organization: The analysis of discrete structural alternatives', *Administrative Science Quarterly*, **36**: 269–96.

——(1993), 'Calculativeness, trust, and economic organization', *Journal of Law and Economics* **36**: 453–486.

——(1996), *The Mechanisms of Governance*, Oxford: Oxford University Press.

——(1999), 'Strategy research: Governance and competence perspectives', *Strategic Management Journal*, **20**: 1087–108.

Winter, S.G. (1964), 'Economic "natural selection" and the theory of the firm', *Yale Economic Essays*, **4** (spring): 225–72.

Wittek, R.P.M. (2000), 'Interdependence and informal control in organizations', doctoral dissertation, University of Groningen, the Netherlands.

Wittgenstein, L. (1976, first published in 1953), *Philosophical Investigations*, Oxford: Basil Blackwell.

Zaheer, A. and N. Venkatraman (1995), 'Relational governance as an inter-organizational strategy: An empirical test of the role of trust in economic exchange', *Strategic Management Journal*, **16**: 373–92.

Zand, D.E. (1972), 'Trust and managerial problem solving', *Administrative Science Quarterly*, **17/2**: 229–39.

Zucker, L.G. (1986), 'Production of trust: Institutional sources of economic structure', in Barry, Staw and Cummings, *Research in Organisational Behaviour*, vol. 8: 53–111.

Index

223